Josephine Ross was educated at Wycombe Abbey School and London University, where she read English. On graduating, she worked for *Vogue* magazine, before being commissioned to write her first book – this study of the courtships of Elizabeth I – for Weidenfeld & Nicolson. Since then, she has written television drama scripts and a number of histories and biographies, including *The Winter Queen* and *The Tudors*, as well as compiling and editing several illustrated books for *Vogue*. Her most recent publication is *Jane Austen: A Companion*. She is married to the historian James Chambers, and lives in London.

THE MEN WHO WOULD BE KING

Originally published as Suitors to the Queen

Josephine Ross

PHOENIX

For James

A PHOENIX PAPERBACK

First published in Great Britain in 1975
by Weidenfeld & Nicolson
under the title *Suitors to the Queen*
This paperback edition published in 2005
by Phoenix,
an imprint of Orion Books Ltd,
Orion House, 5 Upper St Martin's Lane,
London WC2H 9EA

1 3 5 7 9 10 8 6 4 2

A CIP catalogue record for this book
is available from the British Library.

ISBN 0 75381 833 7

Printed and bound in Great Britain by
Clays Ltd, St Ives plc

www.orionbooks.co.uk

CONTENTS

ILLUSTRATIONS

ACKNOWLEDGMENTS

I am deeply grateful to Beatrix Miller, who helped and encouraged me from the outset, and the late Christopher Falkus, whose inspiration and enthusiasm made this book possible. Others who have given me valuable assistance include Dr David Starkey, who kindly read the manuscript, and Francesca Ronan, who edited it. For this Phoenix edition I am indebted to Kate Shearman. I should also like to thank the staff of the Public Record Office; the staff of the London Library; my late parents; John Wilder and Andrew Todd.

The author has quoted mainly from the following sources:

MANUSCRIPT SOURCES

State Papers, Domestic (SP 1,10,11,12)
State Papers, Foreign, General Series (SP 70)

PRINTED SOURCES

Acts of the Privy Council of England, ed. J. R. Dasent, HMSO, London 1890.

Ambassades de MM de Noailles en Angleterre, ed. R. Vertot, Paris 1763.

Burghley State Papers, ed. S. Haynes, London 1740.

Burghley State Papers, ed. W. Murdin, London 1740.

Calendar of Letters and Papers, Foreign and Domestic, Henry VIII, vols VI-XX, ed. J. Gairdner, R. H. Brodie, HMSO, London 1882-1907

Calendar of Salisbury MSS, vol II, Historical MSS Commission, HMSO, London 1888.

Calendar of State Papers, Spanish. Edward VI-Philip and Mary, vols X-XIII, ed. R. Tyler, HMSO, London 1914-54.

Calendar of State Papers, Spanish. Elizabeth I, vols I-III, ed. M. A. S. Hume, HMSO, London 1892-6.

Correspondence Diplomatique de La Mothe Fénelon, ed. C. P. Cooper, Paris and London 1840.

A Chronicle of England, H. Wriothesley, ed. W. D. Hamilton, Camden Society, London 1875.

The Chronicle of Queen Jane and Queen Mary, ed. J. G. Nichols, Camden Society, London 1850.

The Compleat Ambassador, ed. H. Digges, London 1658.

The Diary of Henry Machyn, Citizen of London, ed. J. G. Nichols, Camden Society, London 1848.

Elizabeth I and Her Parliaments, vol I, J. E. Neale, Jonathan Cape, London 1953.

Fragmenta Regalia, ed. R. Naunton, London 1824.

Hardwicke State Papers, ed. the Earl of Hardwicke, London 1770.

John Stubbs' 'Gaping Gulf', ed. L. C. Berry, Folger Shakespeare Library, University Press of Virginia, Charlottesville 1968.

Literary Remains of Edward VI, ed. J. G. Nichols, Roxburghe Club, London 1857.

Memoirs of Sir James Melville, ed. G. Scott, London 1735.

The Progresses and Public Processions of Queen Elizabeth, ed. J. G. Nichols, Roxburghe Club, London 1823.

Queen Elizabeth and Some Foreigners, ed. V. von Klarwill, trans. T. H. Nash, John Lane/The Bodley Head, London 1928.

THE EARLY YEARS

Whoso list to hunt, I know where is a hind
But as for me, alas, I may no more.
The vain travail hath wearied me so sore,
I am of those that farthest come behind.
Yet may by no means my wearied mind
Draw from the deer, but as she fleeth afore,
Fainting I follow. I leave off therefore,
Since in a net I seek to hold the wind.
Who lists her hunt, I put him out of doubt,
As well as I may spend his time in vain;
And graven with diamonds, in letters plain,
There is written her fair neck round about,
Noli me tangere, for Caesar's I am,
And wild for to hold, though I seem tame.

The pursuit of Elizabeth Tudor was the greatest hunt in history. For more than half a century, kings, princes, nobles and knights, Frenchmen, Austrians, Spaniards, Swedes and 'mere English' joined the chase, lured by the magnificent quarry who pranced before them, leaping away, doubling back, sometimes halting and seeming to yield, but always at last disappearing over the horizon. Instinct and experience taught Elizabeth not to surrender, but political expediency, emotional cravings and the exhilaration of the sport combined in her head and heart to keep the great hunt going. From her babyhood into her old age, in spite of her avowals of perpetual virginity, in spite of rich rumours to the contrary, the most splendid men in Europe succeeded one another in the field as suitors to the Queen.

A*

Noli me tangere – do not touch me; it would have been a fitting motto for Elizabeth, but she was not born when Sir Thomas Wyatt wrote the sonnet, bitter with love for her mother, Anne Boleyn. Giddy, seductive Anne had no need of lesser lovers such as Wyatt while Henry VIII, England's mighty Caesar, courted her with exuberant tenderness, drawing hearts and initials on his love-letters like a schoolboy, disrupting the religious and social orders to make her his wife. She was not a classic beauty, but she had the luscious dark eyes and nervy delicacy of a doe, and she dressed with sophisticated, expensive taste; above all, she knew how to make men ache with desire. Women in the London crowds shouted abuse at her and the Imperial ambassador Chapuys sneered knowingly and referred to her as 'the Concubine' in his despatches. After the birth of Elizabeth, in September 1533, he wrote: 'The christening has been like her mother's coronation, very cold and disagreeable both to the court and to the city.' It was a serious blow to Henry VIII that the baby, born eight months after his marriage to Anne, was not a boy; however, the new Queen's ability to bear children was now proved, and the all-important male heir to the throne would no doubt follow. The baby Elizabeth was healthy and indeed had a certain value as bait for a future foreign marriage alliance. But the King's passion for his wife faded as the months paced on and no son was born. Anne's brittle charm cracked into neurosis, her peals of inappropriate laughter sounded hysterical, her shrewishness vented itself in orders to threaten and bully the King's disgraced elder daughter Mary. More than ever Anne seemed 'wild for to hold', carelessly coquettish with any man from the common musician Mark Smeaton to her own brother Viscount Rochford, flirting and teasing and fishing for compliments, seeking reassurance that she was still desirable. Then, in January 1536, she gave birth prematurely to a stillborn boy, and Henry had no more tolerance.

Noli me tangere ... the lascivious incitements by which she roused her lovers included 'touchings', it was stated at her trial. The bald obscenity of the official reports had nothing in common with Wyatt's courtly erotic yearnings, or the King's boisterous love-letters. The world heard from Westminster that the Queen had 'procured and incited her own natural brother, George Boleyn, Lord Rochford, Gentleman of the Privy Chamber, to violate and carnally know her, with her tongue in the said George's mouth, and the said George's tongue in hers, and also with open-mouthed kisses, gifts and jewels'. Five men altogether were condemned to death as her lovers. Anne was judged guilty of carnal adulterous lusts, of despising God's commands and human laws, and Chapuys informed his Emperor that 'she was also charged, and her brother likewise, with having laughed at the King and his dress'.

The mocked King made no secret of his joy at the condemnation of his wife which released him from her. 'Already it sounds ill in the ears of the people', Chapuys reported with interest, 'that the King, having received such ignominy, has shown himself more glad than ever since the arrest of the whore, for he has been going about banqueting with ladies, sometimes remaining after midnight, and returning by the river.' Seven miles up the river Thames, prim, pretty Jane Seymour was lodged in state. Down the river, below London Bridge with its crammed houses and shops, lay the dark bulk of the Tower, where Anne Boleyn was waiting to die. The Constable of the Tower, Sir William Kyngston, reported with surprise that she was 'very merry'; she kept laughing, he wrote, and once she joked: 'I heard say the executor was very good, and I have a little neck,' and then she 'put her hand about it, laughing heartily'. She was beheaded on Tower Green on 19 May, not laughing, but looking 'exhausted and amazed'.

Among the bills left unpaid at Anne Boleyn's death were listed expensive items for her little daughter – caps of satin and taffeta; satin and crimson fringe for the child's cradle. Elizabeth was nearly three when her mother was condemned to death by her father. She had been taken from the Queen shortly after her birth, and a royal nursery had been established, first at the old wooded manor of Hatfield, then at stately Eltham Palace, and later at Hunsdon, in Hertfordshire, but despite the official separation she had seen her parents often during her babyhood. For the first two years of her life Elizabeth was the heir presumptive to the English throne, Henry's eighteen-year-old daughter Mary by his divorced wife Catherine of Aragon having been declared a bastard. There seemed little prospect that Elizabeth would actually inherit, for the King was in his lusty prime, and would surely beget sons to supersede her, but in the meantime she was the 'High and Mighty Princess of England', and both Henry and Anne were proud and fond of her. Two years before he was called upon to act as royal jailer, Sir William Kyngston had written enthusiastically: 'Today the King and Queen were at Eltham, and saw my Lady Princess – as goodly a child as has been seen. Her Grace is much in the King's favour, as goodly child should be, God save her.' In January 1536, only five months before Anne's disgrace, Elizabeth was summoned to Hampton Court to take part in the King's un-bridled rejoicings at the death of his scorned and repudiated former wife Catherine of Aragon. The little Princess was paraded to Mass to the tingling blast of trumpets 'and other great triumphs', and late that evening the King, dressed from head to foot in yellow, except for the white feather in his cap, sent for his daughter and then swung her up in his huge arms and carried her about, boisterously showing her off to the company. By May, however, his elation had evaporated. It was claimed, years later, that just before Anne's arrest he had been seen at a window of Greenwich Palace, staring frozenly out into the courtyard below, while Anne stood weeping beside him apparently pleading with him, holding Elizabeth out to him beseechingly. Such vivid, disturbing scenes outside the familiar nursery world would surely remain in a child's uncomprehend-ing memory, to sink into the layer of impressions with which the subconscious mind is lined.

Incidents remembered; servants' whispers; awkward answers to casual prattled questions; there were many ways in which Elizabeth would have absorbed information. No doubt efforts were made to protect her from the disturbing knowledge of her mother's shocking death, but in a large household consisting almost entirely of servants, with a fond governess – Lady Bryan – who was a cousin of the late Queen, it is not likely that the child remained for long in total ignorance of the event. It might have seemed as unreal as a fairy-story, as personally unrelated as tales of Robin Goodfellow or King Arthur's knights, had the drama not been constantly repeated with living protagonists throughout Elizabeth's childhood, becoming the reality of her own experience. In each of her father's subsequent marriages – Elizabeth was a veteran of five marriages by the time she was ten years old – the same picture was embellished, fresh layers of paint laid on the sketch of her own earliest impressions. The King, her mighty royal father, the image of towering masculinity, possessed utter power over each vulnerable, disposable wife who bound herself to him in wedlock.

The effects of the downfall and disposal of Anne Boleyn were soon felt at the nursery household of Hunsdon. 'The very evening the Concubine was brought to the Tower,' Chapuys wrote, 'when the Duke of Richmond went to say good night to his father, and ask his blessing after the English custom, the King began to weep, saying that he and his sister, meaning the Princess [Mary] were greatly bound to God for having escaped the hands of that accursed whore, who had determined to poison them.' Before the adulteress, whore and poisoner Anne was beheaded, her marriage with the King was annulled, so by the time he married Jane Seymour, at the end of May, Henry had three illegitimate children – his beloved son the Duke of Richmond, by his mistress Bessie Blount; Catherine of Aragon's daughter the bastardized Mary; and little Elizabeth, whose governess Lady Bryan was soon distracted with worry at the poverty and confusion to which her household was reduced. 'My Lady Elizabeth is put from that degree she was afore, and what degree she is of now, I know not but by hearsay,' she wrote, pleading with the King's minister Thomas Cromwell to intercede. When the royal visits ceased, so did the presents of clothes and nursery-stuff; Elizabeth had grown out of all her dresses, caps and underclothes, and Lady Bryan had to beg Cromwell to arrange 'that she may have some raiment', ending her heartfelt plea with the touching revelation that Elizabeth was having pain with her milk-teeth coming through, and therefore they were spoiling her a little, but she added: 'I trust to God an' her teeth were well graft, to have Her Grace after another fashion than she is yet: so as I trust the King's Grace shall have great comfort in Her Grace. For she is as toward a child, and as gentle of conditions, as ever I knew any in my life.'

The royal neglect was remedied, and the former heir pre-sumptive took her official place as the King's younger daugh-ter. Yet she and her grown-up sister Mary remained legally bastards, and with the death of the King's only male offspring, the Duke of Richmond, in July 1536, the succession question became more dangerously uncertain than ever. There were still many Englishmen who could remember the Wars of the Roses, the struggle for supremacy between the Houses of Lancaster and York, which had ended when the first Tudor monarch, Henry VII, laid firm hands on the crown at the Battle of Bosworth in 1485, and nursed the limping country to new strength and wealth. His son Henry VIII had built a magnifi-cently showy structure on firm foundations; under him England's court became one of the finest in Europe. In the words of his own famous song, Henry VIII loved 'pastime and good company', gambling and dancing, and, above all, hunting – he was reported to have worn out eight good horses in a single day's chase – and in a space of three years he managed to spend £3,300 on 'cards, dice, tennis and wagers', in addition to £11,000 which he paid out for jewellery during the same period. At times Henry's personality seemed to be the looking-glass of the Renaissance; he possessed both intelligence and charm, and Erasmus wrote of him warmly: 'He is a man of great friendliness, and gentle in debate; he acts more like a companion than a king,' but the robes and regalia of absolute power could not fail to muffle and distort the informal human-ity in man or woman. As a private individual, a 'Squire Harry', Henry would surely have lived his life in tolerable harmony with his pious foreign wife Catherine and his conscientious daughter Mary, regretful, perhaps, that he had no son, but obliged to be content with his studies, his music, his mistresses and his sport. But as the King, God's anointed representative, with England, Ireland, Wales and a slice of France for his estate, with some four million men, women and children for his dependents, his responsibility was not to accept but to effect, and the future of the great nation which two generations of Tudors had cultivated and guarded was in jeopardy until the next Tudor Prince should be born and the succession estab-lished beyond dispute.

After a quarter of a century of striving, Henry was at last presented with a healthy, legitimate, male heir. On 12 October 1537, eighteen months after the execution of Anne Boleyn, his third Queen, Jane Seymour, gave birth to a boy at Hampton Court, and London went wild with joy. There were bonfires and banquets in the streets, hogsheads of free wine were set out in the City, more than two thousand guns pounded out a salute from the Tower, and there were 'all the bells ringing in every parish church till it was ten at the clock at night'. The baby Prince, 'the whole realm's most precious jewel', was christened Edward in the chapel of Hampton Court. Elizabeth, as the King's daughter, played an official part in the ceremony, carrying the richly-ornamented chrisom-cloth. Being only four years old, however, she herself had to be carried during the proceedings by the Prince's senior uncle, Edward Seymour.

When the customary New Year's Gifts were presented to Prince Edward on 1 January 1538, Henry VIII gave his infant heir sumptuous possessions, including 'a basin all gilt, with a rose in the bottom with the King's Grace's arms in the rose', 'a ewer all gilt', and a 'standing cup with a cover, gilt, wrought with antique work', while the Lady Mary chose for the child 'a coat of crimson satin embroidered with gold, with tinsel sleeves and gold aiglettes'. The Lady Elizabeth, aged five, gave the baby a little cambric shirt which she had laboriously sewed herself. If, as would seem likely, the arrival of a baby brother, and her own part in his christening, had prompted Elizabeth to ask a child's timeless questions about the origins of babies and functions of mothers, the death of Jane Seymour only six days after the birth, when the events were fresh in Elizabeth's mind, would have added another note to the discordant scale of impressions which included her own mother's death.

At six years old, when, according to Wriothesley, she already behaved in public with as much gravity as if she were forty, she was presented with another stepmother, the German Protestant Anne of Cleves, but to the court's bawdy amusement this Anne was so unappetizing that the King proved unable to consummate the marriage, and by the following summer she had been smoothly divorced, bought off with two manors, hangings, plate, fine dresses, a handsome allowance and the title of 'the King's beloved sister', and in her place sat the ravishing young noblewoman Catherine Howard. Sweetly promiscuous, she had been seduced at thirteen and lived in blithe immorality ever since, but at first Henry was too blind with ardour for his nubile 'rose without a thorn' to see the rot beneath the petals. In the autumn of his life he had found again the bliss of springtime sexuality. Catherine was Anne Boleyn's first cousin, and she accordingly made much of Elizabeth, giving her a prominent place at her wedding banquet. A little dizzy with the wines and rich foods, the raucous harmonies of shawms and sackbuts, the smell of hot noisy people in sweaty satin, Elizabeth must have sat in the lofty, crowded banqueting hall of Hampton Court watching curiously as her vast and glorious father greedily fondled her girlish new stepmother. 'The King caresses her more than he did the others,' Chapuys noted. By Christmas 1541, however, the King had awoken from his dream. With fury and misery he learned that his delicious young wife, by whom he could surely have given the nation an infant Duke of York, was no better than a trull, that she had been the paramour of a music master before her illustrious marriage, and had then committed adultery with a Gentleman of the Privy Chamber. 'Yt maketh my harte to dye to thynck what Fortune I have that I cannot be always in your companye,' she had written to her lover, Thomas Culpeper, and added naively that she found writing a very difficult business.

The vague tale of Anne Boleyn's death now leapt into lurid life for the eight-year-old Elizabeth as the court and the country buzzed with interest at the scandal and shocking death of her pretty cousin. On 12 February 1542 Catherine was beheaded, as Elizabeth's mother had been, on Tower Green, and her headless body buried near that of Anne Boleyn, under the flagstones of the Chapel of St Peter ad Vincula, in the Tower.

By the time she was ten years old Elizabeth had had four stepmothers. The installation of a sensible, kind and intelligent woman as the last of Henry's wives, in July 1543, came too late to eradicate the imprints of Elizabeth's childhood experiences, but the new stepmother skilfully brought a semblance of affectionate unity to the King's buffeted family. Lady Latimer, born Catherine Parr, had been twice widowed, but she was still an attractive little woman in her early thirties. A contemporary chronicler recorded that she was 'quieter than any of the young wives the King had had, and as she knew more of the world she always got on pleasantly with the King, and had no caprices, and paid much honour to Madam Mary and the wives of the nobles'. Mary, now twenty-seven, devoutly Catholic, was still unmarried, and since the traumatic time when her own beloved mother's marriage with the King had been pronounced null and she herself declared a bastard, she had been passionately sensitive where her status was concerned. The wanton Catherine Howard, ten years Mary's junior, had slighted her, and the new Queen's tactful respect for her rank and blood was accordingly welcome. For the pale precocious scholarling Edward, Catherine became a 'dearest mother', and to Elizabeth, who spent much of 1544 away from the court, she showed 'care and solicitude'. In public duty as well as in personal relationships Catherine was thoroughly competent; soon after her marriage she efficiently acted as regent while Henry, in temporary amity with Charles v of Spain, was across the Channel commanding the English army in a combined endeavour against the French. The letters between them at this period have the flavour of comfortable domestic affection – 'No more to you at this time, sweetheart,' the King concluded his communication of 8 September 1544, 'saving we pray you to give in our name our hearty blessings to all our children.'

In Catherine Parr, Elizabeth had a fine example of contemporary womanhood: educated, talented, poised, but ultimately submissive to the opinions and authority of her husband. It was fulsomely said of Elizabeth that, when she was six years old, her knowledge was sufficient to make her a credit to her father even if her education were to progress no further. Schooled according to the standards of the Renaissance, which the blaze of New Learning in Italy had ignited throughout Europe, she eagerly studied languages, the classics and philosophy – 'liberal sciences' and 'moral learning' – with music for recreation, and by the age of ten she was an accomplished scholar of French and Italian. 'Her mind has no womanly weakness, her perseverance is equal to that of a man,'

her tutor Roger Ascham was later to report – high praise, to
compare a young woman's talents with the superior capa-
bilities of a man. Education could equip a woman to be the
intellectual companion of her husband, but as Catherine Parr
found, any dispute with him had to be undertaken with
cautious meekness; there was no counteracting the natural
frailty and inferiority of woman. Husband of one highly educated woman, father of two more, Henry could tersely refuse
to permit the Countess of Surrey to join her husband in France
in 1545 on the grounds that the situation there was 'unmeet for
women's imbecilities'. At the beginning of that year the eleven-
year-old Elizabeth's New Year's Gift to Catherine Parr had been
a laborious translation of Margaret of Navarre's mystical work
Le Miroir de l'Ame Pécheresse, bound in a cover which she had
embroidered herself, and accompanied by a tortuously sen-
tentious letter. It was early proof that Elizabeth, like Catherine,
included scholarship among the womanly adornments that she
could offer a husband.

It was not for her personal talents and virtues, however, but
for impersonal political gain that the younger daughter of the
King of England was sought in marriage from her very earliest
years. Before she could even speak English coherently she had
been courted as a wife, in an elaborate negotiation which both
parties exploited to the full and then abandoned, as though in
miniature rehearsal for the courtships of the adult Queen. In
1535, when Elizabeth was not yet two years old, it was proposed that she should be betrothed to the Duke of Angoulême,
the youngest son of Henry's friend and rival, King Francis i of
France. At that time Anne Boleyn was still Henry's 'own sweetheart', and Elizabeth was England's heir-presumptive, only
just weaned, but the most desirable bride in Europe. Chapuys
commented that the King had apparently despaired of be-
getting sons, and concluded, with ironic accuracy, that 'this
last daughter may be mistress of England'. One condition of the
contract was that the young suitor should be brought over to
England and educated in English ways at court. Charles of
Angoulême was nearly fourteen, a swaggering, high-spirited
boy with blue eyes and fair hair, whom Francis loved far more
than his older sons, the cold-natured Dauphin and the stolid

Duke of Orléans. 'He had the favour of his father and the people, child of Fortune,' but he was also highly unstable, liable when drunk to go brawling in the streets of Paris, and at a very early age he took an older woman of the court as his mistress. And it was said that he seemed to be uncertain whether he was a girl or a boy; it was fortunate that Elizabeth, who as an adult liked men to appear aggressively virile, and was scornful of her cousin Mary Queen of Scots for falling in love with the 'lady-faced' lad Darnley, was not tied in infancy to such a husband.

Chapuys and his fellow-envoy at the English court, the Bishop of Faenza, watched the progress of the affair keenly. So close a link between France and England would be detrimental to the power and political manoeuvrability of the Empire; it was a prime condition of the negotiations that neither Francis nor Henry should afterwards treat with the Emperor Charles v. On 5 April Chapuys was maintaining loftily: 'I do not attach much credit to it,' but by the end of that month the Bishop of Faenza had come to the conclusion that the betrothal would indeed take place. Then Chapuys reported a reassuring conversation he had had with Thomas Cromwell, during which the King's minister had confided that he 'felt almost assured that nothing would be concluded at all, skilful as the French were, who asked of them their daughter for the Duke of Angoulême in order to make their profit of them while she was under age, and when they thought expedient, to break all agreements – which never could last long with them, both by reason of their natural fickleness and because the French support the Church of Rome which [the English] will not hear of'. National pride gave rise to a further problem; the relative status of the prospective consort and how he should be styled were sensitive matters, and to the English stipulation that Angoulême should be educated at the Tudor court Francis was reported to have given the haughty response that he would never send his son to reside in England as 'a hostage'. By the end of June the Bishop of Faenza was confident that the affair would come to nothing, and cited the weighty reason that the French refused to defy the Pope and defend 'the cause of the King's second wife'.

Abortive betrothals of royal children were relatively common; Henry's elder daughter Mary had in turn been officially promised to the Dauphin, the Emperor of Spain and the King of France by the time she was eleven years old. But the failure of Elizabeth's first wooing had a prophetic significance, in that at the very start of her long life, in which she was to be courted from cradle to grave, the equivocal circumstances of her religious background thus early served as a hurdle to halt a suitor. Elizabeth Tudor was not only a child of the Reformation, she was *the* child of the Reformation – it was her approaching birth which finally drove the conscience-troubled, heir-craving Henry to defy the Pope, complete the rupture with Rome and effect his own divorce from the menopausal Catherine of Aragon, replacing her with his pregnant love Anne Boleyn. In orthodox Catholic eyes his actions had no spiritual authority; while Catherine lived she was regarded as his lawful wife and Mary his sole legitimate child, so that Anne Boleyn was 'the Concubine', and Elizabeth 'the Little Bastard'. In the Angoulême negotiations Henry stipulated that Francis must give his official approval to the Act of Succession, which flouted the Pope and settled the crown on the issue of Anne Boleyn, but, predictably, the Catholic Francis was not prepared to offer such open defiance to the Pope for the sake of 'the cause of the King's second wife'. The betrothal plan foundered. Angoulême, elevated by the Dauphin's death to the second brother's title of Duke of Orléans, died at the age of twenty-three, while serving against the English at Boulogne, in 1545. According to popular report he entered a plague-infested house, swiped about him with his sword, shouted: 'Never yet hath a son of France died of the Plague!' and was dead within three days.

Anne Boleyn's downfall in 1536, a year after the baby Princess's half-hearted first courtship, further complicated Elizabeth's personal circumstances. Henry declared his marriage with Anne to have been null, and Elizabeth, like her sister Mary, was proclaimed a bastard. Henry never revoked their illegitimacy. Both daughters were subsequently recognized and given official status; in the Succession Act of 1544 they were placed in line to the throne after Edward and any children which Catherine Parr might bear to Henry. But the legal flaw in Elizabeth's rank remained unmended, a potential weakness in her royal status.

The instability of Elizabeth's public role during her childhood echoed the emotional stresses which her early years brought. It was a valuable preparation for her future life; she acquired resilience and a strong sense of self-preservation, she learned to 'seem tame' despite her fiercely independent spirit. She saw the mortal danger of carnal lusts in women: a policy of *noli me tangere* would have saved the life of Catherine Howard. She saw how her royal father, for whom she was taught utter veneration and admiration, was the embodiment of power and manhood, wielder of fate for the women who married him, and thus she acquired abnormal experience of the impotence and disposability of married women.

The observant, quick-witted, receptive child Elizabeth was eight when her mother's distant death was grimly re-enacted in the beheading of her girlish cousin and stepmother, Catherine Howard. Twenty years later the man who was almost successful in the pursuit of the Queen, Robert Dudley, told the French ambassador: 'I have known her since she was eight years old, and from that time forth she has always said "I will never marry".'

2

'THE MATTER OF THE ADMIRAL'

The death of Henry VIII in January 1547 effectively marked the end of Elizabeth's turbulent childhood. She was thirteen years old, gracefully pretty, with a pale skin, red-golden hair and long delicate fingers; the portrait painted in her fourteenth year reveals early maturity, in the shadowy curves beneath her stiff brocade bodice, and in her air of tight, unyouthful guardedness. Attractive, accomplished, confirmed as third in line to the throne by Henry's will, she was a uniquely desirable match for any man of ambition who 'list to hunt'.

The upheavals of Henry's marital career had not produced the longed-for strong succession. The only Prince, Jane Seymour's son Edward, was a pallid child of nine – a frail pin on which to hang a great nation's future. Mary, second in line, was an ageing maiden of thirty, kind-hearted, but dedicated to the restoration of Catholicism in England and deeply attached to her mother's country, Spain. Should Edward die without issue, and Mary succeed, there was every likelihood that supporters of the English Church would revolt in favour of Elizabeth, and the tangled questions of the Tudor daughters' legitimacy and the relative validity of their claims would provide meat in plenty for the monster of rebellion to feed on. It was therefore of immeasurable importance to the security of the nation that Edward should be well protected and guided until he was of sufficient stature to govern as his royal father had.

As the King's life ebbed, factions were forming at court; hopes glowed and flickered like distant torches as men laid plans and whispered of possibilities. 'Remember what you promised me in the gallery at Westminster before the breath was out of the body of the King that dead is,' Henry's influential Chief Secretary Paget later wrote to Edward Seymour, the boy King's senior uncle. 'Remember what you promised immediately after, devising with me concerning the place which you now occupy.' The place which Seymour intended to occupy was that of supreme power. In his will Henry VIII specifically avoided appointing any one man to the dangerously lofty position of Lord Protector of England; instead he delegated sixteen equal Councillors including Seymour and Paget to share the authority of government. But Seymour made his own arrangements, with discreet efficiency, and in the very first meeting of the new Privy Council, held at the Tower on 31 January 1547, the members of that body, after swearing to carry out 'every part and article' of Henry VIII's will, 'to the uttermost of our powers, wits and cunnings', smoothly proceeded to elect Edward Seymour Protector of all the Realms and Dominions of the King's Majesty. He was created Duke of Somerset, and his younger brother Thomas, who had previously been Admiral of the Fleet, became Lord Seymour of Sudeley, Lord High Admiral of England. Within a short time the Protector was using the royal 'We', and addressing the King of France as 'Brother'. Thomas Seymour formed illustrious connections by other means. In secret he married the King's widow, Catherine Parr; and then he became a clandestine suitor to Elizabeth.

The Seymour brothers had climbed from relatively undistinguished origins. They were the eldest and youngest surviving sons of a Wiltshire knight, Sir John Seymour of Wolf Hall. Edward, the heir, did well at court during the 1520s, and became Esquire of the Body to Henry VIII, who evidently liked him, and gambled with him heavily on several occasions, but Thomas merely entered the service of the ambassador to France and received occasional payments for carrying despatches. The brothers' fortunes changed abruptly, however, in 1536, when their sister Jane Seymour, twenty-six years old and 'of no great beauty', captivated Henry VIII as he turned, wearied, from the neurotic and flighty Anne Boleyn. The worldly Chapuys expressed cynical doubts about Jane Seymour's virginity, but her pose of unassailable virtue seems to have been her chief attraction for the King, and the licence for their marriage was taken out on the very day of Anne's execution. Edward Seymour was almost immediately ennobled, and it was as Viscount Beauchamp that he carried the little Lady Elizabeth at the triumphant christening of his nephew Prince Edward in the following year. Three days after the ceremony Edward Seymour became the Earl of Hertford, and Thomas Seymour was knighted. As uncles to England's 'chiefest jewel', the heir to the throne, they had acquired considerable status.

In character the brothers were very different. As Duke of Somerset, Edward Seymour was described as 'a dry, sour, opinionated man', and said to be unpopular. He was clever and high-principled, an able military commander, but he was intolerant of his fellows. Shrewd Paget descriptively reproved him for his 'angry and snappish' behaviour in council meetings, and told him that his sharpness towards those who disagreed with his views had actually reduced one lord to tears. Thomas Seymour, in contrast, had boundless charm. Jovial, boisterous, informal in his manners, he was the embodiment of manly good-fellowship; but, at first unrecognized by Catherine Parr and the girl Elizabeth, beneath his attractive exterior lay selfish ambition.

Since his elevation as brother-in-law to Henry VIII, Thomas had had a colourful career. In 1538, when he was about thirty, there had been a plan to marry him to the powerful Duke of Norfolk's only daughter, the widow of Henry's beloved illegitimate son the Duke of Richmond. It was a gratifying acknowledgement of the Seymour family's new status. Norfolk pronounced that Thomas's 'commendable merits' and advancement by the King outweighed his lack of 'high blood or degree', and Henry remarked with bawdy good humour that in marrying his daughter to Thomas, Norfolk would 'couple her with one of such lust and youth as should be able to please her well at all points'. But despite Thomas's evident sexual prowess and valuable qualities, the plan came to nothing, and within three months of the failed courtship he had begun to serve his King on responsible diplomatic missions abroad. From Vienna in 1542 he sent vigorous reports on the progress of King Ferdinand's war against the Turks, spiced with such exotic information as: 'The King hath had, as they say, 6,000 light horse this two months near unto the town of Buda, who hath sent hither, as yesternight, for a present, a wagonload of Turks' heads, and one, in the same wagon, alive.' In the spring of 1543 he was appointed joint ambassador to Flanders, where he had a special commission to find a first-class gunfounder who would supply the English with brass ordnance for their forthcoming campaign against the French, and in that summer he was honoured with the post of marshal of the English forces, second-in-command under Sir John Wallop. In that capacity he led a detachment against the castle of Rinquecen, took and destroyed it, and for good measure razed another castle, Arbrittayne, admiringly described as 'one of the strongest piles within Boulogne'. Further honours and rewards followed, and then, in the autumn of 1544, he was appointed Admiral of the Fleet, under the Lord High Admiral, John Dudley, Viscount Lisle. While Elizabeth was busy in the schoolroom, studying with her new tutor William Grindall, or working on her New Year's Gift for her stepmother Catherine Parr, Thomas Seymour was on board the 1500-ton flagship *The Great Harry*, eagerly waiting in mid-Channel for the chance to attack the French fleet. For the rest of her life Elizabeth was to be attracted to men of such hearty masculinity and experience.

As long as Henry VIII lived, Thomas's ambition was kept within bounds, and served to spur him to energetic service of the crown. But the King's death and his own brother's easy assumption of power seemed to open up a horizon gleaming with possibilities for a man of his bravado. He had previously experienced great benefits from his late sister's royal marriage; now he intended to gain more from his own.

The thirteen-year-old Elizabeth, officially in mourning for her father, was unaware that Seymour swiftly made a bid for her, and received a firm refusal from Protector Somerset and the Council. She and her household had gone to live with Catherine Parr outside London, in the pretty dower house of Chelsea, bounded by the river Thames and open fields. In that relaxed, affectionate setting, a stealthy love-affair began to develop; someone came riding to the manor under cover of darkness, and was secretly let in through the garden-gate by

Catherine, brimming with love and happiness. 'I pray you let me have knowledge over night at what hour you will come, that your porteress may wait at the gate to the fields for you,' she wrote tenderly, and reminded her lover that he 'must take some pain to come without suspect'. It was only a matter of weeks since the death of her husband the King, an indecorously short time in which to have pledged herself to another man, but that man was Thomas Seymour, and she found him irresistible.

It seemed natural to Catherine that Thomas should have come to woo her; he had been her suitor four years earlier, in 1543, before Henry VIII intervened with his own peremptory proposal, and now, as the Protector's brother and the King's widow, it was God's will that they should marry – 'God is a marvellous man,' she wrote joyously. Thomas sent her loving, confident letters from St James's, grumbling that the weeks when he was not with her seemed far longer than they had 'under the plummet at Chelsea', and addressing his betrothed as 'Your Highness' so frequently as to betray a tinge of gloating. Catherine, who retained the title of 'Catherine the Queen' even after her remarriage, was an excellent match, of royal status, rich, and lovable, and as her husband, Thomas would probably have easier access to her stepson King Edward, around whom he was already forming vague plans. He bribed one of the King's Gentlemen, John Fowler, to ask the nine-year-old King whom he, Thomas, should marry; Fowler reported that when he put the question to young Edward, 'His Highness said, "My Lady Anne of Cleves," and so, pausing a while, said after, "Nay, nay, wot you what? I would he married my sister Mary, to turn her opinions."' Indulgent and jolly with children, a typical favourite uncle, Thomas skilfully obtained his royal nephew's support for his marriage with Catherine, and persuaded the boy to write an official letter counselling them to marry, several weeks after the hasty secret ceremony had actually taken place.

'The Lord Seymour married the Queen, whose name was Catherine, with which marriage the Lord Protector was much offended,' Edward noted in his diary for the month of May. The Lord Protector was offended at his brother's subterfuge, and shocked at the precipitancy of his marriage, which came so soon after the death of Henry VIII that if Catherine immediately became pregnant there might be doubts about the paternity of the child. The Protector's wife, the haughty Duchess of Somerset, was infuriated that the wife of her husband's younger brother would take precedence over herself, and a thoroughly unfraternal atmosphere prevailed. The Protector administered Catherine's lands entirely against her wishes, and tried to withhold the jewels which Henry VIII had given her, even down to her wedding-ring. 'My Lord your brother hath this afternoon a little made me warm,' Catherine wrote to her husband on one occasion. 'It was fortunate we were so far distant, for I suppose else I should have bitten him.' She added with spirit that any man with such a wife as the Protector's ought 'continually to pray for a short dispatch of that Hell'. It was well known that the Duchess, in turn, bore Thomas a deep grudge 'for the Queen's cause'.

Despite their friction with the Protector and his wife, Thomas and Catherine were a delightfully happy couple. Catherine's kind, sensible nature and the Admiral's boisterous ways gave their household a sunny atmosphere; living with them at the dower houses of Chelsea and Hanworth, or at Thomas's London residence, Seymour Place, Elizabeth observed, probably for the first time in her life, a tender, mature love-relationship between a man and a woman of her own rank. When briefly separated from Thomas during her pregnancy in the following year, Catherine sent him news of their unborn baby with touching familiarity: 'Mary Odell being abed with me had laid her hand upon my belly to feel it stir. It hath stirred these three days every morning and evening, so that I trust when you come it shall make you some pastime.' The natural undercurrent of physical enjoyment in evidence during the first weeks of their marriage was made the more overt by Thomas's splendidly virile personality and uninhibited manners. With his hearty oaths – 'By God's most precious soul!' was his favourite – and the aura of sexual vigour upon which Henry VIII had knowingly commented, he must have appeared an awesome, exciting figure to Elizabeth, whose daily life had previously been bounded by her doting governess Katherine Ashley and the gentle tutor Grindall.

Thomas made much of his wife's stepdaughter. He took to bursting into Elizabeth's bedroom early in the morning, before she was ready, and sometimes when she was still in bed. If she were up, 'he would bid her good morrow, and ask how she did, and strike her upon the back or on the buttocks familiarly, and so go forth through his lodgings'. If he caught her still in bed, he would fling open the curtains, 'and bid her good morrow, and make as though he would come at her. And she would go further into the bed, so that he could not come at her'. At Hanworth the games continued. On two occasions Catherine joined Thomas, and together they tickled Elizabeth while she was in bed. Wriggling and laughing helplessly as they tickled her, in the fun which Thomas initiated, or being held by Catherine in the garden while Thomas, in mock anger, cut her black cloth dress to ribbons, was a kind of romping for which Elizabeth was a little too old, with overtones for which she was a little too young.

Katherine Ashley watched the Admiral's behaviour towards her charge with mixed feelings. She was impressed by him; just as he spent money in bribing young King Edward's close servant Fowler, so the Admiral spent time in charming Elizabeth's fond governess, and even before the death of Henry VIII Kat had rewarded him by remarking artlessly that she wished he might marry Elizabeth. But now that he was married to the Queen instead, Kat was perturbed by his familiarities with the thirteen-year-old girl. Once, disturbingly, he tried to kiss Elizabeth in bed, but Kat intervened and scolded him, telling him to 'go away, for shame'. Another time, at Chelsea, a suspicious little incident was reported to the governess; Elizabeth had heard someone fumbling with the lock, and knowing it was Thomas about to come in, jumped out of bed and ran to hide behind the bed curtains with her maids, while he waited determinedly for her to emerge. Worried, Kat met him in the gallery of the Chelsea house, and told him that these things were being talked about, and Elizabeth's reputation was in danger. Defiantly, 'the Lord Admiral swore, God's precious soul! he would tell my Lord Protector how it slandered him, and he would not leave it, for he meant no evil'. It was characteristic of Thomas to take it for granted that his brother would support him, and to persist in doing as he pleased.

Kat Ashley told the Queen of her anxiety; with her customary good sense, Catherine 'made small matter of it', and closed the subject by saying that she would accompany her husband in the romps in future. However, it was Elizabeth herself who eventually quelled them, by taking care to be up and dressed and working at her books by the time Thomas came in to greet her. 'At Seymour Place, when the Queen lay there,' the governess afterwards recalled, 'he did use a while to come up every morning in his night-gown, bare-legged in his slippers, where he found commonly the Lady Elizabeth up at her book; and then he would look in at the gallery door, and bid my Lady Elizabeth good morrow, and so go his way.' Kat remonstrated with the Admiral for coming bare-legged into the girl's bedroom, and on this occasion he was angry, but stopped doing so – an indication that Elizabeth's cooler reception of him was effective.

The girl was unsettled by the unaccustomed physical encounters with a man. If at first she was delighted with the attention paid to her by her stepmother's magnificent husband, and accepted his familiarities as friendly games, it cannot have been long before she became aware of the deeper element which so upset her governess, and, eventually, her stepmother. There was a curious incident at Hanworth, when Catherine Parr told Kat that the Admiral had looked through the gallery window and seen Elizabeth throw her arms around a man's neck. Kat taxed the girl with it, and Elizabeth 'denied it weeping, and bade her ask all her women. They all denied it'. On reflection, the governess knew it could not be true, because no man had been there, except Grindall the schoolmaster, and she finally came to the conclusion that the Queen was jealous of Thomas's interest in her stepdaughter, and had invented this report as a means of warning Kat to keep a close watch over the girl's doings. Catherine was acutely aware of the dangers of scandal, even though Thomas apparently was not.

The spreading ripples of disquiet in an otherwise happy household resulted rather from selfish irresponsibility in

Thomas's nature than from any better defined motive. His wife the dowager Queen, of whom he seemed deeply fond, was a healthy woman in her thirties, so there was no reason to expect that he would ever be free to marry Elizabeth, even had the Protector and Council withdrawn their fierce opposition to such a scheme. That a man newly married to a charming woman should deliberately have courted the death penalty by seducing a virgin of the blood royal also seems highly unlikely. The key to Thomas's behaviour lay in the streak of naïveté beneath his vigorous masculinity; his thought was for immediate benefits rather than the eventual results of a calculated course of action. He was happy with Catherine, but he enjoyed the teasing romps with Elizabeth, which transformed her from a grave, self-contained royal scholar into a giggling hoyden, and he saw no harm in indulging his inclinations and giving her an occasional surreptitious kiss, which he could easily pass off as play. That servants' gossip might endanger Elizabeth's reputation, or that it might be disturbing for her to be prematurely aroused by a man who stood for her in the role of stepfather, seemed less important to Thomas than his apparently harmless wish to gratify thus his strong attraction to the girl.

'The Admiral loved her but too well, and had done so a good while,' Kat Ashley afterwards confided to Thomas Parry, Elizabeth's cofferer, 'in so much that, one time the Queen, suspecting the often access of the Admiral to the Lady Elizabeth's Grace, came suddenly upon them, where they were all alone, he having her in his arms, wherefore the Queen fell out both with the Lord Admiral and with Her Grace also.' The Admiral's flirtation had gone too far; the laughter was hushed. Catherine was angry and unhappy. It was decided that Elizabeth and her servants must leave the Admiral's household, and after a painful interview with Catherine, during which the fourteen-year-old-girl stood almost mute while her stepmother gave her quiet words of advice and warning, Elizabeth, her governess, her cofferer and the rest of her servants set off for Cheshunt, soon after Whitsun, 1548.

Although I could not be plentiful in giving thanks for the manifold kindnesses received at Your Highness's hand at my departure, yet I am something to be borne withal, for truly I was replete with

sorrow to depart from Your Highness, especially leaving you un-
doubtful of health, and albeit I answered little I weighed it more
deeper when you said you would warn me of all evils that you
should hear of me, for if Your Grace had not a good opinion of me
you would not have offered friendship to me that way, that all men
judge the contrary, but what may I more say than thank God for
providing such friends to me.

So wrote Elizabeth to her stepmother. It was a forlorn letter, but
the style and the exquisite, even handwriting showed a control
far beyond her years. The girl who answered little but stood
weighing matters the 'more deeper' was learning, painfully, to
suppress her emotional responses.

   Catherine was pregnant and unwell at the time. During
Thomas's temporary absences she exchanged bantering letters
with him about their 'little knave' – they took it for granted
that their baby would be a boy – and Thomas teasingly
instructed his wife to 'keep him so lean and gaunt with your
walking and good diet that he may creep out of a mousehole'.
Elizabeth wrote, with a sad attempt at light-heartedness: 'If I
were at his birth, no doubt I would see him beaten for the
trouble he has put you to.' Kind and sensible as ever, Catherine
kept up an affectionate correspondence with her stepdaughter
after their parting, and encouraged Thomas to write to her as
well. 'He shall be diligent to give me knowledge from time to
time how his busy child doth,' Elizabeth wrote gratefully. At
the end of August 1548, the child was born; it was a girl. Eight
days later, Catherine died, raving with puerperal psychosis.
There was a pathetic little scene shortly before her death,
when, holding Thomas's hand, she cried deliriously: 'Those
that be about me careth not for me, but stand laughing at my
grief, and the more good I will to them, the less good they will
to me.' Puzzled, the Admiral answered: 'Why sweetheart, I
would you no hurt,' but Catherine drew him close and
whispered sinisterly: 'But my Lord, you have given me many
shrewd taunts.' With the anxious, blundering tenderness of a
strong man in a sickroom, Thomas lay down on the bed beside
her, to see 'if he could pacify her unquietness with gentle
communication', but she only became more anguished.

   For a few days after her death Thomas was dazed with

grief – 'so amazed, that I had little regard either to myself or to my doings', he wrote later. Temporarily he had no heart to carry on with any of his plans, and little Lady Jane Grey, whom he had taken into his household with the intention of marrying her to the young King, was bundled home to her bullying parents, the Marquess and Marchioness of Dorset.

A long, gossipy conversation took place soon after Catherine's death, between Thomas's servant Wightman and Sir Nicholas Throckmorton. Having 'debated the great loss my Lord had by reason of her departure', they went on to speculate about the Admiral's future. Throckmorton said piously that he hoped the loss of 'so notable a wife' would 'make him more humble in heart and stomach towards my Lord Protector's Grace', and added that 'it stood my Lord upon to alter his manners, for the world beginneth to talk very evil-favouredly of him, both for his slothfulness to serve, and for his greediness to get, noting him to be one of the most covetous men living'. Then, significantly, he remarked: 'My Lord Admiral is thought to be a very ambitious man of honour, and it may happen that, now the Queen is gone, he will be desirous for his advancement to match with one of the King's sisters.' Since it was laid down in Henry VIII's will that Mary and Elizabeth might only marry with the Council's consent, it would be treason for Thomas to seek Elizabeth without their permission, and that, as Wightman replied to Throckmorton, 'must needs be his utter ruin and destruction'.

Thomas's grief over Catherine's death did not last long; his defiant swagger soon returned to him. He had no intention of humbling himself to the Protector, or of sweetening his reputation, but on the contrary became more determined than ever to increase his power. On 17 September, within a fortnight of his wife's death, he began to negotiate with the Dorsets for the return of their daughter Lady Jane Grey to his care; the eleven-year-old girl was fourth in line to the throne and as such she was wrangled over like any other piece of valuable property. Thomas intended to marry her to the King – who, unlike his sisters, did not have to have the Council's consent to his marriage, only their advice – and his interest in the matter was heightened by the fact that the Protector hoped to marry her to his own son, the young Earl of Hertford. The Admiral won the child's parents over with what was delicately called 'certain covenants', namely £500 down and a promise of a further £1500, and to Lady Jane herself he acted the role of a kindly, jovial father, for which she was earnestly grateful.

The secret of Thomas Seymour's charm lay in his ability to adopt the tone which would be most pleasing to his hearer. To Elizabeth he was a teasing admirer, to Jane a gentle parent, and to Edward he was a jolly, boyish uncle. He gave his royal nephew continual gifts of money, and instituted a delightful conspiratorial system whereby Edward should leave notes for him under a carpet in the palace. The boy King drew the required contrast between his two uncles, and remarked mutinously : 'My uncle of Somerset deals very hardly with me, and keeps me so strictly that I cannot have money at my will. But my Lord Admiral both sends me money and gives me money.' Thomas stirred the boy's thoughts further, with such artless observations as : 'You must take upon yourself to rule, for you shall be able enough as well as other kings,' pointing out that then he would have plenty of money of his own. The servant Fowler, whom Thomas bribed heavily, 'was always praising of him', and often remarked to Edward : 'You must thank my Lord Admiral for kindness that he showed you, and for his money.' In January 1547, when Edward Seymour had become Protector, there had been some question of Thomas being made Governor of the King's person. 'It was never seen', Thomas afterwards said, ominously, 'that in the minority of a king, when there have been two brethren, that the one brother should have all the rule, and the other none.' It was said that he had researched into precedents in the history chronicles. Understandably, the Protector was thought to be 'in fear of his estate', and to hold his younger brother 'in a great jealousy'.

In the month following Catherine's death, Elizabeth and her large household had moved from Cheshunt, where they had been since Whitsun, to go to the old manor of Hatfield. Her closest female companion now was Kat Ashley, who was well-meaning and devoted, but a fool; dazzled by the Admiral she kept up a misguided campaign to further his suit with her charge. 'You shall see shortly', she said slyly, 'he that would fain have had you, before he married the Queen, will come now to woo you.' Despite Elizabeth's cool-headedness, it became obvious that Kat's talk was secretly pleasing to her. John Ashley, Kat's husband, showed sense; several times he cautioned his wife 'to take heed, for he did fear that the Lady Elizabeth did bear some affection to my Lord Admiral, she seemed to be well pleased therewith and sometimes she would blush when he were spoken of'. But the governess had an ally in the cofferer of the household, Thomas Parry, who repeated to Elizabeth interesting items from his conversations with the Admiral – how he wished she resided at Ashridge so that he could visit her on his way down to the country, how he had inquired about her household expenses and described his own, how he wished her lands could be exchanged for those of his late wife, and so forth. Half-won though the girl was, she would not be drawn beyond a certain limit; when Parry asked her outright whether, if the Council consented, she would marry the Admiral she perceptively demanded: 'Who bade him say so?' and to his reply that 'nobody made him say so, but that he gathered by his asking of these questions before', Elizabeth said snubbingly: 'It was but foolish gathering.'

Around Christmas it was being widely rumoured that Elizabeth was to marry the Admiral. Kat had told her charge of one such report, and Elizabeth 'smiled at it, and said it was but a London news'; but gossip, and the Duchess of Somerset's annoyance, cannot have been diminished by the fact that Thomas offered to lend his house and all his household belongings to Elizabeth and her servants while they were in London. When Parry told her of the Admiral's offer she seemed over-joyed, and Parry, remembering the rumours he had heard, and how Elizabeth looked happy when Thomas was spoken of, 'took occasion to ask her, whether, if the Council would like it, she would marry with him'. To that crucial question Elizabeth gave a reply that was characteristic of her cool, equivocating intelligence. 'When that comes to pass,' she said carefully, 'I shall do as God shall put my mind.'

It was a mind markedly superior to that of her shallow, showy suitor. Parry, unabashed by the girl's guarded reply, continued the conversation with the revelation that the

Admiral wished her to visit the hated Duchess of Somerset and gain her favour in the hope that she would influence her husband the Protector to permit Elizabeth's lands to be exchanged for others more useful to Thomas – 'to entertain Her Grace for your furtherance', he phrased it. Elizabeth was shocked. At first she would not believe that the strong, splendid Admiral wanted her to fawn before an enemy for personal profit. 'I dare say he did not so, nor would so,' she said scornfully. Parry assured her it was true, and she retorted: 'I will not do so, and so tell him.' She 'seemed to be angry, that she should be driven to make such suits', he later recalled, and she swore: 'In faith I will not come there, nor begin to flatter now.'

Hypocrisy was one of Thomas Seymour's failings; indiscretion was another. Like an excited child, he seemed unable to keep safely silent about his hopes and plans, but instead bragged of his intentions. In the autumn of 1548, riding to the Parliament House with Lord Russell, he was warned that rumours were flying that he intended to marry one of the King's sisters. Quickly, he denied it, but two or three days later he brought the subject up again with Russell, and said defiantly that it would be better for the King's sisters to marry Englishmen than foreigners: 'And why might not I, or another, made by the King their father, marry one of them'? The prudent old Lord Russell gave him a strong warning about the dangers of such an ambition, and then added dryly: 'I pray you, my Lord, what shall you have with any of them?' 'Three thousand a year,' Thomas answered promptly. 'My Lord, it is not so,' said Russell, 'no more than only ten thousand pounds in money, plate and goods, and no land,' and he went on to ask Thomas if he could afford to maintain a household fitting a wife of such rank. A vehement argument ensued, which Russell later reported; the Admiral 'answered, "They must have the three thousand pounds a year also." I answered, "By God, but they may not." He answered, "By God, none of you dare say nay to it." I answered, "By God, for my part I will say nay to it, for it is clean against the King's will." '

But neither oaths nor advice could cure Thomas of the ache of swollen ambition. While doing all that he could to disrupt his brother's rule, swearing that he would bring about 'the blackest Parliament that ever was in England', levying troops, winning over nobles and yeomen, and conspiring with the Vice-Treasurer of the Bristol Mint to raise money illegally, he maintained a blind unrealistic faith that his brother would, in the last resort, save him from the consequences of his dangerous play for power. The courtier George Blage made an attempt to reason with the Admiral. 'What if my Lord Protector, understanding your mind, commit you to ward?' he asked urgently, and received the airy reply: 'No, no, by God's precious soul, he will not commit me to ward. No, no, I warrant you.' 'But if he do,' Blage pressed: 'how will you come out?' 'Well, as for that,' shrugged Thomas, 'I care not, but who shall have me to prison?' 'Your brother,' said Blage. 'Which way?' said Thomas. 'Marry, well enough,' retorted Blage promptly, 'even send for you, and commit you, and I pray you, who shall prevent him?' 'If the Council send for me, I will go,' Thomas answered confidently. 'He will not be so hasty to send me to prison.' Blage was so disturbed by this exasperating exchange that he never spoke to the Admiral again.

Thomas Seymour's trust in the Protector's fraternal loyalty was indeed misplaced. On 17 January 1549, he was sent to the Tower of London, almost exactly two years after the death of Henry VIII had set spurs to his hopes. 'I thought before I came to this place that my Lord's Grace, with all the rest of the Council, had been my friends,' he said to his jailer, 'and that I had had as many friends as any man within the realm, but now I think they have forgotten me.' Four days later, on Monday, 21 January, Elizabeth's cofferer Parry and her governess Kat Ashley were also committed to the Tower, on account of 'the matter of the Admiral'. And thus Elizabeth, at the age of fifteen, was left almost friendless at Hatfield, to face alone the first great crisis of her life.

She had been let down badly by those who should have protected her interests, and so again she learned harshly of the need for self-reliance, and the danger of committing her destiny and herself into another's keeping. Her elders were in the Tower, and she, not long out of childhood, had only her own mature and subtle mind to aid her in the frightening situation which her first suitor had created.

Sir Robert Tyrwhitt was sent down to Hatfield to interrogate her. He required proof that the Admiral had, in direct contravention of the Council's wishes, conspired 'to have in marriage the Lady Elizabeth, one of His Majesty's sisters, and second inheritor after His Majesty to the crown'. Evidence of all kinds was accumulating around the Admiral, and at first Tyrwhitt believed his task would not be difficult. 'I have good hopes to make her cough out the whole,' he wrote with grim confidence to the Protector. The pale, aloof girl was 'marvellous abashed' when she learned that Parry and Kat were in the Tower, and she showed her youth by crying miserably for a long time, begging to know whether they had confessed anything or not. Tyrwhitt was encouraged when she sent for him and said she had certain things to tell him, but to his disappointment these turned out to be merely some details of a letter which she had sent the Admiral concerning her chaplain, to which she had added a postscript that she said referred to Durham Place. Such trivialities were not what he wanted, and he ominously reminded Elizabeth of 'the peril that might ensue, for she was but a subject'. He tried to lure her into trustful confession of all that had passed between her and Thomas Seymour by promising that 'all the evil and shame' should be ascribed to Parry and Kat Ashley, and that her own youth would cause the King, the Protector and the Council to treat her leniently, but Elizabeth would not be drawn. 'In no way she will not confess to any practice by Mistress Ashley or the Cofferer,' Tyrwhitt reported to the Protector, 'and yet I do see it in her face that she is guilty, and do perceive as yet she will abide more storms ere she will accuse Mistress Ashley.' He decided to change his tactics with this slippery and resilient little witness; instead of 'more storms' he tried 'gentle persuasion', which he thought brought more promising results. Yet still she would give him no real evidence, merely describing how Parry had asked her whether she 'would be content' to marry the Admiral or not, and resolutely including in her account the all-important clause, 'if the Council would consent'. Embarrassed at seeming to be outwitted by a young girl,

Tyrwhitt wrote earnestly to the Protector: 'I do assure Your Grace she hath a very good wit, and nothing is gotten of her save by great policy.'

Parry and Ashley could not match their young mistress's skilful elusiveness. In the Tower Parry broke down first; he told of the long confiding talk he had had with Kate Ashley, on Twelfth Night, during which the governess had foolishly let him know a good deal too much about the 'familiarity' between the Admiral and Elizabeth. He recalled:

But after that she had told me the tale of the finding Her Grace in his arms, she seemed to repent that she had gone so far with me as she did, and prayed me in every wise that I would not disclose these matters. And I said I would not. And again she prayed me not to open it, as ever she might do for me; for Her Grace should be dishonoured for ever, and I likewise undone. And I said I would not; and I said, I had rather be pulled with horses than I would.

Kat Ashley steadfastly confessed nothing, until she was brought face to face with Parry, and then, when he reaffirmed his statements in her presence, she proved it all by bursting out that he was a 'false wretch', and crying that he had promised that 'he never would confess it to death'. After that she could make no more denials, but revealed what she knew of the Admiral's intimate romping with her charge, of rumours, of titbits of information, of the Admiral's hopes of marriage with Elizabeth.

Triumphant, Tyrwhitt produced the statements for the girl to see, yet even in that daunting moment her courage and presence of mind did not waver. 'She was much abashed and half-breathless,' he reported, but she bought a few vital seconds in which to collect her thoughts by pretending to scrutinize the signatures for forgery – though, as Tyrwhitt commented cynically: 'She knew both Mistress Ashley's handwriting and the Cofferer's with half a glance.' She must have been scared and embarrassed to see set down as cold-blooded evidence the details of the Admiral's behaviour, his bare-legged visits to her chamber, the smacking and teasing and furtive flirting which had ended in her having to leave Catherine's happy household, but still she did not drop her guard; when she had read the confessions, and Tyrwhitt had told her of Parry's betrayal, her only comment was the simple, unassailable truth : 'That it was a great matter for him to promise such a promise, and to break it.'

Tyrwhitt found himself baffled. 'In no way she will confess that either Mistress Ashley or Parry willed her to any practice with my Lord Admiral, either by message or writing,' he complained. Her wilfulness was not to be tolerated; the Council decreed that she must have a new governess, in place of Kat Ashley, and they appointed Tyrwhitt's wife to the task. Elizabeth was furious, snubbed Lady Tyrwhitt, cried all night and sulked all the next day. She was determined to have Kat back – 'The love she yet beareth her is to be wondered at,' Tyrwhitt remarked. The strain had begun to tell; Tyrwhitt went on :

She beginneth now a little to droop, by reason she heareth that my Lord Admiral's households be dispersed. And my wife tells me now that she cannot hear him discommended but she is ready to make answer therein; and so she has not been accustomed to do, unless Mistress Ashley were touched, whereunto she was very ready to make answer vehemently.

Her loyalty and resistance were of no use to Thomas Seymour; on 23 February he was charged with high treason. Among the thirty-three articles produced was the accusation :

It is objected and laid to your charge that you have, not only before you married the Queen, attempted and gone about to marry the King's sister, the Lady Elizabeth, second inheritor in remainder to the Crown, but also being then prevented by the Lord Protector and others of the Council, since that time both in the life of the Queen continued your old labour and love, and after her death by secret and crafty means practised to achieve your said purpose of marrying the said Lady Elizabeth; to the danger of the King's Majesty's person and peril of the state of the realm.

He was condemned to death. The Protector, 'for natural pity's sake', was not present when the Bill of Attainder was put through Parliament, but he headed the Council meeting of 17 March when the date of his brother's execution was to be decided upon. The eleven-year-old King, for whom Thomas had been an endless source of play and presents, gave willing consent to the beheading of 'the Lord Admiral mine Uncle', and so on Wednesday, 20 March, 'betwixt the hours of nine and twelve in the morning', Elizabeth's first love and first suitor was led out of prison to die on Tower Hill.

Londoners were familiar with the scaffold scene – the dull, crunching thump; the head bouncing down, comic and disgusting, from the raw neck; blood drenching the crisp straw and darkening into pools as the crowds, their interest fading, began to move away. 'He died very dangerously, irksomely, horribly,' thundered Latimer from the palace pulpit. 'I have a little neck,' Elizabeth's mother had giggled, putting her elegant fingers around it. 'That woman had never such delight in her incontinency as she shall have torment in her death,' Henry VIII had sworn of Catherine Howard. Love and marriage, love and shame, love and death: the conclusion was inescapable.

Physically Elizabeth was intact, but emotionally she was rifled and despoiled. In addition to all the private pain she had to bear, she was faced with the threat of public ignominy; Tyrwhitt had lost no time in informing her that there were sordid rumours about her, and these she was determined to halt. 'There goeth rumours abroad which be greatly both against my honour and honesty', she wrote to the Protector, 'which be these: that I am in the Tower, and with child by my Lord Admiral. My Lord, these are shameful slanders.' It was masterly diplomacy, to place the damaging allegation after the obviously false and easily disproven assumption. She asked to be allowed to come to court, saying proudly that she wished to visit the King, and, incidentally, to show the world she was not pregnant. Her request was refused, and she became more anxious than ever to rout out public belief in her 'lewd demeanour', pressing the Protector to send out a proclamation declaring the tales to be lies and forbidding the people to repeat them. In her alert, capable mind Elizabeth was conscious of the possibilities which the future might hold, and, unlike her half-sister Mary, she was acutely aware that public opinion was a force which might play a part in shaping that future. Prurient eyes would be peering at Anne Boleyn's daughter as she grew to womanhood; if she were to win and hold the love of the English people, Elizabeth knew she must keep her reputation spotless. That was to be her first concern as the Seymour affair faded into the past. Even at fifteen years old, beset with intense personal difficulties, she was deeply concerned with her public image, and anxious not to gain 'the ill-will of the people, which thing I would be loath to have', as she informed the Protector, with pathetic dignity.

Her first personal encounter with love and courtship had ended in tragedy, like the marriages of her mother and step-mothers, and only her own quick, clear wits had saved her from disgrace. For the rest of her life Elizabeth would carry with her the memory of her first suitor; she would always be attracted to vigorous, ambitious, hardy men such as the Admiral had been. But she would never dare to entrust herself wholly into any man's keeping. *Noli me tangere* would be her safeguard against the tragedies of love and marriage.

3

'THE QUESTION OF
THE DAY'

'Youth must have some dalliance', Henry VIII had written, early
in the century, in the most joyous of his songs, but Elizabeth's
shadowy youth was not a time for dalliance. In the nine years
which followed her first tentative love-affair her constant concern was not to give herself but to guard herself, against threats
to her status, her independence, and her life. She had learned to
fear physical capture, and the disastrous political marriages
which her cousin Lady Jane Grey and her sister Mary were to
make would deepen the scars of her early impressions. She was
a political prize, and as such she was courted, but those who
were to pursue her in her sister's reign, on behalf of a dissolute
English nobleman and a warlike foreign prince, would be
setting nets to catch the wind.

Elizabeth had been profoundly shaken by Thomas Seymour's
emotional and political assault. Under the strain of the affair
and its aftermath her health gave way, and at the country
palace of Hatfield, for weeks and months after her suitor's
death, she suffered from torturing headaches; she was troubled
with catarrh, and often she felt too weak even to write to her
brother the King. 'Whilst I often attempted to write to Your
Majesty, some ill health of body, especially headache, recalled
me from the attempt,' she apologized. Protector Somerset put
aside his sarcastic rebukes and treated her gently, showing that
she was exonerated from blame in his brother's treason by
sending doctors to her, and writing what she gratefully
referred to as 'comfortable letters'. But the pallor, breathless-

ness and fainting persisted, and as she grew older there were constant references to swellings in her face and body. The illness, which almost certainly developed into the serious kidney ailment known as nephritis, was to recur throughout her youth in times of stress.

'She was first sick about midsummer,' Kat Ashley had recalled during the investigation of the Admiral's treason; perhaps it was 'about midsummer', 1548, that puberty had begun for the younger daughter of Henry VIII. She had been 'sick' again immediately after the death in childbed of Catherine Parr, an event which cannot have heightened her desire for marriage and motherhood, and which Kat Ashley tactlessly enlarged upon in a morbid remark which so haunted Elizabeth that she quoted it later, in the sparse confession which Tyrwhitt elicited from her : 'She said she would not wish that I should have the Admiral, because she that he had before did so miscarry.' Relentlessly, the association of the sexual relationship with fear and danger seemed to meet Elizabeth at every turn.

As though to combat the stings of tears and scandal and the ache of illness, she applied herself, when well enough, to long hours of study, finding refuge in books, toiling to build herself a reputation for self-discipline and scholarship that should supplant the old rumours. It was still only twelve years since the scandal and death of Anne Boleyn, and in palace galleries and crowded ale-houses the same colourful comparisons must have been drawn and the same interesting forecasts made for the daughter as for the mother. The Duchess of Somerset had been scandalized to hear that Elizabeth had gone down the Thames by night in a barge, and there were 'other light parts', equally shocking, for which she scolded Kat Ashley. An old country tale was revived, about a midwife who was mysteriously called one night to attend a very young lady with red-golden hair as she gave birth to an unwanted child. The Lord Protector's proclamations could not quench every spark of hot talk, but the fifteen-year-old girl who had been made the subject of such gossip was painfully determined that her own virtuous conduct should give it the lie.

Deliberately rejecting finery, Elizabeth adopted a simple,

virginal style of dress, so that eminent Protestant scholars such
as her own tutor, Roger Ascham, praised her for her admirably
restrained taste in clothes as well as for her intellectual
achievements. Ascham, to whom the lonely Princess clung with
unreasonable dependence after leaving Catherine Parr's household, wrote enthusiastically of his royal pupil: 'Numberless
honourable ladies of the present time surpass the daughters of
Sir Thomas More in every kind of learning, but among them all
my Lady Elizabeth shines like a star, excelling them more for
the splendours of her virtues than for the glory of her royal
birth.' As the pale, quietly dressed girl worked at Greek and
Latin with her tutor in the country, the stains of the Seymour
affair faded; gradually, as she intended it should, the name of
the Lady Elizabeth came to be associated less with the old
scandal than with the New Learning.

In this sober, studious existence she found tranquillity, but it
was a way of life in which the sister of the King of England
could not continue indefinitely. Thomas Seymour's matrimonial manoeuvres had provided bitter proof of her desirability as a wife; she was young, attractive, and second in line to
the throne of England, and others would surely seek her as he
had done. 'He was an ambitious man; I would there were no
more in England,' Latimer had thundered from the pulpit, but it
was a vain hope. While the English succession lay with a
delicate boy and a series of marriageable women, there would
always be bold, unscrupulous men such as the Admiral who
would try to turn the political situation to their own advantage, and their plans would have to take into account the
slender person of the Lady Elizabeth.

It was John Dudley, Earl of Warwick, who came to dominate
English politics in Edward's reign, succeeding where Thomas
Seymour had failed. Dudley, who acquired the title of Duke of
Northumberland in 1551, was as able as he was treacherous; he
ousted Protector Somerset, sending him to the block in 1552,
and he became, in all but name, governor of the boy King and
the realm, with hopes of becoming something greater still.
Those hopes depended, even more than Thomas Seymour's had,
upon his gaining control, through marriage, of a female heir to
the throne.

The rightful heir after Edward was the Lady Mary, but she was of no use for Northumberland's purposes. Fading into her mid-thirties, she was the representative of the officially discarded Catholic faith, chief champion of the smashed saints and gutted monasteries, still defiantly celebrating the forbidden Mass, her short-sighted eyes peering towards her mother's beloved Spain. If she were to inherit the English crown Northumberland's unofficial reign would come to an abrupt end. But her Protestant half-sister the Lady Elizabeth was young and vulnerable enough to be a potential candidate for the new Duke's plans. Curious rumours came to the ears of Scheyfve, the Imperial ambassador; in November 1550 he reported to the Emperor that Dudley was 'about to cast off his wife and marry my Lady Elizabeth, daughter of the late King, with whom he is said to have had several secret and intimate personal communications, and by these means he will aspire to the crown'. The same sinister talk was heard again in the spring of 1553, when the young King was very ill and it was becoming obvious that his life and Northumberland's supremacy would soon be at an end; Scheyfve was informed that the Duke intended to ensure his future power either by marrying Elizabeth to his heir or by obtaining her for himself. Though the report was inaccurate it revealed the nature of Northumberland's intentions, and it showed how Elizabeth might again be made the victim of an ambitious man's political schemes through marriage. However, something in the 'secret and intimate personal communications' which the Duke was said to have had with the Lady Elizabeth must have convinced him that he had nothing to gain from presenting himself or one of his sons as an all-powerful suitor to this pale, resolute, red-haired girl. It was not likely that she would consent to mount the throne as the wife and puppet of an adventurer. So she, like her stubborn Catholic half-sister, was to be set aside, and the Duke's small shrewd eyes came to rest on the Suffolk family, named next in line to the throne by Henry VIII's will. It was the 'very small and short' fifteen-year-old Lady Jane Grey through whom he intended to rule, and marriage was the means to that end. So Lady Jane became the wife of his youngest son, Guildford Dudley.

Whispers of poison seemed to linger round the Dudley family like dirty smoke. The Duke's brood of sons, loyal and disciplined as a wolf-pack, would follow their father in foul dealing or in fair, and it was murmured that the young King had sickened with mysterious rapidity since the Duke's most promising son, Lord Robert Dudley, had been appointed Royal Carver and Gentleman of the Privy Chamber. Dark, handsome Robert, who in later years was to become the dearest and most intimate of all Elizabeth's suitors, would never lose his reputation as an expert poisoner. The death of the boy King was, in fact, almost certainly due to natural causes rather than to Northumberland's orders, but in the light of the events that followed the Duke might justifiably have been suspected of almost any crime. Though Robert Dudley would rise to a position of singular greatness and honour in Elizabeth's reign, he would never be able to rid himself entirely of the shadow of his father's treason.

Little Lady Jane Grey was proclaimed Queen, and Mary and Elizabeth found themselves deprived of their rights and in imminent danger of their lives. In the crisis Elizabeth's health gave way again. It was a timely bout of illness, since it obliged her to stay quietly at Hatfield, uncommitted to either party, but it was almost certainly genuine, for in all such times of stress her sickness returned, sometimes with alarming gravity. Mary, as the immediate heir, was in the greatest danger, but she managed to evade the armed force sent to bring her into captivity, and fled to a stout castle in Suffolk. There the English rallied to her cause. They did not want a spurious Queen Jane and King Guildford, manipulated by the traitor Northumberland, they wanted King Henry's own for their ruler. For a few tumultuous days in that summer of 1553 the hideous spectre of civil war hovered; then it faded, as the support for Mary grew overwhelming. Within a fortnight Dudley's attempt was over. As though by a miracle, the Lady Mary had won her throne against all odds, without foreign intervention, without the spilling of her subjects' blood, while a wave of popularity and loyalty surged around her small, stiff, valiant figure.

For Elizabeth, waiting tensely at Hatfield, the news of Mary's remarkable victory brought confirmation of her own profound

belief in the importance of keeping the goodwill of the people.
All her life Elizabeth would take pains to avoid gaining 'the ill-
will of the people', as she had written, 'which thing I would be
loath to have', but Mary lacked her sister's perceptive wisdom
in this as in so many matters. The people had brought Queen
Mary to her throne, yet soon she would lose their precious love
and loyalty. It was her marriage, above all, that was to alienate
them. If Elizabeth had needed any further proof of the dangers
of royal marriages, she would have it in plenty in her sister's
reign.

The accession of the first Queen since the conquest was
greeted with triumphant rejoicing. 'I saw myself money
thrown out at windows for joy, and what with shouting and
crying of the people, and ringing of the bells, there could no
one hear almost what another said, besides banqueting and
singing in the streets for joy,' one eye-witness wrote. While
London was reeling with relief, the Lady Elizabeth left Hatfield
and made her way, 'well accompanied with gentlemen and
others, right strongly', to her town residence, Somerset Place,
and from there she rode to greet the new Queen.

The half-sisters' first meeting in their new roles as Queen and
heir apparent was very cordial. At Aldgate, Mary, dressed in
purple satin and velvet and gleaming with jewels, embraced the
soberly-dressed Elizabeth with a great show of affection, and
when the splendid procession entered London Elizabeth was in
the place of honour, directly behind the Queen. The princely
cavalcade wound slowly through the streets, accompanied by
cheers and music and halted at intervals by elaborate entertainments, until it reached the Tower, where Mary was received by
the Constable and officials. She passed through the main gate-
way to go to her state lodgings; near the great Norman keep a
little group of prisoners knelt on the grass. She raised them up,
kissed them, and said emotionally: 'These are my prisoners.'
Two of them were familiar figures from her past, her old friend
the proud Duchess of Somerset, whom she used fondly to call
'my good gossip Nan', and the leathery veteran Duke of
Norfolk, now nearly eighty. The Catholic Bishop Gardiner was
there too, imprisoned under Protector Somerset's Protestant
regime; and there was another, a young man, tall and graceful,

with the fair hair and handsome features of the Plantagenets. He was Edward Courtenay, great-grandson of Edward IV; with his combination of royal ancestry and personal attraction he seemed the ideal suitor to a queen – or a princess.

'Yesterday Courtenay, who was thrown into prison fifteen years ago, was released; and there is much talk here to the effect that he will be married to the Queen, as he is of the blood royal,' wrote the Imperial ambassador. It was taken for granted that a queen must marry. The events of the six years since the death of Henry VIII had given grim warning of the dangers of a weak succession; Mary must marry and secure England's future by producing heirs. She was not strong, she was approaching middle age and the menopause, the need for her marriage was urgent, and so the gabbling voice of rumour announced that the ideal candidate had been found already, in the handsome person of Edward Courtenay, 'the last sprig of the White Rose'.

'There is in him a civility which must be deemed natural rather than acquired by the habit of society; and his bodily graces are in proportion to those of his mind,' the Imperial ambassador wrote, in his lengthy report on the young man. Courtenay's youth had been even more constrained and overcast than Elizabeth's, for he had been imprisoned in the Tower since he was a child of twelve, after his father the Marquis of Exeter, a potential claimant to the throne, had been executed for treason by Henry VIII. Courtenay had grown up behind dark walls, and like a plant deprived of sunlight he had grown tall and palely graceful but insubstantial, lacking proper roots, shifting lightly towards any proffered source of benefit, spindly and undependable by nature. His intrinsic weaknesses were not at first apparent, since they were overlaid with charm and accomplishments, and if he appeared somewhat immature for a man of twenty-seven, it was generally felt that he might be forgiven much after his long imprisonment. The Imperial ambassador, the great diplomat Simon Renard, informed the Emperor that Courtenay had 'applied himself to all virtuous and praiseworthy studies' during his years in the Tower, 'so he is very proficient, and is also familiar with various instruments of music'. Bishop Gardiner, who had become devoted to the bright young man while they were prisoners, became his principal champion after their release; the old prelate, reinstated as a member of the Privy Council, was determined to see his protégé married to the Queen, and it seemed at first that he might succeed. It would be a wise diplomatic match, in the tradition of the marriage of Mary's grandfather, Henry VII, to Courtenay's great-aunt, Elizabeth of York; allied to the Queen, Courtenay's Plantagenet blood would reinforce her Tudor muscle to create for themselves and their descendants an impregnable right to the throne. But independent of her, manipulated by skilful men at home or abroad, he might represent a new threat to Mary's security – above all if his claim were to become linked with that of the heir presumptive Elizabeth.

Through the autumn of 1553, as the cheers of welcome died away and the first mutters of discontent became audible, Elizabeth remained at court. Mary treated her with determined affection at first, holding her hand when they appeared together in public, but at heart the Queen was filled with suspicion of the dignified twenty-year-old girl who was the heretical daughter of Anne Boleyn – 'of whose good fame I might have heard', the Imperial ambassador recorded Mary as saying to him sarcastically. As 'contention for religion' spread like a stain across the already frayed fabric of English affairs, Elizabeth's policy of keeping her own colours pale but true became increasingly difficult. To embrace Catholicism, and secure Mary's favour, would be to forfeit her precious position as the shining hope of the numerous Englishmen who inclined towards the reformed religion. But to remain defiantly Protestant would be to declare herself an open threat to the Catholic Queen's security, inviting loss of her status as heir apparent, courting disposal by marriage, imprisonment, or even death.

The nets were spread in every direction. While the French ambassador courted Elizabeth's favour, hoping to use her as a divisive force in the interests of France, Renard was doing his utmost to set Mary against her, uttering repeated warnings about her intentions, seeing in her a dire threat to Mary and Catholicism and the interests of his Emperor. Beneath Elizabeth's caution and subtle quietness he glimpsed something powerful which disturbed him profoundly. 'She is a spirit full of enchantment,' he wrote resentfully.

Not surprisingly, Elizabeth was anxious to leave court for the seclusion of the country. It seemed that allegations against her must always involve talk of a marriage. Renard and his fellow Imperial ambassadors warned Mary:

Many persons are saying that if Courtenay were able to come to an understanding or arrange a marriage with the Lady Elizabeth, the result would be dangerous to Your Majesty as he already has a following, and it is said that Elizabeth's eyes are fixed on him and she also has partisans. The French ambassadors have feasted him in their lodgings.

Courtenay's moment of success was passing. Though Mary had restored him in blood, with the title of Earl of Devonshire, she treated him with nothing more than the indulgent tolerance of an aunt, endeavouring to protect him from his own folly by appointing a gentleman to accompany him everywhere, as a combined social tutor and guardian. However, it became increasingly obvious that his long captivity had left him with graver defects than the mere inability to ride a warhorse or joust like other young nobles. He gave himself exaggerated airs at court and showed off in the streets; he shook off his escort and headed enthusiastically for the stews, dishonouring his rank in the company of London's whores as though hectically determined to make up for his lost years in the Tower. Renard now described him in very disapproving terms, and he informed the Emperor that Courtenay had made himself 'odious and insufferable to the whole court'. Elizabeth especially was making a point of snubbing the young Earl in public. 'Courtenay is in disgrace with the Lady Elizabeth for having spoken otherwise than she had looked for about amourettes said to have passed between them,' Renard sneered, though instead of passing on the circumstantial explanation which gossip had supplied he might have guessed the truth – that Elizabeth, harassed and anxious, was trying to show the court and the world that there was no question of any alliance between Courtenay and herself. Nothing she could do, however, would douse Renard's crackling suspicions, and at the end of November he wrote that he was convinced that it would be best to send Elizabeth straight to the Tower.

She was relegated from her rightful position at court; none of the ladies dared be seen in her apartments, and though she spiritedly encouraged the young gentlemen to visit her instead, de Noailles thought she did so deliberately, 'in the hope of obtaining her dismissal so that she might go to her own house, where she lived formerly'. Early in December she was allowed to leave. The Lords Arundel and Paget gave her final admonishments not to meddle in plots with heretics or the French, warning her frankly of the consequences. Mary put on a show of affection and gave her a beautiful fur wrap, and at last Elizabeth was able to depart for her manor of Ashridge in Buckinghamshire, spied on, suspected, schemed over, but mercifully out of sight of her sister's peering eyes.

'In the beginning of November was the first notice among the people touching the marriage of the Queen to the King of Spain,' a contemporary chronicler wrote. The entry needed no amplification. Mary had turned to the Emperor as to a father, eager to lean on him for advice and support in all things, and in the great matter of her marriage above all; the Emperor's choice for her husband, gradually revealed and subtly urged by Renard, was his own beloved son, Philip of Spain. Mary's acceptance of that choice was the greatest error of her life.

One of Northumberland's most powerful arguments for debarring Mary from the throne had been that she 'might marry a foreigner and thus stir up trouble in the kingdom and introduce a foreign government'. The insular English had grown more suspicious than ever of foreigners in the decades since Henry VIII's divorce from Catherine of Aragon and rupture with Rome had cut them off from religious brotherhood with Europe. The gentleman of Kent who cried that 'the Spaniards were coming into the realm with harness and handguns, and would make us Englishmen worse than enemies, and viler; for this realm should be brought to such bondage by them as it never was before, but should be utterly conquered', voiced the fears of many loyal Englishmen. 'If we should be under their subjection they would, as slaves and villeins, despoil us of our goods and lands, ravish our wives before our faces and deflower our daughters in our presence' ran a desperate call to arms against the 'proud Spaniards or strangers'. But a half-Spanish Queen, who, as Renard put it, did not trust her people, knowing them to be variable, inconstant, and treacherous, was not likely to be influenced by her subjects' street-talk. Nor was she prepared to be dictated to by Parliament; when the greatest peers in England, the Councillors and Members of the Lower House delivered their earnest petition to her to marry, and to choose an English husband, she became so angry that she was obliged to sit down. The Speaker dwelt on the state of the succession, the strife that might arise if she were to die without issue, and the desirability of her leaving an heir of her own, and then began a passionate diatribe against the dreadful dangers of a foreign match. When Mary had regained control of her anger she adopted a benevolent tone, and assured them that though her own inclination was against marriage, she would conquer her feelings for the sake of the welfare of her kingdom. But unlike her keen-eyed half-sister, she lacked the vision to see in which direction the welfare of the kingdom lay.

If the alienation of her own people was one grave consequence of Mary's marriage, the implied rejection of France was another. To tie herself to the Empire was at best to relegate France to the role of secondary ally, at worst to involve the English and French in open hostility – whereas, as de Noailles compellingly argued, by marrying an Englishman she might have become the most fortunate princess in the world, committed to neither of the great rival houses of Europe, and therefore continually sought in friendship by both. The Empire and France were then at war, and though the marriage treaty might provide clauses to safeguard England from becoming involved in Imperial wars, King Henry II of France pointed out to Mary's ambassador, in a long and gloomy interview: 'If the Queen shall marry with him that is my chief enemy, and even during this wartime, although I know it is not my part to appoint her where, nor with whom, nor when she shall marry, yet it must needs be a grief unto me to consider what advantage mine enemies will think thereby to have upon me.' Englishmen at the French court found, gallingly, that they were being pitied 'that we shall now become subjects to Spain', and, even more irritatingly, that the French 'take it to be a great punishment that God hath sent upon us'.

Early in January 1554 the Spanish embassy arrived to conclude the marriage treaty. They were met at the Tower wharf with a mighty salute of guns and greeted by a glittering deputation, amongst which Courtenay, as Earl of Devonshire, was prominent, but their retinue had had a very different reception the day before; as they rode through the streets of London they had been pelted with snowballs by jeering boys. Mary's publicly expressed wish, that 'like humble subjects, for her sake', the people would receive Philip with 'all reverence, joy, honour' was in vain. What followed was open rebellion.

It was very much as de Noailles had forecast, a month before, when Elizabeth left court. He had written to Henry II:

This said Lady Elizabeth is very closely watched, for I can assure you, Sire, that greatly she desires to free herself from control; and from what I hear it only requires that my Lord Courtenay should marry her, that she should go with him to the counties of Devonshire and Cornwall. . . . they could then make a strong claim to the throne, and the Emperor and the Prince of Spain would find it difficult to suppress this rising.

His information was suspiciously accurate in that the rising did indeed begin in Devon, and its primary purpose was to put Elizabeth and Courtenay on the throne together. But though de Noailles was of course right in assuming that Elizabeth longed to be free from control, he misjudged her if he believed that she would willingly forfeit her freedom by marriage to a dissipated young man 'of such a nervous and timid disposition' as Courtenay, when the throne would rightfully be hers alone if Mary were ousted.

Courtenay was far too weak and volatile to conduct his own courtship of Elizabeth and the crown; ironically, it was upon Sir Thomas Wyatt, son of the poet who had loved Anne Boleyn, that the leadership of the armed wooing devolved. While Wyatt's men were boldly mustering in Kent, Courtenay was saying petulantly in London that 'he had been spoken to about a marriage with the Lady Elizabeth, but he would rather go back to the Tower than ally himself to her'. At Ashridge, Elizabeth was ill with anxiety. Though it was to her advantage to see Mary's marriage, and chance of producing heirs, prevented, she had warily avoided giving any direct support to the rebels' cause. But innocent as she was of active participation, she was at the centre of the storm; if the attempt were to fail, Renard would surely have his way at last, and see her imprisoned or executed. Mary wrote her a softly menacing letter, bidding her 'for the security of your person, which might chance be in some peril if any sudden tumult should arise where you now be', to travel to court at once, but Elizabeth, sick and frightened as she was, felt safer at a distance, and sent word that she was too ill to travel. She had her house fortified, and stayed where she was to await the outcome of the rebels' rough wedding plans.

Wyatt came near to success. So great was the general antagonism to Queen Mary's choice of a foreign consort that peaceable Englishmen flocked to take up arms against their sovereign. Forces sent to fight Wyatt chose instead to support him; under the stirring cry 'We are all Englishmen' they marched on London. 'Much noise and tumult was everywhere' as the fighting raged through the streets of the city. But the attempt to 'resist the coming-in of the Spanish King' ended in failure. In the evening of 7 February 1554, Wyatt and his chief supporters were taken to the Tower, where, as they entered, they were greeted with manhandling and taunts; Wyatt, 'holding his arms under his side, and looking grievously with a grim look upon the said lieutenant, said, "It is no mastery now." And so they passed on'.

The mastery was Mary's. 'It seems to me that she ought not to spare Courtenay and the Lady Elizabeth on this occasion,' Renard urged, 'as while they are alive there will always be plots to raise them to the throne, and they would be justly punished, as it is publicly known that they are guilty, and so worthy of death.' On 12 February 1554, Courtenay was committed again to the Tower from which he had so recently been released, and Elizabeth, now very ill indeed, was obliged to set out on the thirty-mile journey to London. The Emperor was informed: 'Wyatt cannot be executed until he has been confronted with the Lady Elizabeth, who is so unwell that she only travels two or three leagues a day, and has such a stricken conscience that she refuses meat or drink. It is taken for certain that she is with child.' It was as though all the austerity and caution of her years since the Seymour affair had been to no purpose. A week later Renard reported triumphantly that French plots had been uncovered involving Courtenay and Elizabeth – 'who, they say, has lived loosely like her mother, and is now with child'. The flirting, giggling, bleeding spectre of Anne Boleyn must have travelled with Elizabeth on the jolting journey from Buckinghamshire to London and the Tower.

'The Lady Elizabeth arrived yesterday, dressed all in white, and followed by a great company. She had her litter opened to show herself to the people, and her pale face kept a proud, haughty expression', Renard reported. Even at such a moment of despair, Elizabeth was intensely conscious of what the people should think of her; the white dress of purity, and the air of regal dignity, may have suggested haughtiness to Renard, but even he could not describe her appearance as being that of a pregnant wanton. In the desperate, stricken letter which she wrote, a month later, when Mary's deputation came to remove her from Whitehall to take her to the Tower, care for her reputation was an anguished theme, as she begged her sister to let her answer the charges before being imprisoned – 'that thus shamefully I may not be cried out on as now I shall be', being 'condemned in all men's sight before my dessert known'. Thomas Seymour pressed upon her memory as she begged Mary to see her, and the words spilled from her pen like unchecked tears: 'In late days I heard my Lord of Somerset say that if his brother had been suffered to speak with him he had never suffered but the persuasions were made to him so great that he was brought in belief that he could not live safely if the Admiral lived and that made him give his consent to his death. . . .' Her pleas were ignored, and on the following day, Palm Sunday, she was taken by barge down the Thames to the Tower of London. In pouring rain she was rowed through the dark arches below London Bridge, to where the water slapped against the slippery steps of the Privy Stairs, at which her mother had landed before her.

A group of Mary's leading Councillors came to interrogate Elizabeth, but she was as alert and elusive as she had been six years before, during the Seymour investigation, and more experienced in self-preservation; and the evidence against her was scanty. There was even a moment when she had the mastery – when the dark-bearded Earl of Arundel suddenly dropped to his knees, and exclaimed: 'Your Grace saith true, and certainly we are very sorry to have so troubled you with so vain matters!' Something of her 'spirit full of enchantment' must have beguiled him, and perhaps in her need for an ally Elizabeth gave him surreptitious encouragement, for when she came to the throne the middle-aged widower Arundel was strangely prompt to present himself as a suitor for her hand.

'The lawyers find no sufficient evidence to condemn her,' Renard reported, with bitter frustration. Bishop Gardiner, in his eagerness to protect Courtenay, served as a shield for Elizabeth too; he conveniently mislaid a valuable letter, intercepted from de Noailles's despatches, which was said to prove 'that Courtenay was to marry the Lady Elizabeth, while the Queen should lose her crown and her life'. Renard claimed it would have served to convict Courtenay and Elizabeth, but without firm evidence Mary steadfastly refused to condemn her half-sister, and before long, to Renard's annoyance, Elizabeth was granted the privilege of walking in the Tower garden.

From those walks, restricted, but precious to a prisoner, arose a little incident that was at once touching, pleasurable, and dangerous. A small boy, the son of one of the warders, took to bringing her bunches of flowers in which, it was said, messages were concealed. The Council heard of it, and forbade it; Renard at once took the improbable view that Courtenay was involved, and reported that he had chosen this means to 'present his commendations to Elizabeth'. Courtenay had neither the inclination nor the ingenuity to send his regards to Elizabeth by such a method, but there was another old acquaintance of hers then captive in the Tower who might well have done so – Robert Dudley.

His father Northumberland had gone grovelling to the scaffold soon after Mary's coronation, and the pitiful young husband and wife Guildford Dudley and Jane Grey had been executed just before Elizabeth was brought to the Tower, but Robert, though sentenced to the horrible death of hanging, drawing, and quartering, was still a prisoner in the Beauchamp Tower with his three remaining brothers. For active young men the Tower offered little occupation; they composed an elaborate poem and design based on their own names, and began to carve it on the wall of the octagonal chamber, but gave up, as though bored, before it was finished; it was quite likely that the resourceful Robert, who always enjoyed dabbling in intrigue, should have whiled away some time in devising a means of communicating with his attractive young fellow-prisoner the Lady Elizabeth. 'Youth must have some dalliance', and even the most closely-guarded inmates of the Tower might find opportunities for clandestine relationships, as was proved in Elizabeth's own reign, when Lady Catherine Grey, a dangerous claimant to the throne, managed to conceive two children by her husband while both were straitly confined in separate prisons within the Tower. To have been near one another and in furtive correspondence, at the darkest moment in both their lives, may have given Elizabeth Tudor and Robert Dudley a sense of affinity from which later developed their lifelong bond of loving intimacy. Perhaps Robert Dudley's resolute pursuit of the future Queen could truly be said to have begun in that walled and sunless spring of 1554.

'The question of the day is: what shall be done with her?' wrote Renard. 'Some people have said the best thing would be to marry her to a foreigner.' On 19 May she was taken from the Tower and sent into less grim confinement in the shabby palace of Woodstock, in Oxfordshire, where she could be strictly guarded until a solution to 'the question of the day' should be found. Disposal by marriage seemed to be the obvious solution – as Paget observed, if there was not enough proof for her to be put to death, the best alternative would be to send her out of the kingdom to be married to a foreigner. The foreigner whom he and many others proposed for her husband was the impoverished royal soldier Emmanuel Philibert, Duke of Savoy and Prince of Piedmont. Commander of the Emperor's army against France, he was the first cousin and friend of Mary's betrothed husband, Philip of Spain.

The Emperor had given his nephew Emmanuel Philibert responsible military posts from an early age, but as commander of the Imperial forces in 1554, the valiant twenty-six-year-old Prince was fighting on his own behalf, as well as that of the Emperor, since the French had occupied his lands and dispossessed him of his patrimony. A marriage with the sister and heir of the Queen of England offered him obvious material advantages in terms of status and possible financial and military support, and it was with considerable hope that he made the arrangements for his visit to London in January 1555. There were, however, certain obstacles lying half-submerged in the path of the stocky, athletic half-Habsburg Prince's pursuit of Elizabeth. She was under grave suspicion of heretical convictions. She was a bastard – her illegitimacy reaffirmed by Mary's Act of Parliament which rescinded Henry VIII's divorce from Catherine of Aragon, making the marriage with Anne Boleyn incontestably illegal. And she was, above all, passionately determined not to marry.

I have always been told that she will not hear of it, unless forced. To strengthen her in this opinion I have bribed one of her mother's near relations, who has promised to make her understand what wrong she would do to her self by marrying a disinherited prince, whom the Emperor merely wishes to use as a tool by which to deprive her of her hopes of the crown. But she is being so badly treated that I am very much afraid she may submit, to regain her liberty thereby.

So de Noailles informed the King of France in June, 1554. But his fears were unnecessary – nobody was more aware than Elizabeth herself of the damage which marriage with a dependant of the Emperor would do to her future independence and hopes. Such a marriage would be no 'liberty', but rather a more permanent and subjugating form of capture. In that dark year of 1554, when Lady Jane Grey's forced political marriage had ended at the scaffold, and Queen Mary's willing political betrothal had already brought rebellion, division, and hostility at home and abroad, Elizabeth could not have contemplated the prospect of diplomatic marriage with anything but anxious distrust.

'I am going not to a marriage feast but to a fight,' Philip of Spain had said before embarking to take possession of Mary and England, in July 1554, and it was as a soldier for Catholicism and his glorious Empire that he arrived to marry the earnest, plain little woman, eleven years older than he, whom he had previously respectfully regarded as an aunt. At twenty-seven Philip was already a widower with a ten-year-old son, Don Carlos, but the incompatibility between himself and his virgin bride must have been obvious, however much the Admiral, Lord William Howard, tried to ease the situation by making the customary bawdy innuendoes as the ill-matched pair sat together at their first meeting – Philip, fair-haired and grey-eyed, a slight but regal figure beside the thin, elderly Queen. Obedient to his Imperial father's instructions, he showed none of the notorious Spanish hauteur, but was all affability and conciliation; he drank beer, and smiled a great deal, and was charming to his wife, and kissed her ladies according to the English custom, to such an extent that his company of Spaniards were infuriated that their mighty Prince should so stoop before the insignificant and uncivilized English. They were already discontented at the terms of the marriage treaty, which had been carefully drawn up so as to exclude the Empire from gaining overt control of English affairs. Philip was to have no active power in England, and his connection with his wife's throne was to cease absolutely if she were to die childless. However, as King Henry II shrewdly pointed out: 'A husband may do much with his wife, and it shall be very hard for any wife to refuse her husband anything that he shall earnestly require of her.' His forebodings were particularly justifiable in Mary's case, for she came to love her fine young husband with the pathetic dependent devotion of a dutiful woman who has been repressed and unloved for twenty years.

Elizabeth met Mary's husband for the first time in the spring of 1555, when she was summoned from her captivity at Woodstock to the red-brick river palace of Hampton Court. The visit of Philip's cousin Emmanuel Philibert at the New Year had passed without major difficulty for Elizabeth; though he was lodged at her London residence, Somerset Place, she was not brought from confinement to meet him, and after three weeks of 'great cheer' in the court, during which he made himself very agreeable to Philip and Mary, he left for the wars again. But a still greater threat to Elizabeth's future was looming when she arrived in April – Mary believed herself to be pregnant, and the country was waiting for news that its three-quarters-Habsburg heir had been born. That event, if ever it took place, would finally debar Elizabeth from the throne; yet a trace of hope still remained, for there were curious undercurrents of uncertainty surrounding Mary's condition. De Noailles scoffed at the notion that the Queen was with child, and the fact that Elizabeth should have been summoned to court at that moment might have been a sign that Philip himself was not entirely confident about his wife's state of health. If Mary, elderly and frail, were to die, and the pregnancy prove to be illusory, it would be of the utmost importance to Philip to be on Good terms with the heir presumptive, the Lady Elizabeth.

In those tense weeks Elizabeth followed her usual policy of seeming tame. She was docile, cautious, charming. But her nimble mind must have followed the direction of Philip's thoughts; with the possibility of Mary's death in the offing, it was to her advantage as well as his to establish amiable diplomatic relations with one another, and it seemed that there was a taste of piquant, illicit pleasure for both in their task. 'At the time of the Queen's pregnancy', the Venetian ambassador afterwards recalled, Elizabeth 'contrived so to ingratiate herself with all the Spaniards, and especially with the King, that ever since no one has favoured her more than he does'. With discreet emphasis the ambassador observed that there appeared to have been 'some particular design on the part of the King towards her'. In after years Elizabeth insisted that the hostile relationship between Philip of Spain and herself had begun with love, and it may have been true. Philip was prudent and discriminating and deeply religious, but he was amorous by nature, and he was weary of his clinging, elderly wife. Elizabeth had the youth, elegance and wit that her sister so markedly lacked; while the elder woman nursed her pathetic delusions of pregnancy, the younger was discreetly displaying her 'spirit full of enchantment' to win the favour of the Emperor's son.

By the summer Mary had to acknowledge, with grief and humiliation, that she was not with child, but Elizabeth's dealings with Philip bore fruit. He could not remain constantly with his wife in England, since he had the business of his ailing father's Empire to attend to in the vast territories of his inheritance, and on 29 August, to Mary's bitter sorrow, he entered his barge at Greenwich and was borne away down the river while she wept uncontrollably at a window. His parting instructions concerning Elizabeth were clear; she was to be treated gently and honourably.

Stiff courtesy and religious conformity tided her over the summer months, and in October she was permitted to retreat to Hatfield, where her life began to follow its old pattern once more. Kat Ashley and Thomas Parry were with her again, and Roger Ascham visited her at intervals. It was not a lively mode of existence for a quick, bright young woman who had just passed her twenty-second birthday, but it offered a refreshing semblance of independence after her long imprisonment and the difficult, unpredictable months at Mary's court, and she was vehemently determined not to relinquish it for any marriage, however glorious. There had been talk of betrothing her to Philip's son, the boy Don Carlos, but as the Venetian ambassador reported in the spring of 1556, Elizabeth was steadfast in her resolution that she would not marry, 'even were they to give her the King's son, or any other prince'.

That autumn the strutting, sulky youth Courtenay died suddenly, in Padua, at the age of twenty-nine, and thus the English 'utterly lost the hope of ever having a king of the blood royal, unless in a very remote degree'. Both Mary and Elizabeth must have been relieved that now there could be no more rebellions to hoist Courtenay and Elizabeth onto the throne as husband and wife; but within weeks the name of Elizabeth's other unwanted suitor, Emmanuel Philibert, was causing fresh contention between the Tudor sisters.

Philip had written to Mary and the Council with urgent instructions to bring about the match between Emmanuel Philibert and Elizabeth. The French had broken the short-lived peace created by the Treaty of Vaucelles, and Philip was in need of English support, both immediately and for the future.

By marrying Mary's heir to his own cousin and satellite the Duke of Savoy, he would tie England to the Empire with lifelong bonds, and, despite Mary's reluctance, he insisted that the knots should be fastened as soon as possible. Obedient to her husband's will, though the marriage was against her own wishes, Mary confronted her half-sister with the proposal. The vehemence and urgency with which the match was announced to Elizabeth were such that for once her subtle weapons of dissembling and equivocation were useless. Instead she burst into frantic tears.

By the end of the interview Mary was crying too, with unbearable anger, frustration, and disappointment. She had no desire at all to see Anne Boleyn's sly, hypocritical bastard make a fine marriage, and be confirmed as heir to the English throne, and she could hardly bear the thought of Elizabeth living with Emmanuel Philibert in Flanders at close quarters with the beloved Philip; but what Philip demanded she would not refuse, and Elizabeth's desperate obstinacy in the face of his express commands enraged her. Elizabeth sobbed, almost hysterically, that she did not want a husband; Mary, whose chief distress was the lack of hers, dismissed the distraught girl back to Hatfield, under guard.

The French war brought Philip back to his wife's side, after an absence of more than eighteen months, in March 1557. By the middle of June England had joined the war against France. By July Philip had gone again.

He had seen his sickly middle-aged wife for the last time; he may have realized that she would not live much longer, and he had to plan for a future in which Elizabeth would be Queen of England by gaining control over her while it was still possible. Since Elizabeth and Parliament were so resolved against the Emmanuel Philibert match, Philip tried to bring it about by the unofficial means of appealing to Mary's conscience, sending his confessor to her to paint a frightening picture of the political and religious chaos that would ensue if Elizabeth were to make a different choice of husband. But Mary herself now proved difficult to sway, for she was utterly averse to countenancing the match and thereby giving Elizabeth hope of the succession. Her resolution in the matter may have been strengthened by the fact that she was again nurturing secret, deluded hopes of pregnancy.

During the years of Elizabeth's youth almost no one seemed to take seriously her protestations that she had no wish to marry. Because her refusal to entertain thoughts of any of the suitors who presented themselves was politic, few people realized that it was also sincere. Thus Mary was surprised and pleased by Elizabeth's rejection of the heir to the Swedish throne, Prince Eric, in the spring of 1558. King Gustavus's ambassadors made a grave tactical error at the outset, for they did not address their suit through Queen Mary, as diplomatic and social etiquette demanded, but presented themselves straight to Elizabeth – thereby enabling her to suit both propriety and her own wishes by summarily dismissing them. Mary, perhaps surprised that Elizabeth should not have seized this opportunity to enter into a secret league with a rich and Protestant monarch, was gratified; she instructed Sir Thomas Pope, who was in charge of Elizabeth at Hatfield, to inform her half-sister 'how well the Queen's Majesty liked of her prudent and honourable answer', and to enquire further into her future intentions. Sir Thomas returned an illuminating report of Elizabeth's response. When he respectfully suggested to his young charge that 'few or none would believe but that her Grace could be right well contented to marry, so that there were some honourable marriage offered her', Elizabeth assured him: 'Upon my truth and fidelity, and as God be merciful unto me, I am not at this time minded otherwise than I have declared unto you; no, though I were offered the greatest prince in all Europe.' But even so, Sir Thomas remained mildly unconvinced, and he remarked knowingly that perhaps this decision was the result of maidenly modesty rather than 'any such certain determination'. To his questions about the Swedish proposal she answered with acid wit: 'I so well liked both the message and the messenger as I shall most humbly pray God upon my knees that from henceforth I never hear of one nor the other.' But that wry prayer was in vain. She was to hear a great deal more of Eric of Sweden's courtship.

During that year of 1558 the long sombre night of Mary's reign was drawing to a close, and daybreak for Elizabeth was at last approaching. Emotionally and politically, the marriage which Mary had insisted on making, in the face of so much opposition, had proved quite as disastrous as had been predicted. No heir had been born to compensate for the loss of the Queen's independent status, but even worse than sterility was the shaming farce of two false pregnancies. Disappointed in her hopes of a child, Mary had been deprived of her adored husband too for much of her married life, alone and yet not independent; neither maiden, wife nor widow, in effect, and without her consort by her side to support her through the surging discontent and rebellion which her marriage had encouraged. The English had become embroiled in the Empire's war, and lost Calais, their last possession in France, for their pains, while at home the human bonfires of Protestants, men and women, priests and peasants, sent the stench of the Inquisition drifting across the damp English air.

> When these with violence were burned to death,
> We wished for our Elizabeth,

proclaimed a fervent contemporary ballad. All comparison with Mary seemed to make Elizabeth shine the brighter. The smudge of possible illegitimacy faded beside the glorious truth that she was 'of no mingled blood of Spaniard or stranger, but born mere English here among us, and therefore most natural unto us', and the Protestant religion which she represented had acquired a new aura of desirable nationalism through the experience of Mary's brand of Catholicism. As Philip's ambassador wrote to him with ruthless frankness: 'They say it is through Your Majesty that the country is in such want, and Calais lost, and also that through your not coming to see the Queen she died of grief.'

Mary died just before dawn on 17 November 1558, and her half-sister stepped from the shadows to become Queen of England, once again the most desirable bride in Europe. Elizabeth was now twenty-five; her youth had given way to womanhood. But her time of dalliance was about to begin.

4

'A GREAT RESORT OF WOOERS'

From the moment of Elizabeth's succession to the throne of England, the hunt was up in earnest. On the afternoon of Mary's death the church-bells were pealing for Elizabeth, and by the evening Londoners were flocking into the streets to eat and drink and make merry in their traditional fashion, while blazing bonfires glowered like beacons near the trestle tables, keeping the chill November night at bay. Some echoes of their cheer, glimmers from those fires, may have drifted through the city to Durham Place, where the new Spanish ambassador, the haughty aristocratic Count de Feria, was in no mood for rejoicing. If England was not to slip from the Empire's grasp, after all Philip's sacrifices and compromises, infinite diplomatic pains and skill would be required, and there was no time to lose. 'It is very early yet to talk about marriage,' Feria wrote distractedly, 'but the confusion and instability of these people in all their affairs make it necessary for us to be the more alert.' No one, however, was quite as acutely alert as the royal prey they sought. Elizabeth had inherited a kingdom beset by difficulties, strained by religious controversy and the threat of foreign aggression, and the caution, the sense of wariness, and the ability to dissemble which she had developed to a fine art during the past ten years were still her most effective defence. 'The more I think over this business, the more certain I am that everything depends upon the husband that this woman may take,' Feria commented to Philip. For the time being, Elizabeth's throne depended upon her ability to stave off that choice, and avoid commitment to one so that she might keep all expectant.

The one great commitment which the new Queen embraced whole-heartedly was to her own people. When Feria tried to claim that she owed her crown to Philip she at once contradicted him; she owed it to her people, she said. All through her youth Elizabeth had known that popularity with the fickle, impetuous crowds was a crop worth cultivating. As a frightened fifteen-year-old she had striven to avoid gaining 'the ill-will of the people'; on her way to imprisonment in Mary's reign she had opened her litter and shown herself to them in her hour of disgrace, white-faced and proud; two years afterwards, when she left court abruptly after refusing to marry Emmanuel Philibert, the crowds who saw her pass were so fervent in their greetings that she had to send some of her retinue to restrain them, lest she should be accused of inciting them to rebellion. But now she was Queen she was free to play up to her subjects with a shameless enjoyment of the whole performance. As she made her grand procession from the state apartments in the Tower through the streets of London on 14 January 1559, the day before her coronation, she 'was received by the people with prayers, welcomings, cries, and tender words, and all signs which argue an earnest love of subjects towards their sovereign; and the Queen, by holding up her hands and glad countenance to such as stood afar off, and most tender language to those that stood nigh to Her Grace, showed herself no less thankful to receive the people's goodwill than they to offer it'. The enthusiastic crowds who jostled excitedly to gain a glimpse of Elizabeth as she passed were 'wonderfully transported with the loving answers and gestures of the Queen'. Richly regal though she was, she had inherited her father's talent for the common touch – calling out a witty reply to one, graciously accepting some humble gift, such as the branch of rosemary which a poor woman gave her in Fleet Street, from another – and though intuitive, the effect was brilliantly contrived to win her subjects' delighted devotion. Her reply to the Recorder of London, who presented her with an ornamented purse crammed with gold, rang out into the crisp snowy air with the shining promise: 'And persuade yourselves, that for the safety and quietness of you all, I will not spare if need be to spend my blood.' Feria did not exaggerate when he wrote disapprovingly to Philip : 'She is very much wedded to the people, and thinks as they do.'

It was his unenviable task to persuade her to think as Philip did. At first, despite his deep pessimism at the way English affairs were tending, he felt that 'with great negotiation and money' this giddy, wilful young woman might conceivably be cajoled or forced into favouring the Empire, and taking whatever husband Philip might think best for her. 'If she decides to marry out of the country, she will at once fix her eyes on Your Majesty,' he told Philip confidently. By the curious destiny which so often decreed that Elizabeth's weaknesses should serve her as well as her strengths, in the vulnerable first weeks of her reign Philip was obliged by circumstances to act as Elizabeth's protector, to ensure that her hold upon her shifting, expectant nation should not be weakened, for if she were to be dislodged from her throne he would be faced with the disastrous prospect of an absolute French takeover of England. When the news of Mary's death had reached France, Henry II had promptly made his intentions aggressively plain, by proclaiming his heir's young wife Mary Queen of Scots Queen of England and Ireland. The pretty Scottish Dauphine had a strong claim, as senior great-granddaughter of Henry VII; if Elizabeth were dispossessed, France would almost inevitably make good that claim by absorbing England and Ireland into the great territories which already included Scotland; and Philip was prepared to go to considerable lengths to prevent so valuable a prize from passing to his rival – a fact of which Elizabeth was quite well aware.

With Mary's death, and her own succession, a new characteristic became evident in Elizabeth. Alongside the familiar caution and dissembling which had brought her through the crises of her austere youth, there appeared a new element of zest, a half-suppressed merriment, as though the laughter and teasing which had been abruptly hushed in her early adolescence were now belatedly breaking out. Circumspect and adroit though she was in her marriage dealings, conscious as she was from the first that the question of whom she would marry was crucial to England's future, there were nevertheless times when she plainly revelled in the role she was so skilfully playing, and more than one ambassador, come with due reverence to treat of royal matrimony, began to feel, disconcertingly, that laughter was lurking somewhere behind the Queen of England's elegant pale countenance.

Feria became increasingly exasperated with her behaviour. When gratified by presents of jewels, or alerted by news of a truce between France and Spain, Elizabeth was charming to the point of coquetry in her behaviour to him, but he found it bafflingly difficult to make any real progress with her. 'The most discreet people fear she will marry for caprice,' he complained. When he broached the subject of religion, anxious to discover straight away what her religion was to be, she answered him gravely that she would certainly not forget God, who had been so good to her – 'Which', Feria remarked with some perplexity, 'appeared to me rather an equivocal reply.' She made a point of informing him, in the sweetest tones, that her sympathies were not with France, and yet he was only too conscious that the current of feeling at court was flowing strongly against himself and Spain. 'They are very glad to be free of Your Majesty, as though you had done them harm instead of good,' he told Philip frankly, and went on: 'I am so isolated from them that I am much embarrassed and puzzled to get the means of discovering what is going on, for truly they run away from me as if I were the devil.' In Mary's time he had had a suite of rooms inside the palace of Whitehall, but now he found himself deprived of this valuable access to the centre of affairs, and when he pressed for the apartments to be restored to him Elizabeth bashfully sent him the explanation that it would not be proper for him to sleep under the same roof as herself, as she was unmarried. 'In return for all my efforts to please I believe they would like to see me thrown into the river,' he wrote bitterly. The English were uncivilized, their ruler was a mere 'young lass, who, though sharp, is without prudence', the kingdom was 'entirely in the hands of young folks, heretics and traitors', and by the end of January 1559, when Elizabeth had been on her insecure throne for less than three months, the Spaniard vented his frustrations in the goaded comment: 'In Scotland I believe they are ill-treating the

English. I am sure they are not doing it so much as I could wish.'

While Feria was trying by every means in his power to convince Elizabeth and her Privy Council that it was essential for her to marry a foreigner, the English, equally anxious that her husband should be an Englishman, were tossing the names of possible suitors into the air like scraps of paper, 'so that nearly every day there is a new cry raised about a husband'. Now that Courtenay was dead it was not easy to judge whom the most eligible suitor to the new Queen might be. The Tudor tendency to produce daughters, coupled with the depletion of the ancient nobility, had helped to bring about a noticeable lack of young peers of old lineage and 'high blood or degree'. The only remaining Duke was twenty-two-year-old Norfolk, who had now succeeded his grandfather, and when Elizabeth came to the throne he was just about to marry for the second time. Since there was no candidate who obviously represented the ideal combination of situation, rank and age, the rumours fluttered freely about, while Elizabeth herself gave no definite indication of whom, if anyone, she favoured. The truth was that nothing could have served her interests better than the uncertainty and the fluctuating reports. After her joyless youth she was finding the attention novel and flattering, and it suited her policy admirably that Spanish apprehensions that she might 'marry for caprice' and succumb to one of her own subjects should be heightened. The more suitors who joined the chase, the longer she might justifiably shy away from giving a firm answer to anyone, and to Philip in particular.

One of the few Englishmen who might have been a fitting husband for the Queen by virtue of his ancient and honourable descent and whom rumour accordingly whirled aloft, was the elderly widower Lord Arundel. He was the twelfth Earl, his title far older than that of his young son-in-law the Duke of Norfolk; he had been Henry VIII's Lord Chamberlain and Mary's Lord Steward of the Household; but he was not a man of much perception, and as so often happens when a middle-aged man pays court to a young woman, he was made to appear rather silly over his apparent hopes of winning Elizabeth. Feria –

understandably, in view of Arundel's eligibility – was particularly scathing about him.

In Mary's reign there had been some talk of a marriage between Elizabeth and Arundel's heir Lord Maltravers, but the young man had died in 1556, and perhaps Arundel had cherished secret hopes of wooing Elizabeth for himself ever since the spring day when she was a friendless prisoner in the Tower and he, sent in stern guise to assist at her questioning, had surprised everyone, and probably himself as well, by falling on his knees and exclaiming that she was innocent. At the time of Mary's death he was in Flanders, taking part in the truce negotiations, but by 7 December he had returned to England, having travelled on the same ship as the suave Spaniard Bishop de Quadra, who had come to assist Feria in the pursuit of Elizabeth. 'I believe the tears of the Earl of Arundel floated them into port,' Feria wrote to Philip, 'for they say the Earl cried like a child.' Whether seasickness or emotion, or both, caused the Earl to weep, his tears were soon dried, and he was to be seen at the palace in fine fettle, 'very smart and clean, and they say he carried his thoughts very high'. Though Feria dismissed him as 'a flighty man, of small ability', Arundel continued to play a prominent part in public affairs, and for her coronation Elizabeth appointed him Lord High Steward, a mark of honour which did nothing to dampen the talk of his hopes; at the lavish ceremonials he strutted about 'with a silver staff a yard in length', commanding everybody in great style. 'The Earl of Arundel has been going about in high glee for some time, and is very smart,' Feria observed at the end of December 1558; late in the following autumn Arundel's personal interest in the Queen was still smouldering with enough warmth to ignite a violent quarrel between himself and another potential English suitor, Sir William Pickering, an old friend of Elizabeth's whom she treated with great favour.

Pickering was not of noble blood such as Arundel's, but he had other qualities which caught the public eye and appealed to Elizabeth. Like Arundel, he was abroad when Elizabeth came to the throne, but unlike the widower-wooer he was unable to hurry back to present himself before the new Queen, as he became ill and was obliged to lie at Dunkirk until the spring.

His absence served rather to heighten speculation about him, however, and talk of the 'very handsome gallant gentleman' who had 'not yet made his appearance' ran so high that in some quarters it was confidently asserted that Elizabeth would marry him when he returned – 'it being well known how much she loved him'. Pickering was a man of sophistication and experience, keenly interested in books and learning, and though at forty-two he was still a bachelor, he was reputed to be 'very successful with women', and to have 'enjoyed the intimacy of many and great ones'. His popularity with men, however, declined considerably after his arrival at Elizabeth's court in May 1559.

The friends of his youth had been the arrogant Earl of Surrey's dashing young set, and for joining in a rowdy escapade through the streets of London with them in the spring of 1543, he had been briefly imprisoned in the Tower to curb his spirits; sentenced with him was another of the boisterous companions, Thomas Wyatt the younger, son of the poet. Pickering and Wyatt remained friends, and eleven years later, in 1554, they worked together in plotting the rebellion to put Elizabeth and Courtenay on the throne. Dangerous as that gesture of loyalty was to Elizabeth at the time, the fact remained that Pickering had risked his life in her cause, and though, having fled abroad, he subsequently undertook some dubious dealings for Philip and Mary, Elizabeth made him welcome when he finally arrived at her court. 'She saw him secretly two days after his arrival,' Feria reported, 'and yesterday he came to the palace publicly and remained with her four or five hours. In London they are giving twenty-five to a hundred that he will be King.'

In fact Elizabeth never seriously considered marrying Pickering, and he knew it, but she enjoyed his company, and as an eligible Englishman he provided a useful weight in the delicately poised scales of the marriage question. She continued to have 'long conversations' with him, and ordered him to be given lodgings in the palace – the privilege which her maiden coyness had denied to Feria – and through the spring and summer of 1559 he made the most of his favoured position, entertaining lavishly, spending a great deal of money, and dining apart from the other courtiers, 'with music playing'. Pickering's attitude caused considerable resentment at court. In September he and the Earl of Bedford exchanged high words at a banquet, which apparently ended in Pickering challenging Bedford to a duel, and that affray was followed a month later by the quarrel with Arundel. 'The other day, when Pickering was going into the chapel, which is inside the Queen's apartments, the Earl of Arundel came to the door, and told him he knew very well that was a place for lords, and he must go to the presence chamber,' reported the Bishop de Quadra. Contemptuously, Pickering answered 'that he knew that, and he also knew that Arundel was an impudent discourteous knave, which the Earl heard, and he went out without answering a word, leaving the other to enter'. Pickering went around telling everyone the story, as though he found it amusing, and he announced that he would not bother to challenge Arundel to a duel 'as he held him of small account'. Bishop de Quadra concluded with a trace of pity: 'It is right that he should refrain, as the Earl is very weak.'

Pickering appears to have been one of the few participants in Elizabeth's marriage dealings who did not take his situation very seriously. It may be that he came closer than any to recognizing her innermost feelings about marriage, which perhaps she herself only half understood at that time; certainly he made a remark which was to prove prophetic during the decades of wooing which followed his own flirtation with the young Queen. While Londoners were putting money on his chances of becoming King, Pickering 'asked after the Imperial ambassador on the day he arrived, and said the Queen would laugh at him, and all the rest of them, as he, Pickering, knew she meant to die a maid'.

To Feria, urgently planning his strategy during the first weeks of the reign, there seemed no likelihood of Elizabeth dying a maid. The crucial question was whether her husband would be an Englishman or a foreigner. The supreme offer, of Philip himself, should not be made yet, he felt – 'It is not a matter that can be spoken of to the Council until more light is obtained as to her own inclinations' – and he explained that he would have to approach the Councillors individually, 'to dissuade them from her marriage with an Englishman, and I am moving in this way as cleverly as I can'. Feria believed he was being most subtle in his methods, which he conceived with a view to taking advantage of the weak points in Elizabeth's character and situation. 'On the one hand she complained to me of her sister's having married a foreigner, and on the other I see she is very vain and as much set against her sister as she was previous to her death. I fancy I can get at her through this feeling,' he informed Philip. His plan was to inveigle her into talking about Philip, and then to remind her that she should not 'hold herself less than her sister, who would never marry a subject'. He would tell her that one of the reasons why Mary had disliked her was jealousy over Philip, and the fear that if she, Mary, were to die, Philip would marry Elizabeth; then he intended to point out how undignified it would seem for her to marry one of her subjects 'while there are such great princes whom she might marry', after which, much to his own enjoyment, he would 'take those whom she might marry here and pick them to pieces one by one, which will not require much rhetoric, for there is not a man amongst them worth anything, counting the married ones and all'.

Feria's view of Elizabeth's personality was clouded by masculine prejudice. Baffled and infuriated by her apparent capriciousness, her wayward, even frivolous, attitude, and her vanity, Feria did not perceive how skilfully the young Queen wielded her weaknesses. 'She is a woman very fond of argument,' he noted, and it was as a conventional clever woman, learned and spirited but curtailed by the natural frailties of her sex, that he regarded her, as he sought to gain the mastery in the crucial issue of whom she would marry and conceive her children by. He acknowledged that she evinced an unusual degree of authority; less than ten days after she had become Queen he had informed Philip: 'She seems to me incomparably more feared than her sister, and gives her orders and has her way as absolutely as her father did.' Yet still he did not grasp how great an adversary he was wooing, and his proposed plan continued: 'We can then remind her of the claims of the Queen Dauphine [Mary Queen of Scots] and the need for her [Elizabeth's] being allied with Your Majesty or with someone

c*

belonging to you,' as though she were a timid woman who might be driven by the French threat into seeking the protection of Spain's strong embrace.

'When she is dissuaded,' Feria went on, 'if she inclines to Your Majesty it will be necessary for you to send me orders whether I am to carry it any further or throw cold water on it and set up the Archduke Ferdinand, because I do not see what other person we can propose to whom she would agree.' He was convinced that there was no hope for Emmanuel Philibert of Savoy now: 'They will not agree to him, for in fact they have a great hatred of war, and they are afraid he may try to recover his estates at the expense of this country.' With the gallant warrior-Duke thus debarred from the chase, it would not be easy to find another suitable candidate whose loyalty to Spain could be relied on. The Archduke Ferdinand was Philip's first cousin, but since 1556, when Philip's father Charles V had abdicated and the title of Emperor had passed to his brother, the Archduke Ferdinand's father, the interests of the two branches of the Habsburg family had become less unanimous, and as Feria had pointed out in his very first letter after Elizabeth became Queen: 'It would be inconvenient enough for Ferdinand to marry here even if he took the titbit from Your Majesty's hand, but very much worse if it were arranged in any other way.' However, if Philip were to decline to enter the chase in person, the Archduke might be acceptable as the Hapsburg representative in Elizabeth's bed, for in the eyes of the English and the Privy Council he had distinct advantages over the Spanish King. As Feria explained to Philip with his customary bluntness:

They think he will always reside in this country and have no quarrel with France, and although some of them understand that the power and grandeur of Your Majesty is of great importance to their security, the short time Your Majesty could reside here and your enmity to France turn them against you.

What mattered above all was that the marriage should go through Philip's hands, and Feria, complaining, expostulating, warning, increasingly convinced that the heretical English were only fit to be dealt with 'sword in hand', tried to impress upon his hesitant King the gravity of the situation. 'The fact is that these people are going on in a way that will end in their coming to grief, and Your Majesty must get the affair in your grasp,' he urged at the end of December 1558. 'We must begin at once to see that the King of France does not get in or spoil the crop that Your Majesty has sown here.'

The fair fastidious King of Spain was no ardent suitor to Elizabeth. When, on 10 January, he informed Feria that he had made up his mind to 'offer to marry the Queen of England', his proposal was outlined to the ambassador in a manner that was far from flattering to his prospective bride. Misgivings and reluctance cast a gloom over his decision, and the happiest note was that of self-satisfaction in knowing himself to be sacrificing personal inclination so as to serve the Lord. The experience of his marriage to Mary had shaken Philip and his courtiers no less than the English, and as he grimly listed the drawbacks of marrying Elizabeth he stressed 'the heavy expense I should be put to in England by reason of the costly entertainment necessary to the people there', and the difficulties that would again arise from his having to live in his own dominions for most of the year, away from his wife in England, which he knew the English greatly resented. 'Besides this such a marriage would look like entering upon a perpetual war with France, seeing the claims that the Queen of Scots has to the English crown,' he wrote regretfully. But there were considerations above these. The 'enormous importance of such a match to Christianity and the preservation of religion' flamed in Philip's soul, fuelled by the political danger that without his guiding presence beside Elizabeth on the throne of England, that country would 'fall back into its former errors which wculd cause to our own neighbouring dominions serious dangers and difficulties'. And so, in spite of the many weighty objections, he was 'resolved to render this service to God' and present himself, for the second time in five years, as a reluctant bridegroom to an English queen.

Though Feria did not fully understand the young woman whom the cause of God and Spain obliged him to court, it was plain that Philip had even less grasp of the changing situation in England and the personality of its new Queen. When he had known that grey, rain-sodden island kingdom it was under stringent Catholic rule, shuffling penitently back to the old faith, while its leading Protestants burned in city marketplaces or fled abroad to nurture their heresies. When he had known the Lady Elizabeth, watched her and talked with her, down the panelled galleries of Hampton Court, or by the gun-grey Thames, loaded with the rainwaters of that flooded summer of 1555, she had been a pale, taut, quietly dressed girl, cautious as a hunted creature, exerting herself to please him, yet with intriguing sparks of wit and spirit flickering behind her cool demeanour. Riding with her through wet green woods, dancing with her by candlelight to the guttural melodious music of sackbuts and crumhorns, Philip must have found his clever sister-in-law a pleasing companion, a little evasive perhaps, but ever ready to defer to his opinions and respect his wishes in all things. Only the lingering memory of a deferential Elizabeth could have led him to write with such confidence three years later: 'She will have to obtain secret absolution from the Pope and the necessary dispensation so that when I marry her she will be a Catholic which she has not been heretofore,' and then to congratulate himself with the words: 'In this way it will be evident and manifest that I am serving the Lord in marrying her, and that she has been converted by my act.'

It was evident and manifest that the King of Spain did not know the Elizabeth who now ruled England. 'His Majesty must be informed of the character of the Queen,' Feria wrote worriedly in a memorandum at the end of February. 'She is acute, depending upon the favour of the common people, detested by the Catholics. . . .' Dark eyes sparkling against a milk-white skin, bright hair twisted into tiny curls, slender lovely hands displayed, she provoked, encouraged, and frustrated Feria through audience after audience, 'very gaily'. No greater match than Philip of Spain could ever be offered to her, and the knowledge that this fair-haired, prim-lipped man of thirty-three, on whose slender shoulders rested half Europe, was awaiting her consent or rejection must have given Elizabeth's feminine nature a thrilling sense of power, even while her clear judicious mind was calculating. There could be no question of her changing her religion and embracing Catholicism, but Philip's suit was of too great a value to be rejected before she had gained as much benefit as she could from it. While Spain's huge hand was seen to be beckoning towards Elizabeth the French would be less likely to make war on her, and as long as Philip hoped to become Elizabeth's husband he would use all his influence with the Pope to oppose France's endeavours to have her denounced as illegitimate and heretical; in England the threat from her Catholic subjects would be reduced if they could fasten their hopes on the coming of a Spanish consort rather than on plots and conspiracies. All the 'power and grandeur' of Spain could not make Philip an accept-able husband for Queen Elizabeth, but they made him a most welcome suitor.

Feria decided it must be the 'excitement of her fresh dignity' that was causing Elizabeth to behave with such 'offhandedness and independence' in such a grave situation, as though she were blind to her own weakness and the splendour of Philip's pro-ffered alliance. He found that all his attempts to press the marriage question were somehow parried, so that the dis-cussions went on from day to day without either a formal proposal on his side or a definite sign of rejection on hers, while her first Parliament sat and dispersed again without having received any conclusive decision from the Queen on the subject of her marriage, and still the rumours tossed lightly on the air – she would wed Arundel, or the Earl of Westmorland, she was in love with Pickering, she would only marry a great foreign prince, she would take none but an Englishman. 'I am afraid that one fine day we shall find this woman married, and I shall be the last man in the place to know anything about it,' Feria sighed.

When, late in February, he tried to broach the matter more forcefully, the Queen at once began to make for cover by 'keeping to her old arguments for not wishing to marry', and so he impatiently cut her short, guessing what she was about to say – 'namely, that she did not think of marrying, and so to shelve the business with fair words'. They talked at length of the peace negotiations that were still in progress at Cambrésis, but always the subject of the marriage hung in the air between them. Once Elizabeth artlessly happened to mention that her commissioners, having encountered such difficulties in treating with the French, were 'proposing certain means of agreement such as marriages and so on', but she only said it casually, and 'appeared to make small account' of the suggestions. She expressed deep gratitude to Philip for his support in the negotiations, and proceeded to work herself up into a furious state about the French and 'the pretensions of the Queen of Scots', which was all very satisfactory for Feria, but when, after much discussion, she chose to sit down, and he realized that she was waiting for him to introduce the subject of Philip's courtship again, he refused to humour her; he merely told her that 'all these difficulties could be overcome if only Her Majesty would do certain things', which she seemed to understand. As he had observed to Philip, the two towering issues of religion and this marriage were 'really only one'.

Though Catholics, in Spain and in England, viewed Elizabeth with gloomy distrust, the Protestant exiles returning from abroad found her to be proceeding at a very slow pace with the great work of restoring the reformed religion. Dr Jewel, later Bishop of Salisbury, wrote to his former host in Strasbourg :

The Queen, meanwhile, though she openly favours our cause, is wonderfully afraid of allowing any innovations; this is owing partly to her friends, by whose advice every thing is carried on, and partly to the influence of Count Feria, a Spaniard and Philip's ambassador. She is, however, prudently, and firmly, and piously following up her purpose, though somewhat more slowly than we could wish.

Elizabeth had long ago learned not to show her hand, she had become experienced in the art of remaining uncommitted for as long as possible, and while the situation demanded that Philip should be kept expectant, she would only proceed by 'a little and little' down the Protestant path.

Her political dalliance with the King of Spain, the greatest of all her suitors, came to an end in March. With the signing of the peace with France in sight she began to treat Feria less archly, and she quoted to him the reasons why she could not wed Philip, which he carefully listed in a memorandum. Significantly, she started with the almost petulant reminder that she had no desire at all to marry, 'as she had intimated from the first'. No one, least of all the sceptical ambassador, took that very seriously, but part of her argument seemed more weighty; she could not marry Philip, she said, since he had been the husband of her sister. Normally in such tenuous cases of consanguinity a papal dispensation was all that was required, but now, to Feria's great disquiet, she 'denied point-blank the Pope's authority, which she had previously only pointed out indirectly'. There were other reasons as well, which Feria recorded for Philip to read, such as the fact that her people did not want her to marry a foreigner, and as though to forestall the most powerful argument in favour of the match, she announced defiantly that it was by no means so clear as Feria made out that Mary Queen of Scots was next in line for the English throne. It seemed, incredibly, that Elizabeth was enjoying flouting the will of Spain; as she produced her final argument, that people were saying that Philip would only stay with her for a very brief time and would then go straight back to Spain, she laughed so much that Feria, unnerved, began to wonder whether his correspondence dealing with this very point had been intercepted and seen by her. He kept his composure, however, and managed to turn the conversation so that her remarks did not seem to have amounted to a conclusive refusal, but there was now no doubt in his mind as to what her final answer, when it came, would be. A further interview a few days later only served to confirm his misgivings. This time there was no laughter; Elizabeth told him flatly that Philip could not marry her, for she was a heretic.

Elizabeth seemed very wrought-up at this meeting, 'disturbed and excited', Feria described her, and it was clear that she was resolved to restore the reformed religion to England. Feria tried to say that he did not believe her to be a heretic, nor that she would dare to change the country's religion, and he told her impressively that Philip 'would not separate from the union of Churches for all the kingdoms of the earth', but to this she gave the unbecoming rejoinder: 'Then much less would he do it for a woman.' Trying to introduce a note of pleasantry, Feria replied: 'that men did more for a woman than for anything else', but it was not the moment for the kind of heady gallantry

which she usually enjoyed. Not only was the Act of Uni-
formity, which Feria called 'the abominable decree', about to be
signed, but the French danger had been temporarily reduced.
As a citizen of London wrote in his diary: 'The eighth day of
April there was a proclamation of peace between the Queen's
Grace and Harry the French King and Dauphin the King of
Scots, for ever, both by water and land; and there was six
trumpeters and five heralds of arms, Master Garter and Master
Clarenceux, proclaimed it.' Philip's suit had served its purpose,
and the time had come for the pretence of wooing to be
converted into a credible friendship.

The rejected suitor bore his disappointment with an equanimity that bordered upon relief; within a matter of days
Elizabeth learned that Philip had contracted to marry another.
His bride was to be Elisabeth of France, the ravishingly pretty
eldest daughter of Henry II and Catherine de'Medici. She was
to have married Philip's son, the deformed and violent Don
Carlos, but the recalcitrance of the Queen of England had made
the King of Spain change his mind and decide to take the
fourteen-year-old French Princess for himself.

The prospect of such a Catholic league was a threatening
one, but all was not lost. When Feria went to see Elizabeth to
condole vindictively with her over 'what she had lost', and to
make sure she was suitably troubled by the prospect of Philip
'in close alliance and relationship with the King of France', he
found she was in one of her moods of perverse gaiety. Elizabeth
'began to say she had heard Your Majesty was married, smiling,
saying your name was a fortunate one, and now and then
giving little sighs which bordered upon laughter'. Feria tried to
chasten her by saying coldly that he could not rejoice to see
Philip married to anyone but herself, 'nor at her refusing to
believe all my importunities and assurances of how desirable it
would be for her to marry Your Majesty', but Elizabeth was
incorrigible. She retorted that it was Philip's fault, not hers,
that the marriage had fallen through, because she had not given
any definite answer yet, and when Feria reprovingly said that
'she knew very well what the facts were', she observed wist-
fully that Philip could not have been so much in love with her
as Feria had pretended, since he had not had the patience to

1 Elizabeth aged about thirteen.

2 Emmanuel Philibert, Duke of Savoy and Prince of Piedmont, the disinherited prince whom Queen Mary pressed Elizabeth to marry

3 (*below left*) Edward Courtenay, Earl of Devonshire, 'the last sprig of the White Rose'.

4 (*below*) Thomas, Lord Seymour of Sudeley, Lord High Admiral of England. Elizabeth's first suitor.

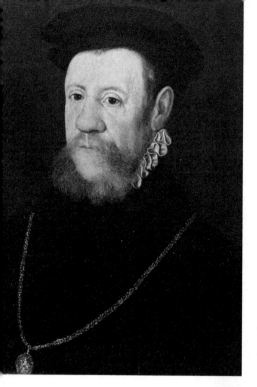

5 Henry Fitzalan, Earl of Arundel. He was of noble birth, but lacked the attractions of Elizabeth's younger suitors.

6 Eric XIV of Sweden. He wooed Elizabeth with lavish gifts, but his suit met with mockery.

7 Philip II of Spain. The enmity of three decades began with a marriage proposal.

8 Archduke Charles of Austria. He was said to be 'for a man, beautiful and well-faced'.

9 Robert Dudley, Earl of Leicester. Elizabeth's great love and the most persistent of all her suitors.

10 Charles IX of France. His mother Catherine de' Medici proposed him for Elizabeth when he was 'but a boy'.

11 Henry, Duke of Anjou (later Henry III of France). He proved a reluctant suitor to the ageing Elizabeth.

12 Robert Devereux, Earl of Essex. The handsome, wilful favourite of the Queen's declining years.

13 Francis, Duke of Alençon, Elizabeth's 'dearest Frog'. Their political courtship turned into a heady romance.

14 Elizabeth I, aged about forty-two.

wait four months for her, 'and many things of the same sort'. The hostile ambassador must have felt that his justifiable triumph was somewhat diminished by her cheerful reception of the news which he had hoped would shock and grieve her, but he was sure that she was really very displeased at heart, and having exchanged some terse words with mild, careworn Secretary Cecil ('who is a pestilent knave, as Your Majesty knows') on the subject of whether or not Philip would care to continue the war against France for England's benefit, Feria was able to conclude with evident satisfaction: 'In short, I left them that day as bitter as gall.'

The mighty King of Spain had withdrawn his suit, and Elizabeth had laughed. For more than three decades Philip and Elizabeth were to face each other across the globe, frowning, smiling, threatening, as they passed from youth to maturity to old age, until the portly galleons of the Armada sailed with their freight of long-hoarded hostility, and beyond. But the enmity of half a lifetime had begun with these few formal steps of courtship, and though Elizabeth had defied Philip in marriage as she would afterwards defy him in war, she never forgot that, had she been so inclined, she might have had him for her husband. Through her childhood and youth, for most of her twenty-five years, she had been a bastard, a pawn and a prisoner; that she was now in a position to dally with and deny the King of Spain himself was exhilarating proof of her power.

Those little spurts of laughter which she hardly troubled to conceal may have welled up from a sense of relief that it was Philip and not she who had been guilty of finally breaking off the marriage negotiations. Now instead of shying away she was free to sigh out her affection for her Spanish brother-monarch, and to make a confidant of his ambassador – and to indulge in hours of chat and speculation about his cousins the Archdukes, so that the wrath of Spain and Rome might continue to be held at bay by the hope that an orthodox Habsburg would yet become King of England. 'If Ferdinand is a man,' as Feria brusquely put it, 'backed up as he will be by Your Majesty, he will be able not only to reform religion and pacify the country, but, even though the Queen may die, to keep the country in his fist.'

As Elizabeth and Cecil were aware, despite his marriage with *la fille de France*, there was still good reason for Philip to maintain a protective attitude towards England – 'namely, the just claims of the Queen of Scots, and the great ease with which the King of France could take possession, owing to the miserable state in which England now is'. It was as central as ever to the interests of Spain that Henry II should not sweep across the Channel to place Mary Queen of Scots on the throne of England, as joint ruler with her husband, his sickly eldest son the Dauphin Francis. 'To let him take the country, which he will do with so much ease that I dread to think of it, would be to my mind the total ruin of Your Majesty and all your states,' Feria pronounced impressively. Though Philip himself had retired early from the hunt, faced with obstacles that prevented him from capturing Elizabeth as he had Mary, by marrying her himself, the saying about his Imperial house, 'Others make war: you, fortunate Austria, marry', would still hold good if one of his cousins the Archdukes should, under his patronage, woo and win the headstrong new Queen of England.

He now enlarged upon this in his instructions to Feria, seeing it as the ideal solution to the question of her marriage. Since the Archduke had no country of his own to rule he could always remain at Elizabeth's side, helping her to bear the burden of government, yet, unlike any of her contemptible English suitors, he would at the same time be in a position to call upon Philip or his own father to 'aid and defend her with all the power of the Empire' in time of need. The match would bring her 'so many connections and of such strength and power that none will dare to offend or vex her, whereas just the reverse will happen if she marry a subject'. Philip the husband had given way to Philip the loving brother, anxious for her welfare, gravely instructing Feria to 'banish any shadow of doubt she may have that because she did not marry me and I have entered the French alliance I shall take any less interest in her affairs'. In time those words would prove grimly ironic; for the next three decades King Philip of Spain would never cease to take the utmost interest in Elizabeth's affairs.

Everyone, everywhere, seemed to be talking of Elizabeth's marriage in that first year of her reign. More and more suitors, old and new, entered the field, while the advantages of one match and the drawbacks of another were constantly weighed up and disputed; some of her Privy Councillors, eager for an English marriage, favoured Pickering, while others pressed for the great foreign alliance that the Archduke would bring; only Elizabeth herself stood a little apart from it all, like a pale flame in the heart of a blaze. But almost no one seemed to find anything significant in that. It was remembered that her sister Mary had been nearly forty when she was made Queen, a devout old maid, yet she had been betrothed within six months, and with every sign of eagerness, whereas Elizabeth was only twenty-five, an elegant young woman, and by 'age and temperament' she was far more fit than Mary to be a wife and mother, as Feria discreetly pointed out. She tended to make modest references to her preference for the virgin state whenever marriage was seriously discussed, it was true, but there was no doubt that she enjoyed the company of men; and diplomacy, or, as her warder Sir Thomas Pope had suggested in the last reign, maidenly modesty, could account for a certain delicate reticence on her part when the matter of her marriage was broached with any forcefulness. It was generally assumed that marriage and child-bearing must be her destiny, both as a woman and as a queen. Only the wordly Sir William Pickering said with conviction that she would laugh at them all and die a maid, and his opinion did not carry much weight.

To her first Parliament, which assembled at the beginning of the year, Elizabeth had given a fair but flexible answer when they 'made request for marriage'. Her reply, written and revised in her own handwriting, was read out in the lofty Parliamentary House, where Thomas Seymour had once sworn to bring about 'the blackest Parliament that has been seen'; her references to the past, to her sufferings in Mary's reign, still so recent, surely stirred her hearers' sense of chivalry. The literary tradition of the distressed virgin was still vivid in a society whose most popular reading included Malory's *Morte d'Arthur*.

If the eschewing of the danger of mine enemies or the avoiding of the peril of death, whose messenger or rather continual watchman, the Queen's indignation, was no little time daily before mine eyes . . . could have drawn or dissuaded me from this kind of life, I had not now remained in this estate wherein you see me.

So Elizabeth wrote proudly. Neither the fear of Mary's wrath nor ambition for a fine marriage had been able to move her then to change her maiden state, she declared, and she was still of the same mind now. But people were not to think there was anything final about that. Smoothly she proceeded to introduce promising phrases such as 'whensoever it may please God to incline my heart to another kind of life', and 'whomsoever my chance shall be to light upon', so that it should be quite plain to her subjects and the world that she was ready to consider matrimony with an open mind. As for the succession question, her response was that if God should wish her to remain in the single state, she believed that he would make provision for an heir to the kingdom – a reminder perhaps that Mary's childlessness had had the happy result of bringing her, Elizabeth, to the throne.

The conclusion and climax to her speech came with the simple yet dramatic force of a vow. 'And in the end', rang her words, in what perhaps she already knew to be prophecy, 'this shall be for me sufficient, that a marble stone shall declare that a Queen, having reigned such a time, lived and died a virgin.' The speech was a masterpiece of subtle diplomacy. Elizabeth was left free to flaunt herself before the desiring eyes of the world, for her own delight and for political gain, but at the same time, with her characteristic gift for creating strengths out of her weaknesses, she had provided herself with an unassailably honourable means of retreat.

'So many loose and flighty fancies are about,' Feria sighed, when spring came and Elizabeth was still as uncommitted as ever. With Philip's suit at an end he had now to begin the irksome process of wooing this 'baggage' of a young woman all over again, on behalf of the unfamiliar Archdukes, which promised long-drawn-out negotiations while other rumours, other ambassadors, jostled him for the Queen's attention. There had been a good deal of talk about the King of Denmark's brother Duke Adolphus of Holstein, a devout Protestant who was also said to be remarkably good-looking, and though Feria had done his best to thwart this contender, by putting it about that he was really 'a very good Catholic, and not so comely as he is made out to be', it was said that he intended to come over in person to plead his suit. Pickering had arrived, and was lounging about the court with a supercilious air, spending a fortune on clothes and entertaining, and receiving an inordinate degree of attention from the Queen; and meanwhile the Swedish ambassador was still trying to win her for Crown Prince Eric. The Swede tried to profit from having brought her a proposal when she was unsought and out of favour in Mary's reign, but he was as maladroit now as then; when he 'told the Queen that the son of the King his master was still of the same mind, and asked for a reply to the letter he brought last year', Elizabeth gave him the curt reply that 'the letter was written when she was Madam Elizabeth, and now that she was Queen of England he must write to her as Queen'. Then, with splendid imperiousness, she added that 'she did not know whether his master would leave his kingdom to marry her, but she would not leave hers to be monarch of the world, and at present she would not reply either yes or no'. Unpromising though that may have sounded, it elicited another magnificent present from the hopeful King of Sweden, and although Elizabeth and her court laughed more and more openly at Prince Eric's lavish wooing, his ambassador continued to scatter money and presents in hopes of eventual success. It was with some justification that Feria observed acidly: 'If these things were not of such great importance, and so lamentable, some of them would be very ridiculous.'

As he had envisaged, the Archduke's suit proceeded very haltingly. 'It is very troublesome to negotiate with this woman, as she is naturally changeable, and those who surround her are so blind and bestial that they do not at all understand the state of affairs,' he wrote, profoundly exasperated. His idea was to drive her into the arms of Philip's candidate by first scaring her thoroughly, showing her the terrible weaknesses and danger of her position, and then soothing her by offering the remedy of marriage with the Archduke which would entitle her to the boon of Philip's protection. But Feria could see that she was as empty-headed as ever. 'Sometimes she appears to want to

marry him, and speaks like a woman who will only accept a
great Prince,' he reported, but 'for my part I believe she will
never make up her mind to anything that is good for her.' It
was with undisguised relief that Feria left his post at Elizabeth's
court at the end of May, and handed over his thankless duties
to the suave, supple-tongued Bishop de Quadra. To the end,
Feria was taken in by Elizabeth's air of wilfulness and inconse-
quential posturing. Had he known her over the years, observed
her progress from difficult childhood through stormy youth to
the position she now held, had he been present at Hatfield ten
years before, when, as a friendless girl of fifteen, she had
triumphed over all the art and experience of her interrogator
Tyrwhitt, he might have seen something more than imprudent
waywardness behind her present dealings. As it was, he left
England with the conviction that the young Queen was not
merely heretical but an irresponsible minx, who deserved only
to be dealt with by force.

At the end of May the Emperor's ambassador Caspar
Breuner, Baron von Rabenstein arrived, and de Quadra
requested an audience for Breuner and himself a few days later.
They were received at one o'clock on a Sunday, and found the
Queen in her presence chamber dressed very elegantly, 'looking on at the dancing', where she kept them for a long while.
Then de Quadra began verbally to open the courtship dance
with the Archdukes which Elizabeth was to pace intermittently,
now slow, now fast, for nine years.

'She at once began, as I feared, to talk about not wishing to
marry,' de Quadra reported, and so he diplomatically cut her
short and left her alone with Breuner. Ambassadors had
learned to expect this from Elizabeth when they tried to talk to
her of marriage; invariably she would shy away with fine
words about preferring her state of maidenhood, so that they
were obliged to coax and lure her into negotiating the matter,
with the knowledge that she might at any moment retreat to
her vantage-point of virginity. 'We find that we have no wish
to give up our solitude and our lonely life,' she was to write to
the Archdukes' father, the Emperor, with exquisite pathos.
'There certainly was a time when a very honourable and
worthy marriage would have liberated us from certain great

distress and tribulation (whereof we will not speak further), but neither the peril of the moment, nor the desire for liberty, could induce us to take the matter into consideration.' Yet her marriageable status was one of her great political assets, and so, as she never failed to add, the matter must remain open to discussion. Slyly she hinted to the Emperor: 'We cannot safely assert anything for the future, nor wilfully predict anything rash,' so that a world of hope might be pinned onto her pious observation that God might 'in his inscrutable wisdom at any time change our thoughts'.

Having left Breuner with Elizabeth, de Quadra, that 'clever and crafty old fox', went outside to exchange a few words with Secretary Cecil. On this occasion Cecil used one of Elizabeth's favourite ploys, innocently telling de Quadra what a great number of suitors the Queen had. It seemed to the ambassador that Cecil was now genuinely anxious that she should marry, but the Secretary confessed to him that as far as the Archduke Ferdinand's suit was concerned, there were certain drawbacks; Elizabeth had been told that he was as devout a Catholic as his cousin Philip, whilst the Archduke Charles was commonly said to be quite unfit to rule.

At this point, Breuner, uninitiated in Elizabeth's wayward and elusive manner of negotiating, came out of her chamber, 'quite despairing of the business'. De Quadra acted with great presence of mind. He at once returned to the Queen himself, and by dint of exceptional skill managed to erase her unfavourable impression of Ferdinand, and win her interest by pretending that she was not being offered Ferdinand at all, but the younger brother, twenty-year-old Charles. It was a masterly stroke. After considerable 'demurring and doubting' she came round to the belief that it was indeed Charles, 'the younger and more likely to please her', who was her ardent suitor, and though as de Quadra put it, 'she went back again to her nonsense, and said she would rather be a nun than marry without knowing whom and on the faith of portrait painters', it was settled that Breuner should be called back again, and so the negotiations began in earnest. Though the young Queen was evidently apprehensive about marriage, and at times seemed to treat the whole subject of her suitors as a great jest, the question was still whom, and not whether, she would finally bring herself to marry. 'For in the natural course of events the Queen is of an age when she should in reason and as is woman's way, be eager to marry and be provided for,' Breuner remarked. 'That she should wish to remain a maid and never marry is inconceivable.'

Elizabeth's delight in the trappings of romance and flirtation, which was to become her substitute for normal sexual fulfilment, until it cracked into grotesquerie in the raddled old virgin, seemed in the eligible young woman to be mere feminine nonsense – somewhat inappropriate, often irritating, but harmless enough while it appeared that marriage would be the final outcome. 'I do not know whether she is jesting, which is quite possible,' de Quadra noted, 'but I really believe she would like to arrange for the Archduke's visit in disguise.' It was a fancy which Elizabeth pursued with some resolution. She was insistent that she could not marry a man whom she had not first seen, for she would not put her faith in portraits; perhaps she remembered the cautionary tale of her second stepmother, dull Anne of Cleves, whom Henry VIII had desired in a picture and spurned in the flesh. In audience with Breuner, who was really not quick or subtle enough to partner Elizabeth in these games, she 'plied him with a thousand silly stories', and then said something which he took seriously but which de Quadra intereperted as a broad hint. One of her jesters, she said, had told her that a member of the ambassador's retinue was really the Archduke Charles himself, come disguised and unrecognized to cast his eyes in secret on the great Queen whom he hoped to win. It is not hard to detect a trace of longing beneath the frivolity of that remark.

Breuner, conscientious but 'not the most crafty man in the world', thought at times that his suit must be progessing well. Elizabeth often made a great fuss of him, and her ladies seemed convinced that she was in earnest. A charming scene took place on the river in June; one evening, after dinner, Breuner took a boat on the Thames, and as he was gliding idly along, past the sprawling palace of Whitehall and the splendid town residences of the nobles, he saw the Queen's barge approaching. Voices called thinly across the water, and then the dip and splash of oars began again as he was rowed over to speak to the Queen. She was in one of her charming moods, gay and bantering; she spoke to him for a long while, told him to take a place in the Lord Treasurer's barge, and had her own boat laid alongside. Then, with the most fetching air, she began to play to him on her lute.

She was evidently much taken with the pretty scene which she had created, and the following evening, by her wish, it was repeated. 'When I arrived there', Breuner reported, 'she took me into her boat, made me take the helm, and was altogether very talkative and merry.' Teasing and chattering on the river on a warm June evening, with the Imperial ambassador nervously steering her barge, Elizabeth was evidently enjoying her proxy flirtation with the splendid young Archduke whom, if she willed, she could have for a husband. She wanted to be desirable – but she wanted also to be unattainable. When matters became serious, and she saw that she was in danger of being trapped, her attitude changed utterly. Only a few months after her encouraging behaviour on the river, when she had long been pressing for the Archduke to come over to England in person, de Quadra proposed to her that he should indeed come, just as she had requested. At this she became almost distracted. She insisted with real anxiety that if he came she could not be bound to accept him. 'When I pressed her much', de Quadra recounted, 'she seemed frightened, and protested again and again she was not to be bound, and she was not yet resolved whether she would marry.' She kept repeating that she could be put under no obligation, and even demanded that this must be put in writing; when de Quadra took that to be a joke she said agitatedly that she 'would write to King Philip herself that he might bear witness that she would bind herself to nothing and had not asked the Archduke to come'. Nothing was certain where Elizabeth's marriage was concerned; ambassadors found themselves hopeful, bewildered, despairing and confident by turns, and de Quadra wrote exasperatedly towards the end of 1559: 'What a pretty business it is to treat with this woman, whom I think must have a hundred thousand devils in her body, notwithstanding that she is for ever telling me that she yearns to be a nun and to pass her time in a cell praying.'

By the autumn of that year there were more than half a dozen ambassadors wooing her at court, competing for her favour and eyeing each other like hostile dogs. 'Here is a great resort of wooers and controversy among lovers,' Cecil wrote, half-amused, but profoundly wishing the Queen would take one of them and settle the business. The Swedish and Imperial representatives were, as Bishop Jewel remarked, 'courting at a most marvellous rate. But the Swede is most in earnest, for he promises mountains of silver in case of success'. The King of Sweden had sent his younger son, Duke John of Finland, to court Elizabeth on behalf of Crown Prince Eric. Duke John had arrived in superb state, bringing a large retinue of noblemen, horses, and many servants, who wore red velvet coats bearing a design of hearts pierced by a javelin, to symbolize Prince Eric's consuming passion for the Queen whom he had never even met. Before long Duke John and Caspar Breuner were at each other's throats. 'The King of Sweden's son, who is here, is fit to kill the Emperor's ambassador, because he said his father was only a clown who had stolen his kingdom,' de Quadra informed Philip. 'The matter has reached such a point that the Queen is careful they should not meet in the palace to avoid their slashing each other in her presence.'

The tragi-comic strain persisted through Prince Eric's court-ship as through his bitter life. From the first moment of his uncouth wooing, when, in Mary's reign, Elizabeth had said she liked his proposal so well that she hoped never to hear of it again, his suit was to be the butt of wit. His father King Gustavus spent a fortune in the pursuit of Elizabeth; gold and silver were scattered among her subjects, and she received magnificent presents of tapestries, furs, horses and money, in return for which it was brought to the Swedes' notice that they were being 'made fun of in the palace, and by the Queen more than anybody'. Once, Duke John was kept waiting to see the Queen so long that he finally gave up, and returned, incensed, to his lodgings. But Elizabeth did not fail to turn the droll affair to her advantage; a rich royal suitor had more than amusement to offer, and so there were occasions when she was charming to the Swedish deputation. As de Quadra once reported:

The Swedish ambassador was summoned the other day by the Queen, who told him she wished to show her gratitude to his master who had sought her in the day of her simplicity, and asked him to tell her whether his ambassadors were coming, as she was being pressed with other marriages. They are constantly getting presents out of them in this way.

It was said that Eric would come in person to plead the constancy and strength of his love for Elizabeth, and Londoners speculated about the number of wagons massed with bullion that he would bring with him. The comedy was to continue for two years, but blond-bearded Eric never came. Having been slighted by the Queen of England he finally married a common soldier's daughter. Having recalled Duke John, believing his brother to be wooing Elizabeth on his own behalf, he was eventually deposed and then murdered by John, through the undignified medium of poisoned yellow-pea soup. From the first to the last, Eric of Sweden was 'of those that farthest come behind' in the pursuit of Elizabeth.

Elizabeth had no more intention of accepting Prince Eric or the Archduke Charles than she had had of marrying King Philip; for her the object of all the splendid courtships which presented themselves was not marriage, the commitment and capture that would take from her her new-found mastery, but political dalliance. By using her superb mental powers in conjunction with her most aggravating feminine weaknesses she could keep her suitors' hopes alive for months on end, to suit her needs both as a queen and as a woman. She had been a victim for so long, dependent on others' humours for her liberty and life, that she found a keen, exultant pleasure in being the coquettish centre of extravagant attentions, with absolute power to encourage or spurn, and even to mock if she pleased. However purely political her suitors' motives, the fact remained that marriage was the most personal of all treaties. And so her demands for detailed descriptions, portraits, personal facts about the wooers were relayed across Europe. There was no hope for the Archduke if he had a big ugly head like the

Earl of Bedford; her ambassador at the Emperor's court must send her a lengthy and exact description of Charles, including his habits and character, and even so she continued to insist she must meet him before she could reach a decision. Her husband must be a real man, she informed de Quadra; one who, in her evocative phrase, 'would not sit at home all day among the cinders, but in time of peace keep himself employed in warlike exercises'. She was describing the type of man to whom she was always attracted; the Thomas Seymour breed, dashing, brave, and virile.

'As she is a woman,' de Quadra wrote in October 1559, 'and a spirited and obstinate woman too, passion has to be considered.' In the coming years passion was not only to be considered, but to play a central role in Elizabeth's life. The Queen had fallen in love, and the man she loved was to become the most ruthless and persistent of all her suitors.

^^^

5

THE QUEEN IN LOVE

While her suitors' ambassadors were jostling hopefully in the antechambers of Whitehall, and speculation was veering from one great name to another, Elizabeth had fallen recklessly in love with a man who was neither a foreign prince nor an eminent English noble, but a mere younger son of a new and tainted family. Lord Robert Dudley, grandson and son of executed traitors, was an ambitious, devious, married man, but he was to be the great love of Elizabeth's life.

For Lord Robert, as for Elizabeth, the wheel of Fortune had turned almost full circle by 1558, when they were both twenty-five. The Dudley family had risen to giddy heights during King Edward's reign; when his able, dangerous father acquired the title of Duke of Northumberland and the position of virtual ruler of England, young Robert had come to the forefront of court life and had a glimpse of power. The Duke of Northumberland dealt out promising official positions to his brood of sons, and Robert became a Gentleman of the Privy Chamber to the boy King as well as Master of the Buckhounds – a post particularly suited to his sporting tastes. At that time he must often have met the Lady Elizabeth when she visited her brother's court. But the plot in which he supported his father after King Edward's death was intended to deprive Elizabeth, as well as Mary, of the throne.

For a few desperate weeks in the summer of 1553, the Duke of Northumberland was poised at the summit of power, his sons, bold and obedient, ranged behind him. If he was to succeed in making little Lady Jane Grey the nominal Queen of England, the rightful heir Mary had to be seized and silenced; it was twenty-year-old Robert who was sent clattering down the stone stairs from his father's council room in the Tower, to ride with all speed to Suffolk at the head of a troop of horse and bring Mary in. That was the beginning of the plunge downwards for Robert Dudley. By the end of July he was back in the Tower, no longer an honoured son of England's most powerful man, but a prisoner under guard. Confined alone, chafing his name onto the wall, ROBART DVDLEY, he waited to die as a traitor.

He was still waiting when the spring came, and the Lady Elizabeth was brought to imprisonment in the nearby Bell Tower. Northumberland had requested at his trial 'that Her Majesty will be gracious to my childer, which may hereafter do Her Grace good service, considering that they went by my commandment that am their father, and not of their own free wills'; as the weeks passed it became apparent that Mary was indeed disposed to be gracious to the traitor-Duke's remaining sons. Vigour and enterprise such as Robert Dudley's were wasted on prison-pastimes, and after more than a year of narrow confinement in the Tower, he and his brothers were released, to do the Queen good service.

Whether or not Robert had succeeded in communicating with Elizabeth while they were both prisoners behind the same dark walls, their old acquaintance developed into a strong bond during Mary's reign. As Robert began to rise to honourable status once again, serving Philip and Mary abroad and distinguishing himself as a valiant and capable Master of the Ordnance at the Siege of St Quentin in 1557, he kept in touch with Elizabeth. A contemporary report said that he gave her generous gifts of money when she was in difficulties; in 1562 the King of Sweden was told by an English visitor to his court that 'in her trouble Lord Robert did sell away a good piece of his land to aid her, which divers supposed to be the cause the Queen so favoured him'. When the news of Mary's death brought the dark days to an end, Robert rode to Elizabeth at Hatfield and was one of the close friends and servants whom she swiftly rewarded with public offices. Kat Ashley became First Gentlewoman of the Privy Chamber; Thomas Parry was knighted and appointed Controller of the Household; William

Cecil was sworn in as Secretary of State, and Lord Robert Dudley was appointed her Master of the Horse. Through all the years of advancement and honour which were to come to him, he would not relinquish that office, Elizabeth's first public favour to him.

The Queen clung to old friends and associates. Even such a fallible servant as Parry was dear to her because he had been with her in times of extreme adversity. But Robert had more than loyalty and proven fellowship to recommend him to the young Queen. He had the superb looks, the aura of sexual vigour and the taste for hardy physical activities which Elizabeth found so intensely attractive in a man. By the spring of 1559 her passion for her Master of the Horse could not be concealed. On 18 April Feria wrote to King Philip:

During the last few days Lord Robert has come so much into favour that he does what he likes with affairs, and it is even said that Her Majesty visits him in his chamber day and night. People talk of this so freely that they go so far as to say that his wife has a malady in one of her breasts and the Queen is only waiting for her to die to marry Lord Robert. I can assure Your Majesty that matters have reached such a pass that I have been brought to consider whether it would not be well to approach Lord Robert on Your Majesty's behalf, promising him your help and favour and coming to terms with him.

In those succinct lines Feria introduced the major themes of Robert Dudley's lifelong relationship with the Queen. Political power, scandal, talk of murder and marriage, and furtive dealings with Spain and other foreign powers were to recur like scarlet threads in the bright, sometimes tawdry, fabric of Elizabeth's greatest love-affair.

For a queen who was so committed to the state of virginity that she had to be coaxed into considering the suits of mighty princes, Elizabeth seemed remarkably abandoned in her behaviour towards her favourite. As she herself said, 'in this world she had had so much sorrow and tribulation and so little joy', that in her new-found freedom she grasped avidly at the pleasure of Robert's company. There was a little flutter of intrigue when Pickering arrived at court, in May 1559, soon after Elizabeth's feelings for Robert had become evident; on one occasion the Master of the Horse went off to hunt at Windsor and the Queen took advantage of his absence to spend some cosy hours with her attractive suitor Pickering. 'They tell me Lord Robert is not so friendly with him as he was,' de Quadra reported ingenuously. But there could be no real doubt as to where Elizabeth's true affections lay, and as though to prove it, at the end of the same month she was reported to have given Robert the enormous sum of £12,000 'as an aid towards his expenses'. Official honours, such as the Order of the Garter, which she bestowed upon him on the first possible occasion, were matched by constant informal signs of love; the Queen smiled at Lord Robert, danced with him, rode with him, made indecorous visits to his rooms with a freedom which could not fail to give rise to gossip. Ambassadors hinted in their dispatches at 'extraordinary things about this intimacy', unspecified goings-on vouched to by nameless witnesses; and the rumours which reached foreign courts were to cause more than one important suitor to express disquieting doubts about the chastity of the Queen of England. Amongst her own subjects whispers of scandal filtered into London streets and country lanes, to be echoed back in garbled form, with folk-song embellishments about a game of legerdemain and a gift of a fine petticoat – 'Thinkst thou that it was a petticoat? No, no, he gave her a child, I warrant thee.' At the heart of all the talk, sophisticated insinuations and illiterate gossip alike, was the one very basic allegation which a drunken inhabitant of Totnes expressed in its simplest form. 'Lord Robert', he asserted, 'did swive the Queen.'

The Emperor, father of the Archdukes, was perturbed by the 'somewhat discreditable rumours' which reached him concerning his son's prospective bride. Breuner was ordered to find out the truth of the matter, and the ambassador's response was illuminating. Informing his Imperial master that 'my Lord Robert is preferred by the Queen above all others, and that Her Majesty shows her liking for him more markedly than is consistent with her honour and dignity', he nevertheless stressed that all his 'most diligent enquiries into the calumnies that are current about the Queen, not only abroad but also here in England' had produced no firm evidence, and all the people who knew the Queen intimately 'swear by all that is holy that Her Majesty has most certainly never been forgetful of her honour'. Then he recounted a dramatic scene which took place early in August between Kat Ashley and the Queen.

Kat, still Elizabeth's most intimate personal attendant, had suddenly fallen to her knees and begged the Queen to marry and put an end to all the disreputable rumours, 'telling Her Majesty that her behaviour towards the said Master of the Horse occasioned much evil-speaking; for she showed herself so affectionate to him that Her Majesty's honour and dignity would be sullied'. Elizabeth gave a restrained reaction to her former governess's exhortations, half-excusing herself: 'If she had shown herself gracious to her Master of the Horse, he had deserved it for his honourable nature and dealings'; half-denying the accusations: 'She was always surrounded by her Ladies of the Bedchamber and Maids-of-honour, who at all times could see if there was anything dishonourable between her and her Master of the Horse'; and working up to a splendidly regal climax: 'If she had ever had the will or had found pleasure in such a dishonourable kind of life, from which may God preserve her, she did not know of anyone who could forbid her; but she trusted in God that nobody would ever live to see her so commit herself.' She had spoken in her own defence, and she had spoken convincingly. Nobody would ever live to see her so commit herself.

Her affair with Lord Robert Dudley was an intensely sexual relationship that was never consummated. The exhibitionism of it all was part of the excitement for Elizabeth; it was a form of acting which required an audience, for the extravagance of her indiscreet familiarity with her favourite was not proof of sexual surrender, but rather a tantalizing, titillating substitute. With his hard eyes and bold air, standing an athletic five feet ten in his tilt-armour, dark-haired Lord Robert typified the masculine splendour which Elizabeth had been brought up to worship in her mighty father. To keep such a strong, desirable man in a state of flattering passion for her without ever quite permitting him to gain the mastery over her was for Elizabeth a heady form of power. She could enjoy all the intimate communion and outward signs of love while clutching, with an instinct beyond the reach of reason, onto the state of virginity which would be her shield against the tragedies that had befallen her mother and stepmothers. It was because the normal physical purpose was missing from Elizabeth's dealings with the man she loved that the preambles became so disproportionately important to her, to the point where she indulged in such antics as mischievously tickling Robert's neck in full view of the court and the Scottish envoy, on the solemn and politically delicate occasion of his creation as Earl of Leicester. With the same Scottish envoy she afterwards enacted a pretty little scene over a portrait of Robert – marked in her handwriting 'My Lord's picture' – which she conspiratorially extracted from her private cabinet and then feigned not to let the Scottish diplomat see, until he played his part in the charade by pressing to be allowed a glimpse of it. There was much in Elizabeth's emotional behaviour and demands that suggested an adolescent girl rather than a mature woman. She felt both passion and tenderness for Robert, but she would never yield herself entirely to him or any man, and in the teasing, posing coquetry for which she became notorious lay the evidence of her lack of fulfilment.

From the very beginning of his relationship with the Queen, even while he was the husband of another woman, Lord Robert's presence was felt in Elizabeth's marriage dealings. At times his very existence seemed likely to hinder the business of selecting a suitable consort for the Queen; reporting on the progress of the Archduke Ferdinand's wooing, in April 1559, de Quadra noted: 'Sometimes she appears to want to marry him, and speaks like a woman who will only accept a great prince, and then they say that she is in love with Lord Robert and never lets him leave her.' In a political situation glittering with possibilities, Northumberland's most promising son would not be content to play a passive role for long. In September, when there was a strong possibility that the Queen might marry the Earl of Arran for the sake of settling the Scottish question, Robert took an active hand in affairs, stealthily approaching de Quadra to offer support and encouragement in the Archduke's cause, to counter Arran's suit. The means by which he negotiated with the ambassador, using his sister Lady Sidney as go-between and ally, was one which he would later employ again, in his own pursuit of the Queen. At first de Quadra succumbed to the young adventurer's charm and air of forthright integrity. 'Lord Robert and his sister are certainly acting splendidly, and the King will have to reward them well,' he wrote warmly. 'Robert professes to be the most faithful servant our King has here.' But disillusionment followed. 'I am anything but pleased with his dissimulation,' de Quadra complained in December, and by the following March he had come to the irate conclusion that Robert was 'the worst and most procrastinating young man I ever saw in my life, and not at all courageous or spirited'. The truth was that the Queen's beloved Lord Robert was, first and foremost, a devoted servant of his own interests.

De Quadra was far from alone in his bad opinion of Elizabeth's favourite. Robert Dudley acquired a vile reputation in many quarters. His obvious ambition and his influence with the Queen made him a figure either to be courted or opposed; those who envied him, resented his undeserved greatness, or genuinely feared his presence at the centre of affairs all contributed to his ill-fame. 'Beware of the gypsy, for he will be too hard for you all. You know not the beast as I do,' warned the Earl of Sussex on his deathbed. There was certainly something gypsyish in Dudley's dark good looks and bold opportunistic nature, but the beastliness alleged in tales of his insatiable lust and predeliction for poisoning people entered the realms of myth. What was real was the dislike which he inspired at court. De Quadra asserted that 'all the principal people in the kingdom' were his enemies, and, even more dramatically : 'Not a man in England but cries out at the top of his voice that this fellow is ruining the country with his vanity.' England's highest peer, the young Duke of Norfolk, was Dudley's chief opponent. He felt his rightful hereditary authority to be undermined by the presence of the powerful favourite, and he was disturbed by the Queen's apparent irresponsibility. 'The Queen and Robert are very uneasy about the Duke of Norfolk, as he talks openly about her lightness and bad government,' de Quadra wrote. Norfolk was heard to say menacingly that 'if Lord Robert did not abandon his present presumptions and pretensions, he would not die in his bed'. Robert's attitude bred mistrust, his advancement aroused fear; even though he was a married man, he was from the outset suspected of aiming at the ultimate prize – the consort's crown. 'I think this hatred of Lord Robert will continue, as the Duke and the rest of them cannot put up with his being King,' de Quadra informed King Philip, and soon after reported : 'He has again been warned that there is a plot to kill him, which I quite believe, for there is not a man in the realm can suffer the idea of his being King.' It was curious, the persistent talk of marriage for a man who already had a wife. Towards the end of November Robert had a furious quarrel with Norfolk, who was urging the match with the Archduke, 'and Robert told him he was neither a good English-man nor a loyal subject who advised the Queen to marry a foreigner'. The question hung in the air: if Elizabeth was to be dissuaded from marrying a foreigner, which Englishman did Robert have in mind for her husband? De Quadra believed he knew. 'Lord Robert has sent to poison his wife,' he asserted. 'Certainly all the Queen has done with us and with the Swede, and will do with the rest in the matter of her marriage, is only keeping Lord Robert's enemies and the country engaged with words until this wicked deed of killing his wife is consum-mated.' The atmosphere was charged with violence.

Mild, wise Secretary Cecil became almost distracted with worry over the situation. Elizabeth showed no signs of making a proper match and providing the country with an heir, but seemed quite given up to reckless dalliance with her unsuitable favourite. 'The Queen, thanks be to God, is in very good health and is now become a great huntress and doth follow it daily from morning to night,' Dudley wrote cheerfully in September 1560, adding that she was sending over to Ireland for some new horses, 'especially for good strong gallopers, which are better than her geldings, which she spareth not to try as fast as they can go. And I fear them much, but yet she will prove them'. While Elizabeth was enjoying thrilling breakneck gallops with her Master of the Horse, her greatest minister, Cecil, was pro-posing to resign, utterly despairing. 'God send Her Majesty understanding what shall be her surety,' he wrote mournfully to Throckmorton, the ambassador in France. To de Quadra, who inferred that Cecil was in disgrace, 'and that Robert was trying to turn him out of his place', he confided a good deal of his anxiety. 'He said it was a bad sailor who did not enter port if he saw a storm coming, and he clearly foresaw the ruin of the realm through Robert's intimacy with the Queen, who surrendered all affairs to him and meant to marry him. He said he did not know how the country put up with it.' With ominous emphasis, reminiscent of Norfolk's threats, Cecil repeated twice 'that Lord Robert would be better in Paradise than here'. His concluding remarks were, in the light of events, still more sinister. According to de Quadra: 'He ended by saying that Robert was thinking of killing his wife, who was publicly announced to be ill, although she was quite well, and would take very good care they did not poison her.' When Secretary Cecil spoke those words to the Spanish ambassador, Robert's young wife Amy Robsart had only hours to live.

She was found dead, with her neck broken, at the bottom of a staircase at Cumnor Place, on 8 September 1560. She had sent all her servants off to the fair that day, her husband was away, as usual, hunting with the Queen at Windsor, and so no one could say for sure how she had died. 'I have no way to purge myself of the malicious talk that I know the wicked world will use, but one, which is the very plain truth to be known,' Robert wrote to a relation, begging him to investigate the accident with the utmost diligence, 'as the cause and the manner thereof doth marvellously trouble me, considering my case many ways.' Elizabeth kept her presence of mind when she learned of it. Lord Robert was sent to his house at Kew, and she told de Quadra the news in a phrase which suggested that she was by no means certain of the facts. But de Quadra's mind at once leapt from murder to marriage. 'Certainly this business is most shameful and scandalous', he wrote, 'and withal I am not sure whether she will marry the man at once or even if she will marry at all, as I do not think her mind sufficiently fixed.'

That Elizabeth had played no deliberate part in the affair was clear, but the 'very plain truth' of the matter was never conclusively proved. The possibility could not be ruled out that Lord Robert had played the beast and fulfilled the expectations of the world by sending assassins to rid him of the frail obstacle which 'stood in his light, as he supposed', barring his way to marriage with the Queen. But physical violence may not have been necessary; perhaps the subtle poison of neglect killed Dudley's wife. According to local opinion, she had been 'a strange woman of mind', and one of her close attendants said she had often heard Amy 'pray to God to deliver her from desperation'. Amy Dudley had lost her husband to the Queen, and in his absence, while she tended his household affairs, the salacious rumours of his dealings at court must have drifted back to her. In a brief business letter, written a year before she died, she included the pathetically revealing phrase: 'I forgot to move my Lord thereof before his departing, he being sore troubled with weighty affairs, and I not being altogether in quiet for his sudden departing.' The love had drained from their relationship, and Amy Dudley was left alone, though not in quiet, until all jealousy, loneliness, and fear ended for her at the foot of a flight of stairs. Some reports had said she was very ill with cancer of the breast; such a condition, in an advanced state, might cause a spontaneous fracture of the spine as a result of even such a mild exertion as walking downstairs. But whatever mental or physical pain Amy suffered at the end of her short life, the husband who had married her for love was not with her to comfort her and see to her welfare. And after it had happened, the murder, suicide or sheer accident that made him a free man, Robert showed no grief, nor any sign of regret, only care for his own reputation. He was, after all, Northumberland's son.

The official verdict was misadventure, but rumour at home and abroad proclaimed Robert's guilt. At the French court Mary Queen of Scots sneered that the Queen of England was going to marry 'her horsekeeper', who had killed his wife to make room for her, and Throckmorton, goaded almost to distraction, wrote from Paris: 'The bruits be so brim and so maliciously reported here touching the marriage of the Lord Robert and the death of his wife, as I know not where to turn me nor what conclusion to bear.' Unnecessarily, considering the recipient's views, he begged Cecil: 'As you bear a true and faithful heart to Her Majesty and the realm, and do desire to keep them from utter desolation, I conjure you to do all your endeavour to hinder that marriage.' He sent his confidential secretary Robert

Jones to England to impress upon the Queen the danger which her reputation was facing. However matters might turn out, however plainly Robert's innocence might eventually be proved, his active courtship of the Queen had begun in the most unpropitious of circumstances.

Elizabeth looked strained and ill in the weeks that followed Amy Dudley's death. When Jones had an audience with her at Greenwich, and told her plainly what was being said about Lord Robert and herself, she moved restlessly in her chair, and covered her face with her hands, then broke into one of her characteristic nervous laughs. She told Jones firmly that the investigations into the affair had utterly vindicated both Lord Robert's honesty and her own honour, and he left feeling somewhat reassured. 'Surely the matter of Lord Robert doth greatly perplex her', he decided, 'and it is never like to take place.' In such an explosive situation, it would have been dangerous folly for Elizabeth to have married Lord Robert out of hand, even if she had wished to. She loved him dearly, and she undoubtedly believed him to be innocent of the crime of murder, but her instinct for self-preservation and her care for the quietness of her realm were stronger than any passion she could ever feel. As early as October de Quadra reported that Cecil had told him 'that the Queen had decided not to marry Lord Robert, as he had learnt direct from her'.

Robert himself was 'all this while, as it were, in a dream', as he wrote to Cecil. In his temporary exile at Kew – 'too far, too far, from the place where I am bound to be' – he had longed to return to court, to wield his personal influence with Elizabeth, instead of remaining, taut with hope and anxiety, at an enforced distance, while his glistening prospects of marriage were darkened by the world's talk of infamy. Yet, once back at court, he found that his return resolved nothing. The Queen loved and favoured him as she had before, but she was both uncertain and unyielding. In November she intended to make him Earl of Leicester, but when the letters patent were brought to her to be signed, with a sudden angry gesture she picked up a penknife and slashed them through, crying that the Dudleys had been traitors for three generations. Active, ambitious Robert, deprived of a reward so nearly within his grasp, fumed with frustration, and again the changeable vane of Elizabeth's humour veered round. She patted his cheek, as though amused by the anger she had roused in him, and smilingly said: 'No, no! The bear and ragged staff are not so easily overthrown.' She could neither accept nor refuse him. Not for years would Robert Dudley give up all hope of winning the magnificent prize, but from the outset of his serious pursuit, in that turbulent autumn of 1560, the Queen had set a wearisome pace.

Amidst the clamour of speculation and slander, the Earl of Sussex raised a rational voice. Though deeply opposed to Dudley as a person, he nevertheless wrote to Cecil from Ireland to recommend that the match between Lord Robert and the Queen should take place. If Elizabeth were allowed to 'choose after her own affections', he urged, it would be the surest way to provide England with the heir that was so desperately needed. 'Whomsoever she shall choose,' Sussex wrote loyally, 'him will I love and honour, and serve to the uttermost.' Behind his words lay sympathy, wisdom and consciousness of the royal prerogative, of which Parliament was to receive such a ringing reminder six years later. The choice of her consort rightfully lay with Elizabeth alone, both as a queen, and, Sussex was intimating, as a woman. The Earl's argument was very sound except in one respect, and that was his basic premise – the generally held belief that Elizabeth's passion for Lord Robert must signify a desire to marry him and find normal fulfilment for her undisguised physical attraction to him. Robert himself based much on that mistaken belief.

Though disappointed, he was not deterred by the setbacks with which his wooing met during the closing months of 1560. 'Whatsoever reports and opinions be,' Cecil informed Throckmorton, on 31 December, 'I know surely that Lord Robert hath more fear than hope, and so doth the Queen's Majesty give him cause.' But with a crown so nearly within his reach, Robert Dudley was not to be dismayed by the humours of a woman so capricious as Elizabeth; fear of losing the prize only served to spur him on to more energetic pursuit. If his 'eminent endowments of mind and body' and unique personal relationship with the Queen would not suffice to persuade her to marry him, then he would find a means to add political weight to his suit. No less a power than Spain should be prevailed upon to support him.

As before, Dudley did not immediately approach de Quadra in person, but sent a relation, this time his brother-in-law Henry Sidney, to open negotiations with the ambassador.

He began by beating about the bush very widely, but at last came to his brother-in-law's affairs and said that as the matter was now public property, and I knew how much inclined the Queen was to the marriage, he wondered that I had not suggested to Your Majesty this opportunity for gaining over Lord Robert by extending a hand to him now, and he would thereafter serve and obey Your Majesty like one of your own vassals.

So de Quadra wrote to King Philip. There was, as the ambassador dryly added, 'a great deal more to the same effect', but the object of Sidney's mission was already quite plain. Since the Archduke's suit had come to nothing there had seemed to be no prospect of Elizabeth taking a husband who represented the interests of Spain, but now Dudley was proposing a pact that should be beneficial to all parties. If King Philip would use his power and influence to persuade Elizabeth to marry her favourite, Dudley would swear to act as a devoted servant of Spanish interests, and to direct Elizabeth in the great work of restoring England to Catholicism. As he put his brother-in-law's case to de Quadra, Sidney was full of fine rehearsed sentiments; above all he stressed that Lord Robert's chief desire was to serve King Philip 'at all times, and in all things, to the full extent of his means and abilities, and more especially regarding religion, as is his duty'. The Queen, Sidney hastened to explain, would not refer to the matter unless de Quadra spoke of it first to her, but he told the ambassador that he 'might be sure that she desired nothing more than the countenance of His Majesty to conclude the match'. Beneath the lofty protestations Dudley's impatience to secure the quarry was evident. That the religious policy of Elizabeth's government should be thus reversed was out of the question, but Robert was prepared to use any inducement that would win him King Philip's support, any means that would make Elizabeth irrevocably his wife. 'He then pressed me still further to write to Your Majesty and

forward the business', de Quadra told King Philip, 'so that Lord
Robert should receive the boon at Your Majesty's hands.' They
would make ill-matched allies, the parvenu traitor's son and the
King of Spain, but de Quadra came to the conclusion that it
would be worth accepting Dudley's proposition. 'It is for Your
Majesty to decide,' he wrote to Philip, 'but I have no doubt that
if there is any way to cure the bad spirit of the Queen, both as
regards religion and Your Majesty's interests, it is by means of
this marriage, at least while her desire for it lasts.'

Lord Robert's ambition, like Elizabeth's love, was blind. He
had conceived his matrimonial coup in the belief that by
combining the advantages both of a foreign alliance and an
English match, and offering both a politically advantageous
marriage and one that would be personally delightful to the
Queen, he could sweep away all resistance. But he was setting
nets to catch the wind. He did not see that all her fanciful talk
of taking a husband, which gave her such intense delight, was
not a preliminary to, but a substitute for, the reality of
marriage.

De Quadra had an audience with the Queen in February to
assess Lord Robert's progress, and came away with encouraging
news for the favourite. Elizabeth had made no secret of her
feelings for him, and she had toyed provocatively with the
notion of marrying him. 'After much circumlocution', the
ambassador reported, she said 'that she was no angel, and did
not deny that she had some affection for Lord Robert for the
many good qualities he possessed, but she certainly had never
decided to marry him or anyone else, although she daily saw
more clearly the necessity for her marriage.' Teasing and
sparkling, she gave it as her opinion that she ought to wed an
Englishman, and then asked gravely what King Philip would
think if she were to marry one of her servitors? Cautiously de
Quadra answered that he knew his King 'would be happy to
hear of the advancement and aggrandizement of Lord Robert',
as His Majesty 'had great affection for him and held him in high
esteem'. Dudley was not the only diplomatic liar at Elizabeth's
court. But the Queen did not find it strange that others should
see fine qualities in the man she loved, and her happiness at
hearing Robert praised was almost undignified. Years before she

had shown similar pleasure when people spoke well of Thomas Seymour.

Indications that his courtship was progressing well made Robert 'excessively overjoyed'. He begged de Quadra to raise the subject again in his next interview with the Queen, insisting 'that it was only fear and timidity that prevented the Queen from deciding', but by the end of March his ruse was obviously failing. 'Robert is very aggrieved and dissatisfied,' de Quadra wrote, and added that he had 'fallen ill with annoyance'. Cecil had intervened in the favourite's manoeuvres, telling the ambassador blandly that the Queen wished to have a letter from King Philip recommending her to marry Robert, which she could openly lay before Parliament. Robert was furious. To be publicly acknowledged as the tool of Spain in this way would do his reputation no good at all; urgently he pressed the Queen to 'free herself from the tyranny of these people', make a stand against the wishes of her own subjects and throw herself entirely on King Philip's favour. Some of Robert's adherents were said to be advising him to give the Queen an ultimatum – either she must marry him before Easter, or else he would leave the country altogether, and go to the wars in the service of King Philip. It was not at all the outcome which Dudley had expected, yet as the fumes of the affair blew away he was seen to be as high in the Queen's favour as ever. 'Lord Robert's recent discontent has ended in her giving him an apartment upstairs adjoining her own, as it is healthier than that which he had downstairs,' de Quadra recorded. 'He is delighted.'

By the spring of 1561 the critical phase of Elizabeth's affair with Dudley was past, and their relationship was set on the path which it was to follow through the greater part of her reign. While Robert was a married man Elizabeth had felt free to pose and flaunt and dally with him to her heart's content, to smile on his victories in the tiltyard, to gallop beside him on the superb Irish hunters he had obtained for her, to provoke him to passion with her sweet indiscreet favours. But with Amy's death that game had come to an abrupt end. Elizabeth was faced with the reality of Robert as a hot, urgent, new suitor, no foreign figurehead courting her by letter and proxy, but at her court, at her feet, in person, to press his cause, and ready to resort to any strategy, political or personal, that would speed his wooing. In the months that followed Amy's death the Queen's inner conflict was clearly visible in her careworn appearance and erratic behaviour towards Robert, but from that difficult period she emerged more emotionally dependent than ever upon him. She would not marry Lord Robert, much as she loved to toy with the idea, but neither could she live without him, and so in her personal love-affair Elizabeth instinctively resorted to the same policy by which she dominated so many of her diplomatic courtships – that of keeping expectations permanently alive yet permanently unfulfilled. As long as she gave Lord Robert grounds to hope that she would one day yield and marry him she could exact from him the unstinting attentions which she craved, until with time and habit their lives became fused together; and without having had to undergo the torments of marriage, Elizabeth obtained from her beloved Robin a more ardent love and unremitting care than she might have had from a husband. It was Cecil's private belief that as consort Lord Robert was 'like to prove unkind, or jealous of the Queen's Majesty'. But as her constant suitor, the ever hoping, fearing and adoring wooer, Lord Robert provided Queen Elizabeth with the greatest emotional satisfaction she ever knew.

It was a curious relationship, composed of rebuffs and caresses, tender intimacy and neurotic posturing. On Midsummer Day, 1561, Robert gave a grand feast; in the afternoon, he, the Queen and Bishop de Quadra found themselves alone together in the gallery of the boat from which they were to watch the festivities. On that heady June day Elizabeth was in high spirits, and she and Robert began joking together, 'which she likes to do better than talking about business', de Quadra commented disapprovingly. He went on: 'They went so far with their jokes that Lord Robert told her that, if she liked, I could be the minister to perform the act of marriage, and she, nothing loath to hear it, said she was not sure whether I knew enough English.' Sharing jokes, teasing one another about marriage – it was a scene to delight Elizabeth's fancy and send Robert's hopes soaring. Such amorous familiarity was characteristic of the Queen's dealings with Lord Robert, and yet she made it very plain that the intimacy which she allowed him was not his right, but a favour which she could withdraw from him and confer upon another at any moment she chose. That he should have developed a proprietorial attitude towards her was understandable, when she encouraged and replied upon him so greatly; in illness it was upon Lord Robert that her tumbling thoughts fastened, and it seemed quite natural when she was suddenly taken ill one night in 1572 that 'my Lord of Leicester did watch with her all night'. When she was in good humour she could find a piquant pleasure in permitting Robert to take liberties with her, as on the occasion when, playing a fast game of tennis with the Duke of Norfolk and 'being very hot and sweating', Robert borrowed her handkerchief to mop his face, 'which the Duke seeing said that he was too saucy and swore that he would lay his racket upon his face'. The upshot of that commotion was that 'the Queen was offended sore' – not with Dudley's presumption, but 'with the Duke'. Yet, privileged though Robert was, neither he nor anyone in the world was allowed to infringe upon Elizabeth's ultimate mastery. Her royalty, like her person, was inviolable.

When Dudley put his power to the test, he found that it melted to nothing. His influence was over Elizabeth the woman; over Elizabeth the Queen he held no sway, as was vividly illustrated by an anecdote which appeared in the following century. According to this story, an adherent of Dudley's had tried to enter the Privy Chamber but was prevented by Simon Bowyer, a favourite Gentleman Usher of the Chamber, whose duty it was to bar the way to all but a select few. Dudley's man argued, and eventually fetched Lord Robert himself, who took the view that his own prestige was at stake; arrogantly informing Bowyer that he would have him dismissed, he strode in to speak to the Queen. Bowyer acted swiftly. He overtook Lord Robert and threw himself at the Queen's feet, imploring her to tell him plainly, whether my Lord of Leicester were King, or Her Majesty were Queen. His question was a spark to a tinder. Elizabeth flared into glittering anger. 'God's death, my Lord, I have wished you well', she blazed at Robert, 'but my favour is not so locked up in you that others shall not participate thereof ... and if you think to rule here, I will take a course to see you forthcoming. I will have here but one mistress and no master.' It was said that 'this so quailed my Lord of Leicester that his feigned humility was long after one of his best virtues'. Elizabeth's declaration: 'I will have here but one mistress and no master,' was not idly spoken in a moment of anger, it was the expression of her deepest feelings. In that moment Lord Robert must have glimpsed the hopelessness of his courtship of the Queen. Yet the 'quailing' of his pride and the casting-down of his hopes were followed, as always, by a renewal of the Queen's lavish favours, and thus the pursuit continued. The prize was so great, success seemed so tantalizingly close; by no means might Robert Dudley draw his wearied mind from the magnificent woman who dominated his life. He could not abandon the chase, as long as the opinion prevailed, in the words of de Quadra's successor, 'that if any marriage at all is to result from all this it will be his'.

The bond between Elizabeth and Robert was often subjected to heavy strain, but it was never entirely severed. Not even infidelity could divide them for long; their jealousies ended in weeping, caressing reunions which brought them yet closer together. When Elizabeth entered into a heady flirtation with the handsome young courtier Thomas Heneage in the autumn of 1565, Robert was both aggrieved and unnerved; Throckmorton, who had become his close confidant, urged him to put the Queen's affection to the test by starting a love-affair of his own in retaliation, watching 'how the Queen took it', and then asking permission to leave the court 'to go to his own place to stay as other noblemen do'. Robert took the advice. The woman whom he chose as the instrument of his vengeance was 'one of the best-looking ladies of the court', the lovely redhead Lettice Knollys, Viscountess Hereford. Tempers and passions rose high; Robert had a furious quarrel with Heneage, then tersely asked for 'leave to go', but Elizabeth too 'was in a great temper, and upbraided him with what had taken place with Heneage and his flirting with the Viscountess in very bitter words'. For three days Robert stayed glowering in his apartments, while the Earl of Sussex and Cecil, although 'no friends of Lord Robert in their hearts', tried to smooth over the unpleasant affair, which was not really very difficult. 'The result of the tiff was that both the Queen and Lord Robert shed tears, and he has returned to his former favour.' Feuding with Norfolk, infuriating Cecil and the wise Councillors, negotiating with foreign powers for their support in his wooing: it seemed that there was nothing Robert could do for which Elizabeth would not forgive him, as long as he remained devotedly hers. As years went by he would hazard a mistress, even a passionate clandestine love-affair, but the prime of his life was dedicated to Elizabeth; marriage, and the lawful heirs for which he longed, were thus denied him. He wrote emphatically, at the beginning of the 1570s, that he would rather never have a wife than marry and lose the Queen's favour thereby. His attraction to Lettice Knollys was not quenched by the joyous tears of his reunion with Elizabeth, but he was to spend fourteen more years in sterile dalliance with the Queen before he could bring himself finally to give the *coup de grâce* to his fallen hopes, and take the voluptuous widow Lettice for his lawful wife.

The constant vigilant presence of Lord Robert cast a long shadow over Elizabeth's other courtships. The true nature of his relationship with the Queen, and the extent of his influence over her, were questions anxiously investigated by prospective foreign suitors. The answers they received were, however, as contradictory as Elizabeth's own declarations. The Imperial envoy reported enthusiastically in 1565 that Lord Robert was 'a virtuous, pious, courteous and highly moral man, whom the Queen loves as a sister her brother, in all maidenly honour, in most chaste and honest love' – a verdict as propitious for the Archduke's suit as the rival French ambassador's equally exaggerated assertion, that Lord Robert had slept with the Queen on New Year's night, was damaging. Elizabeth's own statements only added to the uncertainty; her intentions regarding Lord Robert and marriage seemed to change from day to day. 'Beggarwoman and single, far rather than Queen and married', was the dramatic preference which she expressed to the gullible Austrian envoy, but she also informed him encouragingly that if she were to wed it would be as a queen, and therefore she could only take a great prince as her husband – which, in turn, was in marked contrast to her statement to the Spanish ambassador that she must marry an Englishman, to satisfy the will of her people, and that the most fitting consort would thus be Lord Robert Dudley. It was de Quadra's successor, de Silva, who best summed up the situation when he commented perceptively: 'I do not think anything is more enjoyable to this Queen than treating of marriage, although she assures me herself that nothing annoys her more. She is vain, and would like all the world to be running after her, but it will probably end in her remaining as she is, unless she marry Lord Robert, who is still doing his best to win her.'

In doing his best to win her for so many years, Lord Robert gave Elizabeth the unstinting attention and admiration for which she longed. She dared not rely on the affection of a husband, but from an ever eager, unsatisfied suitor she could expect constant devotion. Though he never achieved his life's desire of taking the Queen of England for his wife, Robert won from her all that she was able to give as a woman, except the ultimate possession of her body and mind. There was in their deep and enduring relationship a sense of underlying reality which set it apart from all Elizabeth's other flirtations, wooings and love-dealings, and above all from the cult of fantastical adoration of the Queen which grew up in the later years of her reign. When the affair began they had been two lively, attractive young people, the King's daughter and the Duke's son, yet when it ended some thirty years later, with his death, their feelings for one another had not greatly altered, in spite of his marriage, and her courtships, and the difficult, demanding temperament of the Queen who was often 'more than a man, and in truth, sometimes less than a woman'. As much as she ever could be, Elizabeth was in love with Robert Dudley, the dearest of all her suitors.

~~~~~~

6

'THE WEAL OF THE KINGDOM'

While there was 'but one mistress and no master' in England, there would be no heirs born to the Queen. Admirable as her desire to remain a virgin might be, it was not royal chastity that would make England secure from wars of the succession, *coups d'état*, and the treacheries which thrived on an uncertain inheritance to the throne. For as long as Elizabeth could remember, the stability of the realm had been threatened by the weak state of the succession; the desperate lack of male heirs that had driven Henry VIII through six marriages had caused even the faded old maid Mary to marry in haste, and now that the last of his line, Elizabeth, had succeeded to the throne the situation was graver than ever. If she were to die young and unmarried, the resultant confusion over the rival claims of Mary Queen of Scots, the sisters of Lady Jane Grey, and others still more distant, would undoubtedly 'divide and ruin the country'. For the sake of her people, for the weal of the kingdom which she was pledged to protect, it seemed that Elizabeth must marry with all speed, and bear children.

A state of crisis came perilously close in the autumn of 1562, when, after three years as Queen, she still considered herself 'as free from any engagement to marry as the day she was born'. At Hampton Court, early in October, Elizabeth began to feel ill, and decided that she would take a bath. It was thought that she caught a chill 'by leaving her bath for the air', then her illness was found to be smallpox, and the ensuing fever was very nearly fatal. Her condition grew steadily worse, until she lost consciousness. 'She was all but gone,' it was reported. While the Queen was lying close to death her Council was hurriedly

meeting, trying to reach a decision about the succession. No
one spoke for Mary Queen of Scots, who already regarded
herself as Queen of England and Elizabeth as a bastard usurper;
the lovely Scottish Queen was the senior great-granddaughter
of Henry VII, but she was an alien and a papist, and had been
passed over in Henry VIII's will in favour of the Suffolk line –
Lady Jane Grey and her sisters Catherine and Mary Grey. Some
believed that King Henry's will should be obeyed and Lady
Catherine named heiress, while others supported the Earl of
Huntingdon, who was descended from Edward III. Opinions
were dangerously divided. As de Quadra reported: 'There was
great excitement that day in the palace, and if her improve-
ment had not come soon some hidden thoughts would have
become manifest.' But before discussion could erupt into
aggression the Queen's condition began to improve, and as she
regained consciousness her flickering thoughts focused on her
kingdom. The first words she managed to speak astounded her
anxious hearers. She asked that Lord Robert Dudley should be
made Protector of the realm, with a title and an income of
£20,000.

Weak and feverish though Elizabeth was, she knew what a
flood of speculation her demand would unleash, and she roused
herself to defend her honour and her suitor's character as
though for the last time, protesting feebly but earnestly 'that
although she loved and had always loved Lord Robert dearly, as
God was her witness nothing improper had ever passed between them'. With death still lurking amongst the hangings of
her bedchamber it was not an oath that she would have taken
lightly. Hiding their dismay, hastening to soothe her, the
Council promised to carry out all that she asked.

The Queen recovered and life at court returned to normal,
with Lord Robert enjoying greater favour than ever, but Elizabeth's illness had left deeper marks than the smallpox scars on
her face. It had been a 'great terror and dreadful warning', and
Englishmen took heed of it. They had seen how fine the thread
was upon which England's security hung, they had glimpsed
the confusion which would follow if that thread were to snap
while the succession question remained unresolved, and now
there was a new urgency in their talk of 'the Queen's marriage,

and succession of the crown'. Just before Parliament met, in January 1563, Dr Nowell preached a sermon in Westminster Abbey in which he publicly exhorted Elizabeth to marry. 'For as the marriage of Queen Mary was a terrible plague to all England,' he declaimed, 'the want of your marriage and issue is like to prove as great a plague,' then, his rhetoric swooping between the dynastic and the personal, he argued: 'If your parents had been of your mind, where had you been then? Or what had become of us now?' Though Parliament addressed the Queen in very different tones from Nowell's ill-advised harangue, they developed his theme. Humbly but fervently, Parliament petitioned Elizabeth to secure the succession, and marry.

The Commons' petition boldly stressed 'the great dangers, the unspeakable miseries of civil war, the perilous inter-meddlings of foreign princes with seditious, ambitious and factious subjects at home' which would rend the kingdom if Elizabeth were to die without an acknowledged heir; the Lords dwelt rather on the pleasures and benefits which marriage would bring to herself and her realm, before making subdued reference to their grave fears during her recent illness. The Lord Keeper, Sir Nicholas Bacon, drafted a speech in which he appealed to the Queen's maternal feelings, begging her to 'imagine the comfort, surety and delight that should happen to yourself by beholding an imp of your own, that should in time to come by God's grace inherit and enjoy the imperial crown of this realm, to the great rejoicing of all your loving subjects'. The Queen to whom all their pleas were addressed was not yet thirty years old; she was a lively, elegant young woman whose liking for male company was only too well known. That she should marry and have babies appeared to be both a natural and a necessary solution to the whole question.

Elizabeth's reponse to the petitions of this Parliament was characteristically moving and impressive. Though she committed herself to nothing, she implied a great deal – observing, somewhat tartly, that 'none other tree's blossom should have been minded ere ever hope of my fruit had been denied you', and declaring that any who thought she was bound 'by vow or determination' to remain unmarried were entirely wrong. 'For though I can think it best for a private woman, yet do I strive with myself to think it not meet for a prince,' she conceded. 'And if I can bend my liking to your need, I will not resist such a mind.' She brought her speech to a climax with an assurance about the succession: 'I hope I shall die in quiet with *nunc dimittis*, which cannot be without I see some glimpse of your following surety after my graved bones.' Her profound antipathy to marriage, her fear of naming a successor who could become the focus of constant plots, as she herself had been in her sister's reign, were thus hidden for the time being beneath fine non-committal pledges, while she sought to find a means by which the 'following surety' of her people would be secured. Evasive though her reply was, her profound concern was unfeigned; as she reminded the Commons: 'This matter toucheth me much nearer than it doth you all, who, if the worst happen, can lose but your bodies; but if I take not that convenient care that it behoveth me to have therein, I hazard to lose both body and soul.' What Parliament did not know was that even while they were debating the tortuous question, Elizabeth, harassed, isolated and perplexed, had taken a tentative step towards solving it, by a proposition so utterly unexpected that at first it seemed outrageous. In audience with the Scottish envoy, Maitland of Lethington, in March, she had casually suggested that Lord Robert Dudley should be married to Mary Queen of Scots.

The idea seemed in every way preposterous. Maitland, taken quite unawares, 'could not reply for confusion' as the Queen of England, curled and jewelled and shining with smiles, sweetly informed him that 'if his mistress would take her advice, and wished to marry safely and happily, she would give her a husband who would ensure both, and this was Lord Robert'. Mary Stuart of Scotland had been Queen of France and was now contemplating marriage with the heir of Philip of Spain, while other princes of noble houses vied for her attention; that she should marry the cast-off favourite of her greatest rival, a man who was the son of traitors and had once been condemned as a traitor himself, a courtier of blemished reputation, whose wealth and position had been given to him like lovers' favours by Elizabeth, was a proposal that amounted almost to an insult. It was with difficulty that Maitland rallied his wits and tried to turn aside her words with chaffing compliments. Elizabeth had announced that Lord Robert was endowed with such graces that if she herself had wished to marry he was the man whom she would take rather than all the princes in the world; Maitland responded that 'this was a great proof of the love she bore his Queen, as she was willing to give her a thing so dearly prized by herself'. Gallantly he told her that even if his mistress Queen Mary loved Lord Robert as dearly as she, Elizabeth, did, Mary would refuse to marry him, since that would deprive Elizabeth 'of all the joy and solace she received from his companionship'. But Elizabeth was not to be deterred; she went on to say that she wished to God that the elder Dudley brother, the Earl of Warwick, had as great an abundance of 'grace and good looks' as Lord Robert, for then she might have married one brother and Mary the other. Elizabeth was obviously enjoying herself, but for Maitland it was all very difficult and embarrassing. At last, longing to escape, he steered the conversation round to the succession, 'which he knew would shut her mouth directly', and suggested, with calculated facetiousness, that since his mistress Queen Mary was still very young, Elizabeth might first marry Lord Robert herself, and have children by him – 'which was so necessary for the welfare of the country' – and then when God should call her from this life she could leave Mary both her kingdom and her husband. Maitland can hardly have intended that joke to afford Elizabeth much amusement.

Astonishing as the Queen of England's proposal might have appeared, she was almost certainly in earnest. Beneath the fine cloak of diplomatic affection which covered Elizabeth's formal dealings with her cousin Mary Stuart lay hostility and fear. As Queen of France Mary had represented a grave threat to the security of England and Elizabeth; now, back in her northern kingdom as an eligible young widow of legendary charms and powerful connections, blatantly eager to enforce her claim to the English throne, she was potentially a still greater menace. As Feria had once said of Elizabeth: 'It all depends on the husband that this woman may take,' and just as Philip of Spain had then been willing to sacrifice his private feelings and marry

Elizabeth, so Elizabeth was now prepared to set aside personal emotion for the sake of her country. Married to a foreign prince, Mary would remain a constant danger, perhaps become the focus of a Catholic league against Elizabeth. But married to a minor English nobleman, a Protestant, in whom Elizabeth had absolute trust, she would be curbed, watched over and reported on. The political wisdom of offering Mary such a husband was obvious, and so, in Elizabeth's eyes, was the choice of Lord Robert. Because of the intimate bond between herself and Dudley she believed that she could rely utterly on his devotion, she 'was quite certain that he would sacrifice his life for her', and she did not doubt that he would defend her interests with unswerving loyalty, so that as the husband of Queen Mary he would remain the servant of Queen Elizabeth. It was an honour and a responsibility of which few would be worthy, but Elizabeth's faith in her beloved Lord Robert was boundless. Mary Stuart need not scorn to be offered a man of such notable abilities and attractions, who although not himself of royal blood, would bring Mary the assurance of Elizabeth's favour and the likelihood of the succession – and whom, as Elizabeth proudly declared to Maitland, she herself would prefer to any prince in the world if she had a mind to marry. That she was offering him to her rival instead was a tacit admission that she never would have 'such a mind'.

Yet she had assured Parliament that she would try to 'bend her liking' to her country's need in the matter of marriage, and as though to honour that pledge, in the autumn of 1563 Elizabeth re-opened matrimonial negotiations with the Archduke Charles of Austria. 'Marriage can bring Your Majesty and your realm nothing but advantage, weal and blessing,' an enthusiastic envoy told her in the following January, during an audience at Windsor. Had he substituted the word 'courtship' for 'marriage', Elizabeth's agreement would have been unfeigned.

The youngest of the Emperor Ferdinand's three sons, twenty-three-year-old Charles, had small power or wealth of his own to make him a match worthy of the Queen of England, but he was a Habsburg, and first cousin to Philip of Spain; a leisurely and protracted courtship with such a prince could be of great service to Elizabeth at this time. It would demonstrate an apparent willingness on her part to marry and produce heirs, so that she would be less harried by her anxious subjects, and to some extent it would deflect Catholic hopes, both at home and abroad, from Mary, Queen of Scots. Mary was showing great interest in the idea of marrying Philip's own son and heir Don Carlos – evidently she did not know that the youth was as sick and savage in mind as he was illustrious in blood – and King Philip, approving the suggestion, had commented menacingly: 'The bringing about of this marriage may perhaps be the beginning of a reformation in religious matters in England.' But while there seemed to be a strong possibility that his Catholic cousin the Archduke might be peacefully established as King-Consort in England, Philip would stay his arm from violent interference in Elizabeth's affairs. As usual, Elizabeth was using courtship as a means to almost any end except that of marriage.

The most devoted of her suitors, Lord Robert, was not at all willing to be used as a mere political pawn. However beautiful and fascinating the Queen of Scotland might be, he had no desire to be banished to the far north as her husband; however great the benefits to his own country would be, he had no wish to sacrifice his glorious hopes of marrying Elizabeth. It was plain that her feelings for him were still very strong, and in the autumn of that year, 1563, she presented him with the magnificent castle and parklands of Kenilworth in Warwickshire – yet, to his chagrin, she proceeded determinedly with the scheme of marrying him to Mary, Queen of Scots, while at the same time re-opening her own marriage negotiations with the Archduke. The need to hinder Mary from embracing 'such alliance as may bring trouble to this realm' was greater than any personal consideration in Elizabeth's eyes, but Robert Dudley was not prepared to go so far in the service of his Queen as to wed her rival while he still believed that he had some chance of winning Elizabeth herself.

The affair proceeded haltingly, but Elizabeth's resolution to subordinate passion to political necessity was further strengthened by the 'troublesome chance' which occurred in the following spring. A pamphlet came to light, Hales' *Dis-*

course on the Succession, in which a member of Parliament named John Hales put forward the arguments in favour of the Suffolk line, thereby pronouncing Lady Catherine Grey to be the rightful heiress to the crown. Lady Catherine was a sly, silly young woman, with none of the qualities of her tragic sister Lady Jane, but under the terms of Henry VIII's will she was indeed the heiress presumptive to the throne of England. Her clandestine marriage to the young Earl of Hertford, the late Protector Somerset's heir, had been officially declared invalid, and both she and her husband had been long imprisoned in the Tower, where two sons had been born to her. The existence of those two little boys of Tudor descent and Protestant parentage gave further weight to her claim, if, as Hales had sought to prove, the marriage was really legal. Hales' activities smacked of sedition and conspiracy, and the effects of his arguments upon public opinion could have been far-reaching; Parliament, increasingly anxious to see the succession finally established, might, thus incited, have proved hard to restrain. Elizabeth was frighteningly angry over the affair. Hales was later sent to the Tower, Lady Catherine was kept in strict custody, and Elizabeth pressed ahead with the plan that would, if successful, make Mary Stuart a suitable heiress presumptive to the throne, 'second person' in England as long as Elizabeth remained unmarried.

In the autumn of 1564 a special envoy from Scotland, James Melville, arrived in London, and was received with great charm and dissimulation by Elizabeth. 'The old friendship being renewed,' Melville somewhat ingenuously wrote in his memoirs, many years later, 'she enquired if the Queen had sent any answer to the proposition of marriage.' He gave the dampening reply that Mary 'thought little or nothing thereof', but added that she had referred the matter to the body of commissioners, both Scottish and English, who were soon to meet on the border. Elizabeth's tone became confiding. She told Melville that before he returned home he should see her create Lord Robert a very great earl: 'for she esteemed him as her brother and best friend, whom she would herself have married, had she ever minded to have taken a husband. But being determined to end her life in virginity, she wished that the Queen her sister might marry him'. The two Queens' formal references to one another as 'sister' and their diplomatic assurances of affection could not veil the mistrust and jealousy which existed between them. With a genial air, Elizabeth proceeded to tell Melville bluntly that if Mary were matched with Lord Robert, 'it would best remove out of her [Elizabeth's], mind all fears and suspicions, to be offended by any usurpation before her death – being assured that Lord Robert was so loving and trusty that he would never permit any such thing to be attempted during her time'. There lay a frank enough admission of how far she trusted her 'good sister' Mary of Scotland, and there was more to come.

As she had gaily promised, during Melville's visit Lord Robert was at last given an earldom. It was ironic that this honour which Dudley had long desired, as constituting a notable step forward in his courtship of Elizabeth, should at last have been given to him to fit him for an unwanted marriage with another queen, so that Mary 'might have the higher esteem of him'. Earl of Leicester and Baron Denbigh were his new titles; the ceremony was performed at Westminster, 'with great solemnity', and Elizabeth helped to put on his ceremonial garb as he knelt before her 'with a great gravity'. But there was nothing solemn or grave in the way she suddenly slipped her fingers inside his ruff and teasingly tickled his neck, smiling, in full view of the French ambassador and Melville. It was an erotic little gesture, implying a singular degree of familiarity between her and the man whom she was proposing as the husband of another reigning queen; it was nothing short of offensive to Mary. Yet, though she could not resist that possessive caress, she abruptly abandoned her frivolity a moment later. Turning from the resplendent new Earl of Leicester, she asked Melville what he thought of him. The Scot, unsuspecting, replied with some conventional compliments, and then Elizabeth, as though she could read his thoughts, delivered the startling pronouncement: 'Yet you like better of yonder long lad.' She was pointing to the tall, slender figure of young Lord Darnley.

It was a bad moment for Melville. As he afterwards recounted: 'I had no will that she should think I liked him, or had any eye or dealing that way – albeit I had a secret charge to deal with my Lady Lennox, to endeavour to procure liberty for him to go to Scotland.' Eighteen-year-old Darnley was the son of Lady Lennox and thus the great-grandson of Henry VII; though it had been officially established that his mother was born out of wedlock, he had enough royal blood in his veins to entertain great hopes, and it was Lady Lennox's dearest wish that he should be married to his half-cousin Mary, Queen of Scots. Undoubtedly Melville was disconcerted by Elizabeth's perception, but he returned a clever evasive reply, flavoured to suit her taste in men; glancing from Robert Dudley's virile appearance to the delicate pointed features of young Darnley, he answered 'that no woman of spirit would make choice of such a man, who more resembled a woman than a man. For he was handsome, beardless and lady-faced'. There was talk of the pretty youth Darnley becoming Mary's husband, as Elizabeth well knew; as a Catholic and a descendant both of the Tudor and Stuart lines, he was not, from her point of view, a very safe man to see set up as King-Consort in unneighbourly Scotland, though he would at least be preferable to 'the children of France, Spain and Austria'. No one, however, would be so satisfactory for English interests as her own ardent suitor the new-made Earl of Leicester. As she told Melville, her chief cause for displeasure with Mary was that she seemed 'to disdain the marriage of my Lord of Leicester'.

During his visit Melville had some remarkably illuminating conversations with the Queen of England. He proved himself skilful in dealing with her, and she seemed to respond to him with unusual condescension and warmth. Fencing carefully with her over the subject of the succession, he remarked: 'You are certainly convinced you will never have any children, seeing Your Majesty declares yourself resolved to die a virgin.' With dignity Elizabeth replied: 'I am resolved never to marry, if I be not thereto necessitated by the Queen my sister's harsh behaviour towards me.' Disregarding that thrust, Melville commented, with singular perception: 'I know the truth of that, Madam, you need not tell it me. Your Majesty thinks, if you were married, you would be but Queen of England, and now you are both King and Queen. I know your spirit cannot endure a commander.' The woman of such rare spirit, who was resolved to keep her mastery and never to marry, and who was prepared to give up even her 'loving and trusty' Leicester for the sake of the weal of her kingdom, had nevertheless no wish to be thought unfeminine, especially in comparison with the celebrated beauty Mary Stuart. And so she determinedly subjected Melville to displays of her charms and accomplishments throughout his visit. She changed the style of her dress every day, appearing in the fashions of one country after another, and asking him gaily which became her best. He cleverly told her that the Italian clothes did, which implied a compliment to her abundance of curling reddish-golden hair. There was something childlike, and even faintly pathetic, in the persistent questions which she put to Melville about her looks as compared to those of Mary, as though she was uncertain of her own attractions and personal lovableness. The contrast between her mental and emotional powers was very great. 'She desired to know of me', Melville afterwards recalled, 'what colour of hair was reputed best; and whether my Queen's hair or hers was best; and which of them two was fairest.' Perhaps a little embarrassed, Melville attempted a joke, saying: 'The fairness of them both was not their worst faults,' and then, when she pressed him: 'She was the fairest Queen in England, and mine the fairest Queen in Scotland,' but still Elizabeth was not satisfied. She enquired which of them was the taller, to which the Scot replied without hesitation: 'My Queen.' 'Then,' said Elizabeth firmly, 'she is too high, for I myself am neither too high nor too low.' In similar decided tones she was later to tell the Imperial envoy, who had praised Mary Stuart, 'that she was superior to the Queen of Scotland'. She continued to ask question after question about Mary, about her interests, her sports. She learned that 'when her more serious affairs permitted, she was taken up with reading of histories'. When she heard that Mary played the virginals 'reasonably well, for a queen', Elizabeth promptly arranged a pretty scene whereby she might show off her own considerable talent for music, feigning to be unaware that Melville was in the room while she played. She pretended to slap him for his presumption in listening to her performance, but was plainly gratified when, in answer to her predictable question as to which of them played better, she was assured that she herself did. She showed off her languages too, and made Melville prolong his stay so that he might have the pleasure and privilege of seeing her dance. 'Which being over', he later recounted, 'she enquired of me, whether she or my Queen danced best. I answered, The Queen of Scotland danced not so high or disposedly as she did.' It was unfortunate for Elizabeth's plans that her compulsive personal interest in Mary, Queen of Scots was not shared by Leicester.

Leicester showed as plainly as he could that he had no wish to be sent away to marry Mary. The prize he sought, and believed he was close to winning, was Elizabeth, and he was not prepared to give up the pursuit and be satisfied with a lesser quarry, not even for the sake of England. Still hoping for eventual success, he preferred to remain a suitor to the Queen of England than become the husband of the Queen of Scots, and in characteristic Dudley fashion he quietly manoeuvred to achieve his ends. He sought out Melville, and invited him to go down the river with him in his barge; gliding down the Thames on that late autumn afternoon Robert tried to inveigle the envoy into telling him what Mary thought of him and the marriage proposition. Melville 'answered very coldly', as he had been instructed, and Leicester began to explain volubly that he was not responsible for the proposal, declaring dramatically that he was not even worthy to wipe the Queen of Scotland's shoes, and asking Melville 'to excuse him at Her Majesty's hands, and to beg, in his name, that she would not impute that matter to him'. Later Melville wrote: 'My Lord of Leicester, beside what he had spoke to me, did write to my Lord of Murray to excuse him at the Queen's hands.' In his determination not to be debarred from the pursuit of Elizabeth, Leicester went still further. According to Mary herself, he sent word to her that the proposal was merely a 'fetch', a deceit, conceived to hinder her from concluding a marriage alliance with any foreign prince – though if that had really been the case Leicester would have had nothing to fear from willingly participating in the scheme. Elizabeth afterwards told de Silva that it was because Leicester 'had not consented' that the proposal had come to nothing. It may have been chiefly through his influence that early in February 1565, Elizabeth suddenly made the fatal decision that young Lord Darnley should after all be granted permission to go north to join his father in Scotland.

Within weeks of his arrival Mary was utterly infatuated with the tall girlish youth, 'the properest and best-proportioned long man that ever she had seen'. Elizabeth's permission for Darnley to travel to Scotland had been unexpectedly, unaccountably, perhaps unwillingly, given, and was now bitterly regretted. But all her furious endeavours to oblige him to return to England were useless. For Robert Dudley, however, the affair had come to a fortunate conclusion. Resplendent in his new rank of Earl of Leicester, acknowledged as worthy to match with a reigning queen, he was free to pursue his courtship of Elizabeth with renewed hopes.

If Mary had obeyed Elizabeth's wishes, and married Leicester, the English succession would surely have eventually been settled upon their issue. As it was, the Scottish Queen's impending marriage to another man, a descendant of the Houses of Tudor and Stuart and one who was by no means certain to have English interests at heart, left Elizabeth's situation as weak as ever. Spain, France and the Pope displayed their goodwill towards Mary, while at home the succession question remained dangerously unresolved. Thus it was that when the Imperial envoy Adam von Zwetkovich arrived in London in May 1565, he found to his satisfaction that the Queen of England was graciously disposed to entertain a renewal of 'the matrimonial negotiations with His Princely Highness the Archduke Charles'.

The new Emperor Maximilian II had cautioned Zwetkovich that the Archduke Charles 'would not, as on the last occasion, suffer himself to be led by the nose'. But earnest, gullible Zwetkovich was unable to prevent it. It was Elizabeth, not he, who set the pace, sweetly encouraging the wooing one minute, coldly pointing out obstacles the next, and he did not know her well enough to see through her duplicity and recognize the core of reality beneath the layers of pretence. If Robert Dudley, who had known the Queen so long and so intimately, still believed, despite her frequent protestations to the contrary, that she might eventually yield and marry one or other of her suitors, then Zwetkovich, a novice in the art of courting Elizabeth, could not know that whilst she was delighted to entertain the Archduke Charles as a suitor, she had no intention of accepting him or anyone else as a husband – that he was simply being used for her own political ends.

In the presence of the sovereign of England and Ireland, this thin woman of thirty-two whose face was as white and smooth as an egg, adorned with great pearls like drops of water that quivered above the heavy riches of her dress, the envoy was deeply impressed. He had been given orders to make the most diligent enquiries into Elizabeth's moral character before proceeding with the negotiations; if there appeared to be any doubts as to the Queen's chastity, the Emperor had pronounced, he was not to say one single word about the Archduke wishing to marry her, but to pretend that he had no instructions on any such subject. Zwetkovich's investigations led him to conclude enthusiastically 'that she has truly and verily been praised and extolled for her virginal and royal honour' and that 'all the aspersions against her are but the spawn of envy and malice and hatred'. As for the Earl of Leicester, he was found to be a man of the highest moral principles, whom the Queen esteemed as a faithful servant and regarded as a brother, and the idea that she might desire to marry him was confidently dismissed as 'quite out of the question'. Everything looked propitious for the Archduke. Elizabeth explained modestly that her own preference was for the virgin life, but at the behest of her people she had decided to set aside her private wishes. Dramatically, she 'called God to witness that she was willing to marry only for the sake of her realm. She would prefer to die a maid and end her days in a convent, for she verily never had any desire to marry'. Her dedication to the weal of her kingdom was Elizabeth's principal theme in this wooing.

Yet even in so avowedly political a courtship, the deeply personal nature of the intended alliance could not be disregarded. Ponderous touches of romance were introduced; Zwetkovich ventured to suggest that the Archduke should write a friendly loving letter to the Queen, and chide her for not writing to him more often, as though they were fond acquaintances on the verge of falling in love. Such a letter, he went on, would show Elizabeth 'how greatly the Archduke loves her and yearns for her', despite the fact that he had not so far met her. Elizabeth managed to create a major obstacle by insisting that she must see this prospective husband in person before she could give him a definite answer. It would not be becoming for the Archduke to travel to England on such conditions, she was told, since the dignity of himself and his august House would be seriously affronted if he were then to be rejected, but Elizabeth was insistent, saying over and over again that she could not accept a man whom she had not seen. 'One great obstacle is that the Queen's Majesty will needs see before she marry,' Cecil noted worriedly. The Emperor seemed shocked by the suggestion. 'Among Kings and Queens this is entirely novel and unprecedented', he wrote to Zwetkovich, 'and we cannot approve of it.' When the envoy reported optimistically that 'the Queen becomes fonder of His Princely Highness and her impatience to see him grows daily. Her marriage is, I take it, certain and resolved upon', the Emperor commented that the affair seemed to him 'to be still very dubious and questionable', if Elizabeth insisted on this condition which could not be fulfilled. Throughout the negotiation the Emperor was inclined to be suspicious of his prospective sister-in-law; he assessed the progress of his brother's wooing according to 'the logic of facts', in a way that his envoy in London, under the compelling influence of Elizabeth's glib, impressive charm, could not.

To all appearances the Archduke's suit seemed to be progressing well during the summer of 1565. Elizabeth was on bad terms with Leicester at this time; perhaps she had still not forgiven him for thwarting her over the Mary, Queen of Scots marriage. 'The Queen's Majesty is fallen into some misliking of my Lord of Leicester, and he therewith much dismayed,' Cecil wrote with satisfaction in August. He went on to say that Elizabeth was making it plain that she regretted having wasted so much of her precious time on Leicester. 'She is sorry of her loss of time, and so is every good subject,' he wrote, silently expressing his hearty agreement. He recorded in his diary for the same month: 'The Queen's Majesty seemed to be much

offended with the Earl of Leicester, and so she wrote an obscure
sentence in a book at Windsor.' Lovers often have private
words and allusions which are understandable only to themselves. Whatever the meaning of the 'obscure sentence', whatever the real cause of the rift between Elizabeth and her
constant favourite, there was a moment when, after six years
of energetic wooing, Leicester 'lost hope of his business', and
Cecil was able to express the fervent hope that 'we shall see
some success' with the Archduke's suit.

Cecil, perhaps the most selflessly devoted of all Elizabeth's
servants, was convinced of the necessity for her to marry for
the sake of the realm and the succession, and he believed that
the Archduke would be the wisest choice. His opinion of
Leicester as a prospective husband for the Queen of England
was very low. When, as always happened, Elizabeth's anger
with her beloved Robert passed, and he was reinstated in his
former favoured position, Cecil gloomily drew up comparisons
between the English suitor and the Austrian. If, as Elizabeth so
often declared, she was willing to set aside her private inclinations and marry as a queen for the sake of her kingdom, the
arguments in favour of a speedy marriage with the Archduke
were very strong; Cecil's memoranda effectively disposed of
Leicester as a worthy alternative. The Queen's situation was
very weak, he pointed out, for no ruler 'ever had less alliance
than the Queen of England hath, nor any prince ever had more
cause to have friendship and power to assist her estate'. Of
Leicester he wrote grimly : 'Nothing is increased by marriage
of him, either in riches, estimation, power. It will be thought
that the slanderous speeches of the Queen with the Earl have
been true.' He went on to observe that Leicester would raise all
his own friends and adherents to high offices, if, in spite of the
grim facts that 'he is infamed by the death of his wife', and 'he
is far in debt', he were to become King-Consort. Scrupulously he
drew up his lists comparing the eligibility of the two. Charles
was brother of the Emperor, Leicester, 'Born son of a knight,
his grandfather but a squire'. Charles was 'an archduke born',
Leicester merely 'an earl made'. In age and beauty Leicester was
admitted to be 'meet', but in wealth sadly lacking : 'All of the
Queen, and in debt.' In friendship the Archduke could offer 'the

Emperor, the King of Spain, the Dukes of Saxony, Bavaria, Cleves, Florence, Ferrara and Mantua', a mighty list beside which Robert's entry, 'none but such as shall have of the Queen', looked the more sickly. He was the Austrian Prince's equal in nothing. Reviewing the likelihood of each suitor to beget heirs, Cecil noted that the Archduke's family showed a tendency to be 'blessed with multitudes of children', whereas no brother of Robert's had had any, and his own marriage to Amy Robsart had been childless. Of that marriage Cecil had more to say. He did not believe that Leicester would prove a kind or loving husband once he had achieved his goal, and in the category, 'In likelihood to love his wife', he wrote in Latin: 'Carnal marriages begin in pleasure and end in strife.' In reputation, Cecil wrote, Charles was 'honoured of all men', but of Leicester he recorded the cryptic words: 'Hated of many. His wife's death.' It was a clear, businesslike assessment, and of course the conclusion was overwhelmingly against Leicester as a fitting husband for Elizabeth. But there was one fact which Cecil, his mind on politics, not passion, had left out – the human element. Elizabeth loved the adventurer Robert Dudley; loved, needed and relied upon him. That was the consideration which gave weight to his suit, and kept the scales of her courtships quiveringly poised.

Encouraging reports of the Archduke's physical appearance were sent to Elizabeth in the summer of 1566, to increase her interest in his wooing. Thomas Dannett, the English agent in Vienna, wrote that the Austrian Prince was courteous, affable, just, liberal, and wise, and greatly enjoyed sports; mindful of Elizabeth's liking for handsome, athletic men, he described him as 'for a man, beautiful and well faced, well shaped, small in the waist, and well and broad breasted; he seemed in his clothes well thighed and well legged'. Though he appeared slightly round-shouldered, Dannett reported, in the saddle he sat as straight as anyone. It was an attractive enough verbal portrait, but still Elizabeth was determined to see her suitor before she would give him a definite answer. There was little or no doubt in her secret mind as to how the negotiations would end, but as long as they were proving useful – as well as gratifying – she was very willing that they should be prolonged, in spite of her

E

protestations that such matters were not at all to her liking. 'She always repeats her dislike to marriage and even to talking of it,' wrote de Silva, who was not taken in.

It was obvious to him that Elizabeth derived great pleasure from her suitors. Her vanity was not that of satisfied self-assurance, but that of restless uncertainty, ever clutching at compliments, avid for praise. Because she lacked the normal inward satisfactions of sexual love, the external signs and rituals assumed an unnatural importance in her life, developing, over the years, into an ever more elaborate code of pretence. For her maternal instincts she found a just and absorbing outlet in care for her subjects. 'Though after my death you may have many stepdames, yet shall you never have a more natural mother than I mean to be unto you all,' she had proclaimed to the Parliament of 1563, and she was to keep that pledge. But for romance she required the glittering sham of her courtships. With Leicester she found an approximation of real loving intimacy, but whatever rank she bestowed on him he would always remain her subject, dependent on her for his very life. As Queen of England she revelled in the purportedly amorous homage of her foreign equals in blood and power. The notion of the Hapsburg Archduke coming to England to woo her in person held a particular fascination for her – and indeed the one royal suitor who did come over the sea to court her, more than a decade later, was almost to succeed in winning her. Once when she spoke to de Silva of the Archduke's possible visit, the Spanish ambassador teased her by asking meaning-fully whether she had noticed an unfamiliar face amongst the Imperial envoy's retinue, 'as perhaps she was entertaining more than she thought, only she must be told so in a way not to disconcert her'. Her reaction was one of real shock. 'She turned white, and was so agitated that I could not help laughing to see her,' de Silva recounted. But she recovered her dignity, and said: 'That is not a bad way for the Archduke to come,' adding untruthfully: 'I promise you plenty of princes have come to see me that way.' She seemed to take particular pleasure in listing the great princes who had wooed her and been rejected; she proudly enumerated them on more than one occasion when entertaining envoys. Even though she was perfectly conscious of the political nature of royal courtships, and indeed openly referred to the personal incompatibility which had been so evident in her own sister's political marriage to Philip of Spain, she nevertheless found real pleasure in such wooings. De Silva reported that she even tried to revive Eric of Sweden's much-mocked suit early in 1566, saying that 'she wished to treat of marriage with him again, so that the Archduke was not the only one'. He went on to say perceptively: 'The Queen would like everyone to be in love with her, but I doubt whether she will ever be in love with anyone, enough to marry him.'

Leicester's brother-in-law Sir Henry Sidney once told de Silva that he himself 'was always sure that the Queen did not mean to marry, and that they were in the most troublous state that ever was known in England, especially if the Queen were to die, as they were all so divided that no three persons were entirely of one opinion'. Elizabeth's isolation as an unmarried, childless queen was made the more striking by the birth of Mary's son James in June 1566. Now the two chief contenders for Elizabeth's throne, Lady Catherine Grey and Queen Mary, both had fine baby sons to give their claims additional weight. According to Melville, who was sent in all haste to England with the news, when Elizabeth was told of the birth of the Scottish Prince, 'all her mirth was laid aside for that night', and, sitting down, she put her hand to her face, 'bursting out to some of her ladies, that the Queen of Scots was mother of a fair son, while she was but a barren stock'. Though she afterwards recovered her equanimity, and 'seemed very glad of the birth of the infant', she would have been less than human had she not suffered a brief pang of envy for her beautiful cousin who seemed to represent every desirable feminine attribute and now had a son, the baby prince that was regarded as the primary purpose of a Queen's existence. There was no apparent physical reason why Elizabeth should not have children. The whispers of 'some womanish infirmity' which would make it impossible seem to have no real foundation. The illness which troubled her throughout her youth and early maturity was probably nephritis, which, amongst other side-effects, can cause a disturbance of the monthly periods, but that trouble would have rectified itself when the acute phase of the nephritis subsided, and as late as 1579, Cecil wrote in a memorandum on the subject of her likelihood of having children, that she had 'no lack of natural functions in those things that properly belong to the procreation of children'. He of all people would have known if the Queen had had anything physically wrong with her. The question of her ability to produce heirs was so central to the matter of her marriage that he could not have afforded to overlook any evidence that she might be unlike other women in that respect. Living surrounded by her attendant ladies as she did, any unusual physical symptom would not have gone unnoticed. In 1566 her own physician swept aside all such speculation as nonsense, and asserted confidently that he would guarantee her having ten children. There was indeed an abnormality in Elizabeth's ability to become pregnant, but it was seated in the mind, not in the body.

Melville had accurately diagnosed a great part of the hindrance when he said to Elizabeth that if she were married she would be but Queen of England, whereas now she was both King and Queen. 'I know your spirit cannot endure a commander,' he had observed perceptively. As the negotiations with the Archduke continued it became plain how far the Hapsburg Prince would expect to have a hand in Elizabeth's affairs. The Emperor made it plain that Charles would naturally expect to 'share the pains, cares and exertions of government with the illustrious Queen' and also to 'participate in the fruits and benefits of the realm', and that 'as regards the realms and dominions which appertain to the Queen, the Archduke shall in common with Her Royal Highness not only nominally bear and enjoy the honours and titles of royalty, but shall assist the illustrious Queen in her happy administration of these realms and dominions'. For twenty-five years of her life Elizabeth had been subject to the will of others; her desire never to place herself in such a position again was central to her reasoning where marriage was concerned. That was one advantage that marriage with Leicester would bring – unlike a foreign prince, he would be unquestionably her inferior.

There was all too much of the commander in the attitude of the Parliament which met in October of 1566. The hopes of marriage which Elizabeth had held out to them in 1563 remained unfulfilled, and the succession question was by no means resolved. Elizabeth was now thirty-three years old, and every year that passed was making childbirth a more hazardous prospect for her; she must marry soon, and she must settle the troubled matter of the succession, her people were saying, made bold by fear. In both the Upper and the Lower Houses Englishmen regarded this Parliament as their opportunity to press their case to their curiously recalcitrant Queen.

According to the French ambassador, a council meeting on 12 October set the tone for what was to follow. The Duke of Norfolk, who strongly advocated the Austrian match, addressed the Queen on behalf of the nobility, and asked that Parliament should be permitted to discuss both the question of her marriage and that of the succession. Elizabeth was furious at such presumption. The succession was entirely her concern, she told him; she wanted none of their advice. With passionate conviction she referred to her own situation during her sister's reign, when she herself, as the heir, had been courted by those who were her sister's subjects. It was obvious that those times of fear and faint hope were still all too vivid in her memory. She knew what had happened then, and she did not wish to see it happen again, with herself in Mary's role. As for her marriage, she told the Council haughtily that it was not far off.

Elizabeth's spirit and power – the Tudor force of personality of her grandfather and father – were rarely so impressively displayed as during this autumn when Parliament threatened to interfere with her royal prerogative. To the deputation from the Lords she 'addressed hard words' which had the more weight for their direct, almost homely flavour. When Pembroke mildly observed that it was not right to 'treat the Duke badly, since he and the others were only doing what was fitting for the good of the country, and advising her what was best for her', she told him 'that he talked like a swaggering soldier'. She turned on Leicester and cried reproachfully 'that she had thought that if all the world abandoned her he would not have done so'. He answered 'that he would die at her feet', and she snapped 'that that had nothing to do with the matter'. When the Queen talked later with the Spanish ambassador, he noticed

that she was particularly upset about Leicester having joined
with the others, after she had shown him so much kindness
'that even her honour had suffered for the sake of honouring
him'.

The speech which she drew up for delivery to the Commons
was magnificent. 'I need not to use many words, for my deeds
do try me,' she declared proudly, though there were a good
many words in the whole. Towards the end of the part where
she spoke of her marriage, she affirmed: 'I will never break the
word of a prince, spoken in a public place, for my honour's
sake. And therefore I say again, I will marry as soon as I can
conveniently, if God take not him away with whom I mind to
marry, or myself, or some other great let happen.' She went
on: 'And I hope to have children, otherwise I would never
marry.' Many of those present, she observed, would be just as
vehement in opposing whomever she might wed as they now
were in urging her to marry. Turning to the matter of the succession, she again returned to the crucial factor of her own
experiences as heir to the throne during her sister's reign.
Noting acidly that her petitioners seemed unconcerned for her
safety, but were thinking only of themselves, she stated: 'I
stood in danger of my life, my sister was so incensed against
me; I did differ from her in religion, and I was sought for divers
ways. And so shall never be my successor.' As usual, she
brought her speech to a superbly compelling climax, in which
simplicity tempered grandeur with dramatic effectiveness:

I care not for death; for all men are mortal. And though I be a
woman, yet I have as good a courage, answerable to my place, as
ever my father had. I am your anointed Queen. I will never be by
violence constrained to do anything. I thank God I am endued with
such qualities that if I were turned out of the realm in my petticoat,
I were able to live in any place in Christendom.

She ended by telling them that she could make no immediate
statement about the succession: 'But as soon as there may be a
convenient time, and that it may be done with least peril unto
you – although never without great danger unto me – I will
deal therein for your safety.' But, she warned, she would not do
so at their request, 'for it is monstrous that the feet should

direct the head'. The image of society as a body, of which the ruler was the head, was one which Elizabeth's subjects would hear again later in the reign – flowing not from her pen but from Shakespeare's.

Yet the matter did not rest there. It was proposed to print her promise to marry and name a successor as soon as she could. On the bottom of the paper which bore this draft the Queen, enraged, wrote her angry comments, furious that 'such audacity should be used to make, without my licence, an act of my words'. At the end of the session, however, her tone mellowed, as she cautioned them: 'Let this my discipline stand you in stead of sorer strokes never to tempt too far a prince's patience.' She had clearly promised to marry soon, if nothing should hinder the outcome of her negotiations with the Archduke; it was a promise she could make with confidence, because it was becoming increasingly obvious that a matter of great importance would almost certainly make the marriage impossible. The 'great let', or obstacle, was the fact that the Archduke was a staunch Catholic, and would not relinquish his faith even to win Elizabeth. With her mind still full of the happenings of Mary's reign, Elizabeth would never bring another Catholic Habsburg into her realm to be King of England, though the existence of her negotiations with him served to show her good faith to her subjects on the matter of marriage.

As Elizabeth had declared, the weal of the kingdom was in her keeping. Like her ministers and subjects, her care was for England's good, but in her means of achieving it she differed from them. Whereas the majority of Englishmen believed that the greatest good must come from her marriage, Elizabeth, directed by her emotions, as well as by her mind, saw that her realm might be equally well served by her courtships.

7

THE BROTHERS OF FRANCE

'The French, having got wind of the Archduke's affair, may wish to divert it by bringing their own King forward,' de Silva observed in the spring of 1565. His tone was justifiably sceptical. The King of France, Charles IX, was then not quite fifteen years old, an undergrown lad, dominated by his widowed mother Catherine de' Medici; it seemed certain that the marriage negotiations entered into on his behalf were no more than a defensive measure, designed to hinder Elizabeth from concluding a match with the Habsburg Archduke – as de Silva expressed it : 'The French may be trying to beat her at her own game.' It was an unpromising beginning, yet France's wooing of the Queen of England was to span the next eighteen years, as, in turn, each of the three surviving sons of the sickly, degenerate brood born to Henry II and Catherine de' Medici took up the pursuit of Elizabeth, until the suit of the youngest culminated in a whirl of gallantry and feigned romance that almost swept the ageing Queen into marriage. The disparity of age between the young men and the woman they wooed was almost comically great, but though her personal charms dwindled and faded, her political desirability did not, and the youthful Valois brothers were to dominate the later years of Elizabeth's courtships.

When the boy King Charles IX was tentatively put forward in 1565, Elizabeth was nothing loath to add another royal suitor, however unlikely, to her list. She bashfully 'held down her head a little and laughed' when de Silva made a pointed reference to rumours he had heard about her marrying the King of France; though she repeated her disinclination for marriage it was evident that she loved to hear her powerful suitors named, just as she enjoyed quite broad sexual teasing if it implied a compliment to her femininity. Joking about the rival suitors, the Queen's jester declared: 'She should not take the King of France, for he was but a boy and a babe; but she should take the Archduke Charles and then he was sure that she would have a baby boy.' The Imperial ambassador, reporting the incident, added solemnly, 'I told the Queen that babes and fools speak the truth and so I hoped that she had now heard the truth, but she only laughed.' Though she was seventeen years older than the young French King, Elizabeth was still only thirty-one, and retained enough of her looks for the endless talk of love and marriage not to seem entirely inappropriate; she had never been a beauty like Mary Queen of Scots, but with lavish dresses and jewels to set off her white skin and bright hair, flourishing her lovely hands and showing off her wit and spirit, she was a more attractive match for a young bridegroom than her pious half-sister Mary Tudor had been. Her own exacting requirements concerning the physical attractions of her suitors had become well known, and in offering her Charles IX Catherine de' Medici took care to assure her that she would find as much to please her in his body as in his mind. The English ambassador in France was more guarded in his description of the boy King's personal attributes, however, reporting somewhat ambiguously that Charles was likely to grow tall, since his knees and ankles were at present disproportionately large for his legs, and adding uncertainly that his fast, thick speech no doubt denoted a hot and active nature. For Elizabeth there could be little appeal in the match, and the disparity of age was rather an advantage than otherwise, since it provided her from the outset with excellent grounds for her eventual refusal. But for the time being the King of France made a splendid addition to her list of mighty suitors.

With many sighs she told the French ambassador Paul de Foix that she only wished she were ten years younger. He, primed with bland reassurances, declared that she would have many children, that Charles would come to her in the flower of his youth, and that any disadvantages must be on his side, for she had nothing to lose and would remain all powerful. Difficulties could easily be dealt with in advance by drawing up contracts. At this Elizabeth went a little too far. With an innocent air she asked who would bring the King to justice if he should break them. De Foix became very dignified; taking this to be a refusal, he replied that he could see her affections were engaged elsewhere. Elizabeth certainly did not intend to refuse the Valois King at this stage, however, and so she exerted all her charm to mollify the ambassador; she told him this was not a refusal, she merely wished that the difficulties she foresaw should be pointed out to Queen Catherine, and before the interview ended she had a stool brought for him, and thanked him winningly for the flattering reports of her which he had sent to his King and the Queen-Regent. There were times when Elizabeth's motives were transparently clear.

When she heard that the ominous meeting between the Queens of France and Spain was about to take place at Bayonne, her behaviour to de Foix could not have been more sweetly encouraging. The reunion of Catherine de' Medici and her darling daughter Elisabeth, Philip of Spain's wife, threatened to result in the Catholic league that loyal Englishmen most feared; at such a moment it behoved Elizabeth of England to show great interest in the possibility of marrying the King of France. Almost girlishly she told de Foix that she wished she had had the good fortune to be present at Bayonne as a third Queen, then passing to the subject of the marriage she observed that there was really only one difficulty, that of age. But she went on to say that in her ambassador's last report he had written that Charles was so wonderfully grown that after a mere absence of three weeks he had been scarcely recognizable, and it seemed he would become as tall as his father had been. At dinner de Foix was seated at the Queen's side; she seemed full of happiness, and drank to the King's health. After dinner she kept the Frenchman by her, and chattered to him about France, its glories and its court – 'like someone', de Foix recorded, 'who is relishing things they expect to possess one day'. Catherine de' Medici was shrewd and guileful, but she was not so accomplished an actress as the Queen of England.

At Bordeaux, in April, the English ambassador Sir Thomas Smith had an audience with Catherine, in which she told him plainly that there were only three serious objections to the match. The first was the age of her son, but she assured him that if Elizabeth would put up with that, she herself would put up with Elizabeth's age. At this point the young King Charles broke in, exclaiming eagerly: 'I find no fault. I would she could be as well content with me as I am with her age.' The other difficulties which Catherine spoke of were the question of Elizabeth having to reside in France at times, and the discontent of the English people and nobility which might result, but she pointed out that England and France united would be so strong that they would have nothing to fear from anyone. Smith answered discreetly that his limited instructions did not permit him to give a reply to that, but he had a few dry words for the youthful suitor. 'If the King had three or four years more, and had seen the Queen's Majesty, and were fallen in love with her,' he observed, 'then I would not marvel at this haste.' 'Why, I do love her indeed,' protested Charles, to which Smith answered blightingly that he did not yet know what love was, but he would soon go through it; 'It is the most foolish thing,' said Smith, 'the most impatient, most hasty and disrespectful that can be.' Understandably, the young King blushed, and Catherine intervened on his behalf, saying: 'This is no foolish love.' Smith courteously assented, but he added some weighty comments about the serious nature of such a marriage, with a degree of conviction that was generally lacking from the tone of the negotiations.

As the Bayonne meeting drew nearer Catherine pressed for an answer, while Elizabeth played for time, offering evasive protestations of friendship and then expressing doubts about Catherine's sincerity. All such doubts were amply justified, since, ironically, both she and Catherine had entered into marriage negotiations with the House of Austria. A match between one of the Emperor's daughters and Charles IX was being discussed, while Elizabeth was complaisantly receiving the renewed advances of the Emperor's brother the Archduke Charles. The matrimonial game was a complex one, but Elizabeth was an experienced player. The Hapsburg Archduke was the suitor with whom she desired to dally at length; the immature King of France was a welcome, but dispensible, makeweight.

'She is so nimble in her dealing, and threads in and out of the business in such a way that her most intimate favourites fail to understand her,' the Spanish ambassador wrote vexedly in the following year. Though the Archduke's suit seemed to be prospering, Charles IX was still talked of, while Elizabeth herself veered between appearing resolved to marry some great prince for the sake of her country and declaring herself resolved never to marry at all. The most intimate favourite of all, Leicester, by no means confident that his own suit would ever succeed, was smiling and scheming between the lodgings of the rival ambassadors. He made a convincing show of supporting the Austrian match at first, but his serious dealings were with the French. While Cecil, Norfolk and the weight of reason were giving strong support to the Hapsburg suit, Leicester was endeavouring to thwart it by encouraging the French; it was in his interests as well as theirs to hinder Elizabeth from concluding a marriage with the Archduke. In the spring of 1566 Cecil's learned, intelligent wife told de Silva that in her opinion, 'the Queen will never marry Lord Robert, or, indeed, anyone else, unless it be the Archduke, which is the match Cecil desires'. It was with the intention of altering that situation that Leicester had joined forces with Catherine de' Medici's ambassador, to lend some heat to Charles IX's tepid wooing while it lasted and thereby to acquire France's support for his own suit when they should need a new candidate with which to counter the Archduke. As de Silva remarked to Cecil: 'These Frenchmen are in a fine taking when they see the Archduke's own suit progressing, and at once bring their own King forward to embarrass the Queen. When they see that this trick has hindered the negotiation they take up with Leicester again, and think we do not see through them.' Amidst the tensions and rivalries which accompanied Elizabeth's first French courtship a note of farce was discernible.

Elizabeth herself seemed well aware of the absurdity of a match with so young a suitor as Charles IX. In the summer of 1567, when she was nearly thirty-four and the boy King of France just seventeen, de Silva reported: 'The Queen told me this afternoon on my introducing the matter as a joke that it was true the French had again addressed her, but it would not result in people seeing such a comical farce as an old woman leading a child to the church doors.' In similar tones she observed that people would say she was marrying her son, just as they had said King Philip was marrying his grandmother when he took her half-sister Mary Tudor for his wife. Though she could speak lightly of that grim marriage it was obvious that it haunted her still, as a vivid warning of the ills that a wrong choice of consort might bring to herself and her realm. 'She knew very well how the King of Spain had cursed the painters and envoys when he first beheld Queen Mary,' she told the Archduke's ambassador; to be emotionally rejected as Mary had been by her fine young husband was a prospect which Elizabeth, with her craving for constant male admiration and attention, could not endure. To marry a young consort, and above all a young French consort, would be to invite dis-illusionment. It was delightful to her to be courted by eligible men of almost any age, but to put their professed adoration to the test of a lifetime of marriage she neither dared nor desired to do.

'She seems to regard it as profitable to create delays some-where or somehow in order to gain an advantage, and this we have long suspected on the logic of facts,' wrote the Emperor that summer, in a private letter to his brother the Archduke. He was finding Elizabeth more perplexing than ever to treat with over 'this most difficult affair' of marriage. The Earl of Sussex had arrived in Vienna, to present the Emperor with the insignia of the Order of the Garter which Elizabeth had en-couragingly conferred upon him, and also to pursue the subject of the marriage; to the Emperor's disquiet, Sussex 'spon-taneously laid stress upon the fact that should these nego-tiations lead to no result, the illustrious Queen, who is still being wooed by many others, is firmly resolved to marry the Most Christian King of France, in spite of the disparity of age.' Uncertain though he was of Elizabeth's real intentions, the Emperor had no wish to see the great matrimonial prize fall to the young French King, and in his note to his brother he repeated his earnest hopes that the Archduke would at last 'contract this honourable and splendid marriage, which without doubt will redound to the great profit of the entire glorious House of Austria' – and, he might have added, to the great loss of the rival House of Valois. But the Archduke's own scepticism extended further than the Emperor's. 'If the English Orator threatens that should the marriage negotiations with me make no progress his Queen would marry the King of France,' he wrote back, 'I take this to be but an attempt to accelerate the negotiations.' Doubt and distrust were in the air, and Elizabeth's long dalliance with the Habsburg Archduke was drawing to an end.

She found an effective shelter in the very real obstacle of the Archduke's religion. He was too conscientious a Catholic to doff his faith for worldly gain, and Elizabeth, the head of the English Church, would not recall the dark days of her sister's reign by inviting a Catholic Habsburg to share the throne of England. 'I prize quietude of conscience and the continuance of the peaceable reign which I have begun and desire to pursue higher than all the favours which princes of the world and all kingdoms can confer upon me,' she wrote proudly to the Emperor. It was one of the few clear sentences in a letter which the Emperor irritably described as 'most obscure, ambiguous, involved and of such a nature that we cannot learn from it whether the Queen is serious and sincere, or whether she wishes to befool us.' The Archduke showed no great regret at the prospect of losing the glorious prize which had been held out to him for nearly eight years. 'My opinion of the affair is that it will result in nothing,' he wrote judicially to his brother in January 1568, and could not resist adding, albeit respectfully, 'and may it please Your Majesty to remember that this opinion always deterred me.' The courtship was dead, though not buried.

The noble, loyal Earl of Sussex came back to England from the Imperial court full of grieved disappointment at the failure of the match, and convinced that Leicester's malevolent influence was responsible for it. 'If it should ever please God to put into my dear mistress's heart to divide the weeds from the grain ... she may, if she will, make a happy harvest,' he sighed, his devotion to the Queen unimpaired by his bitter dislike for her favourite. It was partly out of dogged loyalty to her that he was led to hold Leicester accountable for her apparent errors of judgement; for those who, like Sussex, sincerely longed to see Elizabeth conclude an honourable marriage alliance, and could not understand her continuing failure to do so, ambitious, devious Leicester made a convenient whipping-boy. The blame for the Queen's neglect of what they regarded as the country's urgent need of a king-consort and an heir could convincingly be attributed to his influence. Certainly Leicester welcomed the disappearance of the Archduke from the field, and there was no doubt that he had done all he could to thwart the match in the face of its formidable supporters, Cecil, Norfolk and their adherents on the Council. But in the last resort he was as powerless as they to force the Queen's hand when it came to the final irrevocable step of marriage. His self-seeking manoeuvres and their sincere advice could influence the course of a courtship, but no conscious persuasions in the world could have any real bearing on Elizabeth's decision not to marry, for that was the product of her own unreasoning instincts. Sussex did not perceive that her emotional dependence on Leicester was not a cause of that decision, but an effect.

Elizabeth's deep-rooted antipathy towards marriage, however advantageous, her fear of tying herself to one man, however attracted she might be to him, could only have been strengthened by the horrifying outcome of Mary, Queen of Scots' marriage to Lord Darnley. Never was Cecil's observation that 'carnal marriages begin in gladness and end in strife' more vividly proved; the 'long lad' with the delicate features and royal blood whom Mary had found so irresistible had degenerated into a vicious, physically repulsive nuisance to the Scottish Queen, and in February 1567 had ended his short life as a strangled corpse in the garden of a blown-up house. There were parallels with the early days of Elizabeth's affair with Robert Dudley, when Amy Robsart had met her mysterious, violent death amidst whirling rumours, but Mary did what Elizabeth had not done – promptly married the principal suspect, Lord Bothwell. The storm rose higher; the Scottish crowds roared 'Burn the whore!' as Mary was hustled through the streets of Edinburgh under guard; battle, imprisonment, escape, flight followed, and then the ominous stillness of captivity in England, where she was to remain a prisoner for the rest of her life. 'The daughter of debate, that eke discord doth sow', Elizabeth called her in verse, but loyal Protestant Englishmen were blunter. She was 'a killer of her husband and an adulteress', as well as 'a common disturber of the peace of this realm'. The list of Queens whose marriages had ended in shame, grief and death had grown longer; Elizabeth's mother, her stepmothers, her cousin Lady Jane Grey, her half-sister Mary, now her lovely cousin Mary Stuart. The woman who had cried as a child of eight: 'I will never marry!' had been given little cause to change her mind as an adult.

The threatening situation which had made Elizabeth's marriage seem so necessary at the time of the Parliament of 1566 had taken on a different aspect by 1568, when the Archduke's courtship was finally abandoned. In February of that year Lady Catherine Grey died. Her two sons had been declared illegitimate, and her only remaining sister, Mary, was a stunted little creature who had so far forgotten herself as to marry – without the Queen's permission – a burly sergeant porter. She was not a prepossessing figure to put forward as a successor to the throne, and nor, in the eyes of loyal subjects, was Mary, Queen of Scots, imprisoned as she was under suspicion of the gravest of crimes. 'The Queen expresses sorrow to me at Lady Catherine's death,' wrote de Silva, 'but it is not believed that she feels it, as she was afraid of her, so that both on this account and on the Scotch side she is now without misgiving.' The relentless pressure on Elizabeth to name a successor lifted, and in the coming months the whole question of marriage was laid aside for a time, for the Habsburg and Valois rulers had more pressing affairs to deal with than courting the elusive Queen of England. Spain was beset by the problems of the discontented and rebellious Netherlands, while France was again rent by bloody civil war. Elizabeth too was occupied at home, with the first grave bouts of Catholic plotting, as supporters of the troublesome Scottish Queen rallied to Mary's cause, and even the Duke of Norfolk turned traitor. It was a period of 'manifest danger' such as Elizabeth had not faced since the darkest days of her sister's reign, and the seriousness of the threats to her life and England's peace made her appear more precious than ever in the eyes of loyal Englishmen. By 1570, when she was nearly thirty-seven, a perceptible change was taking place in their attitude to her; the members of the first two Parliaments of the new decade showed themselves to be concerned rather with protecting and cherishing her all-important existence than with harassing her to name a successor or provide heirs by marrying. In comparison with the villainies attributed to Mary, Queen of Scots — 'as vile and naughty a woman as ever the earth bore' – Elizabeth's virtue gained in lustre. Significantly, a member of the Parliament of 1572 chose to refer to Mary in the symbolism of chivalric legend, calling her 'the monstrous and huge dragon'. It was an early hint of the powerful psychological importance that Elizabeth's virgin state was to acquire in the years to come.

Though she was well past her youth in 1570, the Queen of England remained the most eligible woman in Europe, and her advancing middle age in no way deterred her from exploiting that advantage to the utmost. As France's civil wars of religion came to an uneasy halt in the spring of that year, Elizabeth's thoughts turned again to marriage, or rather to courtship. Young Henry Cobham was sent to the Imperial court as Sussex's successor, to see whether the Archduke Charles could be induced to renew his suit, but the Emperor's patience had been tried too far already, and Elizabeth's new overtures did not meet with a warm reception. The suspicion that the dignity of the House of Austria had been trifled with gave a chilly tone to the Emperor's response; since Elizabeth had allowed three years to elapse, he explained, his brother the Archduke had not taken her to be in earnest, and he was accordingly negotiating to marry another princess, the Duchess of Bavaria, 'with whom', the Emperor said pointedly, 'there could be no differences on the subject of religion'. The Archduke himself offered courteous professions of regret and brotherly esteem, but Elizabeth was piqued. It was said that she declared with great spirit that if she had been a man she would certainly have challenged the Emperor to a duel. She could no longer turn to Charles IX as an alternative suitor, for he too was married in

that year, to a daughter of the Emperor. But Charles's two
brothers, the Dukes of Anjou and Alençon, were still available,
and just as Elizabeth had need of France's friendship now, so
Catherine de' Medici had much to gain from allying one of her
sons to Elizabeth. It was the turn of the Duke of Anjou to
become a suitor to the Queen of England.

Dissolute, homosexual, sinisterly good-looking Anjou was
Catherine's favourite son, and she rejoiced in the prospect of
his wearing the crown of England. But there was more than
maternal love to recommend the match. With the ending of the
recent eruption of France's internal religious wars, concessions
had been made to the Huguenots, and a moderate coalition
government was now in power; the presence of Anjou, who
was a figurehead of the extreme Catholic Guise faction, could
only be a disruptive force, and it was highly desirable that he
should be removed from France by the magnificent expedient
of making him King of England. Though Elizabeth had no
intention of thus sharing her throne, still less did she wish to
see Anjou share it with Mary, Queen of Scots. The powerful
Guise family were Mary's near relations, and she had been their
protégée since her childhood and marriage with the Dauphin,
Anjou's eldest brother who had died young; by enmeshing
Anjou in negotiations with herself Elizabeth might keep French
intrigues on behalf of the captive Scottish Queen at bay. At the
same time she would be securing France as an ally against the
increasing menace of Spain. Though the Spanish ambassador
wrote sourly in January 1571: 'Her matrimonial intentions are
of no use any longer for deceiving people,' Elizabeth proved
herself well able to sustain the fiction that she was seriously
contemplating marriage, for quite as long as it suited her to do
so.

Leicester evidently did not believe she was in earnest, however, since he at first seemed very willing to assist the negotiations. Shortly before Christmas 1570 he brought the French
ambassador de La Mothe Fénelon to the Queen's apartments,
where they found her dressed even more splendidly than usual
and evidently expecting them. The ambassador broached the
subject by recalling how she had often expressed regret at not
having married sooner and how she had said she would only

take a husband from a royal house, which made him think she would permit him to speak to her of the Duke of Anjou. Graciously Elizabeth answered that she had understood the Duke's affections to be lodged elsewhere, an allusion to rumours that he might marry a great Catholic princess, but then she unbent and went on to say, with becoming modesty, that she was already old, and if it were not for the consideration of leaving heirs she would be ashamed to talk of a husband, being one of those who were courted for their kingdoms and not for themselves. French princes, she added pensively, had the reputation of being good husbands, and greatly honouring their wives, but of loving them not at all. When, in a later conversation, the ambassador declared lyrically that he would advise any princess who sought true happiness to take a husband of the House of France, she could not resist introducing a sly reference to some of the more celebrated mistresses of recent Valois kings.

Elizabeth's half-concealed fears of being neglected and unloved were often visible during this courtship. She relished the teasing compliments on her sexual and maternal prospects which it inspired, pretending to disparage herself and pointing out the difference in age between herself and Anjou so as to elicit reassurances from her listeners; if they were not forthcoming she was instantly offended. Leicester knew how to treat her – when the Queen demurred that Anjou would always be so much younger than herself, he answered with a broad smile: 'So much the better for you.' Lady Cobham, less tactfully, ventured to remark that the most successful marriages were usually between people of a similar age, to which the Queen said sharply: 'There is only ten years difference between myself and the Duke; I trust he will find compensation in the other advantages.' That the difference was really eighteen years Elizabeth knew very well, since she constantly expressed anxiety on the subject to de La Mothe Fénelon. At a grand dinner at the end of January 1571 she told him again that she was forced to marry to oblige her subjects, but she was frightened of not being loved by her husband. With great gallantry the ambassador replied that he knew someone by whom she would be both loved and honoured, and told her that at the end of nine months he hoped to see her the mother of a fine baby boy. Elizabeth was delighted with that remark, and smiled and talked of it vivaciously for a good while. Her pleasure in such speculation seemed only to increase as time passed.

The great diplomat Walsingham, negotiating the affair for Elizabeth in France, knew how much importance the Queen attached to the physical appearance of her suitors, and he scrutinized Anjou carefully. To Leicester, who was keeping in close touch with the progress of the affair, he sent a description of the Valois suitor which was not over-enthusiastic. Anjou was about three inches taller than himself, 'his body of very good shape, his legs long and slender but reasonably well proportioned'. He added cautiously: 'What helps he has to supply any defects of nature I know not. Touching the health of his person I find the opinion diverse, and I know not what to credit, but for my part I forbear to be over-curious in the search thereof, for divers respects'. Opinions of the young Duke seemed to vary greatly. A Venetian diplomat wrote frankly: 'He is given up to voluptuousness, it dominates him; he covers himself with scents and perfumes; he wears at his ears a double row of rings and pendants; he spends fantastic sums on his shirts and clothes; he charms and beguiles women by lavishing the most costly jewels and fripperies on them.' But a more partial sketch was delivered by a member of the French court, who wrote Walsingham a glowing account of Anjou's beauties of body and mind, declaring that neither pen nor paintbrush could do justice to the Duke's eyes, to the charming line of his mouth when he spoke, or the sweetness which won the hearts of all who met him. If this courtier's lengthy praises of the Duke were intended to speed his suit with Elizabeth, the latter part of the description was misconceived, for the writer went on with equal enthusiasm to affirm Anjou's unswerving devotion to the Catholic faith, swearing that he would live and die in his religion. It was ironic that he should have concluded: 'If the Queen your mistress is not satisfied with so worthy a person, she will never marry; there is nothing she can do from now on but take a vow of perpetual virginity.'

Anjou had no more personal inclination to marry Elizabeth

than she felt to have him. He was under strong Catholic pressure not to forward the match; the Spanish ambassador and the Guises constantly represented its evils to him, pointing out that Elizabeth was a confirmed heretic, excommunicated by the Pope, and that she was not only far too old for him and unlikely to have children, but a woman of scandalous reputation. They urged a glorious armed conquest of England rather than the shameful compromise of such a marriage, and the moody, unstable Duke became increasingly recalcitrant under their influence. The spectre of Philip of Spain's marriage to Elizabeth's half-sister was summoned up again, and it was said, with every truth, that if Anjou were to marry Elizabeth he would not be King, but only the husband of the Queen. 'My son has told me', Catherine wrote despairingly to de La Mothe Fénelon, 'that he wishes never to marry her, having always heard her honour ill spoken of by all the ambassadors who have been in England.' To spur de La Mothe Fénelon to do whatever he might to salvage the situation, Catherine added dramatically: 'So, Monsieur de La Mothe, you are on the point of losing such a kingdom as that for my children.' But with so much at stake for both parties the affair could not end thus. Under Catherine's dominating influence Anjou was brought to a state of grudging compliance for the time being; although the two Queens doubted one another's sincerity in the affair, Catherine could not afford to let the negotiations founder through the reluctance of her favourite son.

Elizabeth seemed anxious to allay suspicions that she might not be in earnest by showing a convincing degree of interest in the marriage. 'I do perceive Her Majesty more bent upon marrying than heretofore she has been,' Leicester wrote. The long list of disappointed suitors to the Queen, which included his own name, was evidently in his thoughts, as it was in Elizabeth's; her history of failed courtships had made prospective husbands wary. Catherine de' Medici expressed fears that her son was being mocked, as others had been, and at one point Anjou said mulishly that the Queen of England's only aim was to dally with the French for a time, which they would soon regret. To combat such talk Elizabeth adopted a pose of injured innocence, instructing Walsingham to explain to the Queen mother that her rejection of Philip of Spain, early in her reign, had been from the highest of motives, but that she was now quite determined to marry. Catherine was to be offered the most earnest assurances of Elizabeth's sincerity in this courtship, anything that would spin out the negotiations for as long as possible without her having to give any specific pledge. 'We pray the Queen mother not to be over-curious in requiring so precise an answer', Elizabeth instructed, 'until the matter may be further treated of and explained, and not to think it any touch to the honour of her son to be named as a suitor to us as others of as great degree have been, though the motions took no effect, rather for other impediments than for any mislike of their persons.' Elizabeth gave the flattering appearance of being far from misliking Anjou's person, and as usual was very eager that he should pay her a clandestine visit; she conceived a romantic plan by which she should await Anjou at the coast while he slipped across from France on the morning tide to meet her. Though that encounter never took place, a pretence of personal contact was established, in florid, formal compliments which passed between the Prince and the Queen. Elizabeth praised Anjou's beauties, mentioning the elegance of his hands, in which respect she knew he could return the praise; in conversation with de La Mothe Fénelon she whispered coyly that she found the Duke very desirable. The response she hoped for was immediately forthcoming – the ambassador promptly assured her that they were both very desirable, their only fault being that they had not already made themselves possessors of one another's perfections. Elizabeth's greed for such gallantries was insatiable. She wanted to know whether de La Mothe Fénelon had told the Duke about the charms of her arm, her foot, and other parts which she discreetly refrained from naming, and altogether she presented the appearance of an unmarried, middle-aged woman excited at the prospect of acquiring a fine young husband. She could afford to indulge her love of being wooed, and to encourage this courtship by seeming to be enamoured of all that she heard of Anjou, for there were 'other impediments' great enough to halt the affair when it should become necessary.

Though the French wished Anjou to be settled abroad, they

had no intention of allowing the English to dictate the terms on which they would have him. When a draft of proposed conditions was brought to England, in April, by one of Catherine de' Medici's most trusted Italian servants, Guido Cavalcanti, Cecil and Leicester had the task of examining the proposals, but it would not have taken a detailed scrutiny to show them that the French were making demands that Elizabeth could not submit to. The draft stipulated that the marriage ceremony was to be performed by Catholic rites alone, and the Duke and his servants were to practise their religion freely and openly at all times; Anjou was not only to be crowned King but to govern jointly with Elizabeth; he was to receive £60,000 a year from England's revenues, even if no children were born of the marriage, and if the Queen were to die before he did – which seemed likely, considering the difference in their ages – the payments were to continue. It was evident that in this courtship, as in the Archduke's, the gaping problems of religion and the consort's status would provide grounds for lengthy diplomatic dispute.

Skilful, prudent Cecil suggested compromises. Ever anxious that Elizabeth should take a husband and secure the succession, and conscious that every year her chances of marriage and child-bearing grew slighter, he patiently endeavoured to forward the Valois match in spite of its notable drawbacks. 'I see no continuance of her quietness without a marriage,' he had written in March. Cecil was encouraged by the belief that the Queen was at last sincerely disposed to marry, however, and for a time it seemed that the match would succeed. In a letter to Leicester, Walsingham had argued forcefully that unless Anjou married the Queen it would be most dangerous, for 'if England refuse, then is Scotland more ready to receive him'. To keep that threat at bay Elizabeth was happy to appear fascinated by her young Valois suitor, while her ministers loyally laboured over the terms of a contract which was never to be signed. Leicester, who gave the impression of supporting the match, knew very well how her mind worked and what the outcome was likely to be, and some of the observations in his letters to Walsingham offered clues for the initiated. The Queen was resolved to marry, he wrote, but she wished to deal 'as privately as may be devised', for less reproach to both parties if nothing should come of the negotiations. He reported that Elizabeth found Anjou most acceptable in person and situation, but she was determined not to be swayed on the religious issue – a decision of which Leicester truthfully expressed cordial approval, his piety and self-interest united. Elizabeth could safely inform Catherine de' Medici that she was ready to accept Anjou, as long as certain difficulties could be settled, just as she had been able to assure the discontented Parliament of 1566 that she would marry unless 'some great let happen'. The great let, the hindrance which still barred the path of Elizabeth's suitors, was religion, and behind that immovable obstacle she could always take shelter from the chase.

Soon after Cavalcanti returned to France with the English amendments to the draft contract, de La Mothe Fénelon had to face an unpleasant scene with Elizabeth. It had come to her ears that a notable French courtier had been joking at her expense, publicly mocking the courtship with Anjou by saying in front of a large number of people that she had a sore on her leg which was incurable, and that this would be a good pretext for Anjou to give her a potion that would make him a widower and thus enable him to marry Mary Queen of Scots and become the absolute master of the isle. De La Mothe Fénelon denied it energetically, and demanded to know who had spread such a tale, so that the miscreant might be punished, but Elizabeth would reveal no names. In the first heat of anger and chagrin she swore she would take up with Spain again, to France's cost; though reason prevailed over rage, the story continued to rankle with her, and for some time after she would make haughty references to it when she saw the French ambassador, telling him on one occasion that she was sorry he had not seen her dance at Lord Northampton's ball, since he would have seen that the Duke of Anjou was in no danger of marrying a cripple. For a woman accustomed to ceaseless extravagant flattery any hint of mockery was doubly painful, and to this, as she was acutely aware, she would always be vulnerable while her love-dealings were with a suitor whose age was so laughably different from her own.

But the threat of another, far deeper, discord hung over the match, which no diplomatic reassurances could smooth away. 'I prize quietude of conscience and the continuance of the peaceable reign which I have begun and desire to pursue higher than all the favours which princes of the world and all kingdoms can confer upon me,' Elizabeth had written to the Emperor, with proud sincerity. To marry Anjou would almost certainly be to forfeit that quietude and disrupt that peace. Anjou could not be permitted to go to Mass publicly and practise his faith openly, since that would be against the laws of Elizabeth's realm; to allow him to do so would be to expose England to the kind of religious strife that had so recently torn France apart. But, Catherine urged, the strength and assistance of the King of France would be Elizabeth's best protection against all such troubles. Walsingham told her diplomatically that he believed more good than evil must come from the match, and added that in England civil wars tended to be sudden and violent but short-lived, as there were no strongholds or walled towns that could hold out over long periods. Perhaps, in the months following the massacre of St Bartholomew's Eve, he would remember that remark, as the gallant Huguenot inhabitants of La Rochelle held out against their King's besieging forces, with Elizabeth's tacit support. For the continuance of her peaceable reign she needed protracted negotiations with France for a marriage which would almost certainly have brought an end to her quietude.

Of all the suitors who ever paid court to Elizabeth, Anjou was the most reluctant. Representatives of the aggressive Catholic faction such as the Spanish ambassador and the papal nuncio counselled him to resist the match at all costs, while on the other side Charles IX and Catherine de' Medici demanded his obedience to their own authority. The simmering hostility between the royal brothers more than once flared into heat; in June, Charles IX accused Anjou of accepting bribes from the Catholic clergy to remain in France as the champion of the Roman faith. 'I tell you plainly, I will have no other champion here but myself,' he swore and threatened to make some of the priests shorter by the head, at which Anjou rushed to his rooms in tears and stayed there for the rest of the day weeping. Catherine tried to keep Walsingham from hearing anything about the incident, but there was no concealing the prospective bridegroom's dissatisfaction with his role, even though he had, in one of his more amenable moods, been induced to tell Walsingham that he regarded Elizabeth as 'the rarest creature that was in Europe these five hundred years'.

By the autumn of 1571, when Walsingham became ill and had to leave his post at the French court for a time, Elizabeth's situation appeared alarming. As more and more strands of the web of plotting that had been spun around Mary, Queen of Scots came to light, English relations with Spain deteriorated dangerously, while the Spanish and the Guises wooed Charles IX and Catherine. There were even plans afoot for marrying Anjou to a Polish princess instead of the Queen of England. At all costs Elizabeth wanted to preserve her courtship with the Valois Prince; in an endeavour to breathe new life into the dying negotiations she went so far as to instruct Walsingham to give way over the religious issue. But by now Anjou had become so obstinate that the English ambassador could see little hope of a satisfactory outcome to the affair, whatever concessions Elizabeth might offer to make, and it was clearly impossible that the crucial question of the religion of England's prospective King-Consort could be set aside for long. When Catherine blandly apologized for Anjou's insistence that he must be free to hear Mass in public with full ceremony, and his refusal to accept any form of compromise, Sir Thomas Smith came out with a reply that spoke for all loyal Protestant Englishmen. 'Why', he exclaimed bluntly, 'then he may also require the four orders of friars, monks, canons, pilgrimages, pardons, oil and cream, relics and all such trumperies. That could never be agreed to.' And he proceeded to outline the reasons for the unpopularity of Catholicism amongst Elizabeth's subjects, telling Catherine of the cruelties of Queen Mary's reign and the treacheries of the present time. It was obvious that Elizabeth could not take a fervent Catholic for her husband, and it was obvious too that Anjou would never be prevailed upon to sacrifice his religious loyalties for the sake of marriage. There was, however, still a means by which Elizabeth might protract her dalliance with France, and Catherine hope to see a Valois prince at last acquire a magnificent share of the rule and revenues of England. Catherine's youngest son, the Duke of Alençon, would soon be eighteen years old; he had reached an age when he too might be considered eligible to become a suitor to the Queen.

It was to be the most remarkable courtship of all, and Alençon was almost to succeed in winning the garish old virgin for whom he sighed out his torments of impatient desire; yet at the outset, in the early spring of 1572, Elizabeth showed a marked lack of interest in the youngest Valois Prince, for he was known to be undersized and badly scarred by smallpox. It was ironic that the wooing which was to be distinguished by its erotic nature should have begun with Elizabeth disdaining her suitor for his personal appearance. She considered herself slighted by Anjou's reluctance to become her husband, and Alençon seemed a poor substitute for the elegant elder brother. 'To be plain with Your Lordship,' Walsingham wrote worriedly to Burghley, 'the only thing I fear in this match is the delicacy of Her Majesty's eye and the hard favour of the gentleman, besides his disfiguring with the smallpox, which, if she should see with her eye, I misdoubt much it would withdraw her liking to proceed.' Catherine kept giving assurances that Alençon would grow taller, and that his beard was beginning to show, and in conversation with the envoy Sir Thomas Smith she indulged in some optimistic speculation about the number of children her son and the Queen of England would have; when Smith expressed the humble hope that Elizabeth might bear an heir, Catherine answered confidently: 'No, two boys, lest the one should die, and three or four daughters to make alliances with us again.' But her maternal zeal could not disguise the fact that the young Prince now being offered as a suitor to the Queen was a puny fellow with a big nose and pitted skin, who in no way resembled the hardy, handsome male type that was Elizabeth's ideal.

The difficulties on which Elizabeth officially based her objections were Alençon's age and religion. He had strong Huguenot connections, she was assured, and the English envoy wrote that he was 'not so obstinate', so 'papistical', or 'restive like a mule as his brother', adding innocently that for some reason people thought Alençon more likely to beget children than his brother, the perfumed dandy Anjou. Sir Thomas Smith urged the marriage, consoling Queen Catherine for her son's low stature by reminding her that Pepin, father of mighty Charlemagne, had scarcely reached up to his wife's waist, and imploring Burghley to ensure that Elizabeth did not dally and waste time in this courtship 'as is commonly her wont'. But Elizabeth had no intention of hurrying into marriage with an unattractive French prince twenty years younger than herself. The signing of the defensive Treaty of Blois, in the spring of 1572, gave her the firm alliance with France which she needed, and while that held she could afford to vacillate over the marriage question, sending contradictory letters to Walsingham, one day declaring herself unable to marry so young a man, and the next announcing that she was very well disposed towards the match. To the French envoys who arrived in England in June for the ratification of the Treaty of Blois, she gave 'neither yea or nay' on the subject of Alençon's suit, and in July she informed Walsingham that although she had withheld her consent to the envoys' proposal on the grounds of the disparity of age, a greater cause for dislike was the disfigurement of the Prince's face by smallpox, which she had heard was very extensive. She was angling for the return of Calais to be included in the bargain, as compensation for the prospective bridegroom's extreme youth and reputed lack of personal attractions. She wrote to tell Walsingham that considering 'the youngness of his years' she could not bring herself 'to like of this offer, specially finding no other great commodity offered to us with him, whereby the great absurdity that in the general opinion of the world might grow, might be in some manner recompensed'. The inducement of Calais was not proffered, but soon Elizabeth began to find that there might be other compensations in a French courtship.

Alençon's friend La Mole arrived in England at the end of July, and set himself to charm away the Queen's disdain, with considerable success. He was an attractive young man with engaging manners, and Elizabeth was 'full of graciousness and caresses' for him. She talked excitedly of receiving a visit from Alençon himself, eager to see the master of such a servant; she publicly drank La Mole's health at a banquet, and as usual she showed off shamelessly, playing the virginals to him with much display of her beautiful white hands. She was delighted with the handsome young envoy's wooing; the flattering attentions of a man who represented a prince of the illustrious and powerful House of Valois held a special pleasure for her which all the customary compliments of her own courtiers could not provide. She found this foretaste of French gallantry very sweet, and it did nothing to diminish her appetite for such delights.

Dalliance was in the air, and Alençon's suit seemed to be prospering, until the events of 24 August, St Bartholomew's Eve, flung a blood-soaked pall over all dealings between England and France. On that day thousands of Huguenots were slaughtered in the streets of Paris, men, women and children alike, in an indiscriminate massacre that began with the consent of Catherine and Charles IX and accelerated, beneath the blades and blows of the mob, into a frenzy of human butchery, until by nightfall the gutters ran red and the Seine was choked with bobbing naked corpses. In the palace of the Louvre the royal family waited for the roaring hubbub to die down, while in Walsingham's lodgings in the Faubourg St Germain the terrified English Protestants who had taken refuge with the ambassador huddled together in prayer. It was several days before Walsingham could send word to Elizabeth, and then he dared only write guardedly. But the boatloads of Huguenot refugees fleeing to the English shores carried all the vivid details of the horrors that had spread across France, and as the news of the 'horrible universal massacre' became known Englishmen cried out for vengeance. The old familiar prejudices against France blazed out again, refuelled with revulsion and fear. The relatively new distrust of papists had received a baptism of blood. After St Bartholomew's there were few of Elizabeth's loyal subjects who would have welcomed the coming of a Catholic consort for their Queen, and least of all would they accept one who was the brother of the blood-stained King of France.

It was some days before Elizabeth would receive the French ambassador. When he was finally shown into her presence, on 8 September, he found that she and her court were in mourn-

ing, and all were silent as he approached. With regal solemnity
Elizabeth accepted the official explanation of the atrocities
which he brought from Charles ix; and the diplomatic bonds
between England and France held, visibly frayed though they
were. Within a matter of weeks, Catherine de' Medici – who
was said to be looking quite ten years younger since the
massacre – was again talking optimistically of the Alençon
marriage, and towards the end of September the young suitor
wrote a humbly affectionate letter to Elizabeth, concluding
with a postscript in his own bad handwriting. Though Elizabeth expressed the gravest of doubts about the match, pointing
out in tones of sad reproof that a brother of a monarch who
was so clearly determined to 'root out all the possessors' of the
Protestant religion would scarcely be a fitting husband for her,
she nevertheless could not afford to break off her dealings with
France. The massacre which had so shocked and affronted
Elizabeth and the Protestant English had placed Mary, Queen of
Scots' relations, the ultra-Catholic Guises, in the ascendant
once more; it had won the hearty approval of the Pope, and
Philip of Spain was said to have laughed appreciatively when he
first heard of it. The marriage negotiations with France were as
necessary as ever, and through the middle years of the 1570s
Elizabeth was to dance high and disposedly with the Duke of
Alençon, with all the skill of an experienced performer, until at
the end of that decade the tune changed and the steps
quickened and she almost fell headlong into her partner's
arms.

The years of Elizabeth's halting political courtship with
Alençon, before the affair turned into the hectic personal
relationship, saw great changes in the lives of the three
brothers of France. As Catherine had so ardently hoped, a
foreign throne was obtained for Anjou; in the spring of 1573 he
was elected King of Poland. But in the following year Elizabeth's other former suitor Charles ix died of consumption at the
age of twenty-four, and Anjou returned from his Polish kingdom to become King Henry iii of France. The ugly undersized
Alençon was now next in line to the throne, and as well as his
brother's former title of Duke of Anjou he inherited his
brother's former role, that of dissident and royal troublemaker.

Before the death of Charles IX, while Anjou was away in Poland, Catherine had thought it wise to keep her youngest son under virtual house-arrest in the Louvre; as the hope of the Huguenots and potential claimant to the throne of France, he remained closely watched over by Catherine and Henry III, until at last, in September 1575, he succeeded in escaping from the confines of the court and fled to take command of the Huguenot rebel forces. It was ambition rather than religious zeal, however, that burned in Alençon's breast and impelled him to endeavour great deeds, and by the following spring he had come to remunerative terms with Henry III and an appearance of amity had been established between the royal brothers, though jealousies and rivalries continued to erupt between them and their followers. Worldly gain was a greater incentive to Alençon than any hope of spiritual rewards, and while such discontented ambition smouldered within him it was clearly desirable that he, in turn, should be found occupation abroad.

Hopes of finding him occupation as King-Consort of England faded away in 1576. Elizabeth was forty-three now, and though she had no lack of attractive Englishmen eager to praise her beauty and virtue in adoring speeches and languishing letters, her chances of marriage seemed to be dwindling rapidly. At the close of the Parliament which met in that year, the Speaker referred to the realm's great need of an heir of Elizabeth's line, and humbly 'besought Her Majesty as shortly as might be to incline herself to marriage', but Elizabeth's response showed her to be as little inclined to marriage as ever. 'If I were a milkmaid with a pail on my arm,' she told the assembly, 'whereby my private person might be little set by, I would not forsake that poor and single state to match with the greatest monarch.' She went on to assure them lovingly that she was prepared to sacrifice her private inclinations for the sake of her subjects' well-being, but Parliament had been receiving such assurances from her for nearly seventeen years, and many of those who heard her words on this occasion must privately have concluded that their Queen would never marry.

But the days of her political wooings were not yet ended. When, three years later, the young Duke of Alençon again took up the pursuit of the elderly Queen, England was to tremble with the passions aroused by the courtship of the youngest of the three brothers of France. In her forty-seventh year, on the brink of the menopause, Elizabeth was to come within kissing distance of a marriage.

▰▰▰▰▰▰▰▰▰▰▰▰▰▰▰▰▰▰▰▰▰▰▰▰▰▰▰▰▰▰

8

A FROG HE WOULD A-WOOING GO

'The pock holes are no great disfigurement,' Elizabeth's ambassador had written from Paris, early in 1573, 'because they are rather thick than deep or great. They upon the blunt end of his nose are great and deep, how much to be disliked may be as it pleaseth God to move the heart of the beholder.' There had been little in such descriptions to arouse Elizabeth's interest in Alençon, and it was not out of love for the pock-marked Prince that she began to smile anew on his suit towards the end of 1578. The courtship was to become an emotional affair, but it began as a matter of expediency. Alençon had found himself occupation out of France, aiding the rebel leaders in the turbulent Netherlands, in return for a title and lands there; though it was a lone venture of Alençon's, rather than an official French undertaking, Elizabeth found it disturbing. She had no wish to see a prince of France, the heir presumptive to the French crown, gain control in the Netherlands to the exclusion of English interests there, and it accordingly seemed wise for the negotiations for her marriage with the young Valois to be revived once more. If Alençon was to fight in the Low Countries, it should be as her knight.

For Alençon himself the prospect of English aid and support was alluring, and he set about his renewed courtship of the Queen with an enthusiasm such as none of her foreign suitors had ever shown before. She was his *belle Majesté*, he was her slave; he wrote that he was more devoted to her than anyone else on earth could be, and to speak – and act – on his behalf, he sent over his best-loved servant, Jean de Simier, at the end of December 1578. Simier was the ideal man for the task of

F

making love to the Queen as proxy for Alençon. He approached Elizabeth with a combination of servile passion and erotic dexterity, flattering and flirting as eagerly as if she had in reality been the 'perfect beauty' which he called her, and the Queen, predictably, was delighted. This was the lovemaking for which she had always longed, humble adoration spiced with sexual insinuations, proffered on behalf of one of the most illustrious young princes in the world. Simier naughtily stole her nightcap from her bedchamber to send to his master; evidently the Prince set great store by such intimate trophies, for he already had one of her handkerchiefs, and a similar theft took place three years later, on the occasion of Sir Francis Drake's knighthood, when Elizabeth's ornate purple garter slipped down and was promptly claimed by the French ambassador. Far from taking exception to Simier's amorous liberties, Elizabeth was full of praises for his behaviour, describing him as 'sage and discreet beyond his years in his conduct of the case'. Not everyone was so impressed with his sagacity and discretion, however. There were whispers of love-philtres and charms having played a part in his success, and ripples of scandal began to spread. Some of the salacious talk eventually reached the ears of the captive Queen of Scots, through her guardian's wife, the hard-bitten Countess of Shrewsbury, who enjoyed passing on titbits of malicious gossip about the vanity and immorality of Queen Elizabeth. Leicester had been the subject of such rumours for long enough to know truth from falsehood where Elizabeth was concerned, but he had no cause to smile on Simier's artful wooing, which, if successful, would surely oust Leicester at last from his position as Elizabeth's most favoured and intimate companion. It was not long before the envoy had been given a nickname; in a pun on the associations of 'Simier' he had become her 'Monkey', fondly referred to as nostre singe in her letters to his master Alençon. The political courtship had acquired the atmosphere of a seduction, and according to the French ambassador the Queen of England had never looked more radiant.

Through the spring of 1579 the subject of the Alençon marriage was being debated, with Walsingham and Leicester opposing the match while Cecil and the Earl of Sussex supported it. As always, Burghley approached the question in a methodical and judicious manner, weighing 'objections' against 'benefits'. 'Her Majesty's own mislike to marriage' was noted down, as well as 'the difficulty in choice of such a person as in all respects might content Her Majesty's mind and satisfy her eye.' More serious still was the danger of child-birth at Elizabeth's advanced age, but as the memorandum was for the Queen to read, Burghley offered lavish reassurances on this point. Referring to the Duchess of Savoy, 'a woman of sallow and melancholy complexion, and in all respects far inferior to her Majesty', who had been older than Elizabeth, yet had borne a fine baby son, he concluded encouragingly that it was likely that Elizabeth, 'a person of most pure complexion, of the largest and goodliest stature of well-shaped women, with all limbs set and proportioned in the best sort, and one whom in the sight of all men nature cannot amend her shape in any part to make her more likely to conceive and bear children', would have no great difficulty in producing an heir to the Tudor throne. A graver problem lay in 'the mislike of the people to be governed by a foreign prince and especially by the blood of France'. But Burghley argued that 'no marriage offered by any stranger hath been liked', and concluded that since Elizabeth had made it plain that she would never marry one of her own subjects, those who opposed her marrying a foreigner must intend that she should never marry at all. In Leicester's case that was probably true. The Spanish ambassador reported that the King of France had 'assured Leicester on his word of honour that his authority and position should not be injured in any way by the marriage, as he would be the guide and friend of his brother', but the man who had been Elizabeth's supreme favourite for nearly twenty years could not fail to be disturbed by the threat to his position that her marriage must bring. And he had a special reason now to fear for his place in Elizabeth's favour. He was hiding a guilty secret, one which, if disclosed to the Queen, might well destroy for ever the royal relationship which he had so long enjoyed. In this delicate situation the arrival of a consort for Elizabeth was the last thing Leicester wanted.

But despite his opposition, and that of Walsingham and many others on the Privy Council, the French Prince's suit continued to prosper. 'Everybody here is full of the marriage and the coming of Alençon,' wrote the Spanish ambassador in April. 'Many people who were wont to smile at it now see that appearances are all in favour of it taking place and believe it.' Appearances had ever been misleading where Elizabeth's court-ships were concerned, but there was no doubt that the Queen's interest in Alençon had been aroused, and for once diplomacy was deliciously mingled with romance. No foreign suitor had ever paid court to her with such passion before. In March the young Valois Prince had informed her that his only misfortune lay in the fact that he was at present unable to sacrifice his life to do her some slight service, but if he should ever be in a position to do so he would regard himself as the luckiest man on earth – a chivalrous vow which no stolid Habsburg suitor would have been prepared to make. Alençon was particularly anxious that Elizabeth should know that his love was dis-interested; his feelings for her had 'nothing to do with avarice or ambition', but were inspired by her beauty, virtue and good-ness. Elizabeth might say deprecatingly to the Spanish am-bassador that 'it was a fine idea for an old woman like her to talk about marriage', but she was intoxicated by her young suitor's skilful lovemaking and she was undoubtedly allowing herself to indulge in fancies of taking a husband at last, even if at heart she knew she never would. It was obviously the last chance that she would have.

In May the Spanish ambassador reported that there had been an unpleasant scene involving the Privy Council and Simier. Elizabeth had ordered the Council to discuss the marriage, he wrote, and after objections had been raised on such grounds as the 'great confusion' that might be raised by the 'coming hither of Catholics, and above all Frenchmen, who were their ancient enemies', Simier was eventually summoned and in-formed that Alençon was making exorbitant demands – 'such things have never been proposed by any prince who treated for marriage with the Queen'. According to the Spaniard's inform-ation, Simier became extremely angry at the Councillors' opposition, and flung himself out of the door, 'which he

slammed after him in a great fury'. When the Queen learned of
this she was full of regrets, he went on, and that night she said
twice: 'They need not think that it is going to end in this way;
I must get married.' But however brightly she smiled on Simier,
however tenderly she wrote to Alençon, she still continued to
insist on her customary stipulation; she would never marry a
man she had not seen. On this occasion, when the suitor in
question was reputed to be so remarkably unattractive, her
freedom to see and refuse was particularly important to her.
Somewhat maliciously, the Spanish ambassador reported that
Elizabeth was 'largely influenced by the idea that it should be
known that her talents and beauty are so great, that they have
sufficed to cause him to come and visit her without any
assurance that he will be her husband'. Whether it was for the
Queen of England's talents and beauty, or for hope of political
advantage, Alençon, unlike her previous royal suitors, was
prepared to hazard his dignity to gain his desire, and even
without a firm promise of eventual success he was ready to
cross the seas to woo Elizabeth in person.

For weeks the English court stirred with anticipation of his
coming. Londoners were laying bets; the odds were given as
two to one against Alençon's coming and three to one against
his marrying the Queen. But the atmosphere throughout the
country was not by any means festive. 'Alençon's coming may
cause disturbances in this country,' the Spanish ambassador
had prophesied in June. The hatred of the English for the
French had lost none of its bitterness in the seven years which
had elapsed since the massacre of St Bartholomew's Eve – 'If
they went up to the knuckles in French blood, they will up to
the elbows in English blood,' a fervent English Protestant was
to warn. The Huguenot leanings of the youngest Valois Prince
counted for less than his close kinship with those who bore the
responsibility for the massacre, and as heir presumptive to the
French crown he was, despite his flexible conscience, officially
a Catholic, 'a prince and good son of Rome, that anti-Christian
mother city'. At court the atmosphere was strained by
Leicester's opposition to the match, though his resistance was
based on personal, rather than religious motives. When he
heard that Elizabeth had finally signed the passport that would

bring her suitor over to England, Leicester was filled with despondency, and he retired to his house at Wanstead, determined to win her sympathy. It was a trick that always worked. Missing him sorely, anxious about his health, Elizabeth hastened to his side; she made the journey to Wanstead and stayed there for several days, consoling him. It was a moment of stillness before a mighty storm in their relationship.

Some weeks previously, while Simier was on the Thames with Elizabeth and Leicester, shots had been fired at the royal barge. The shooting was judged to have been accidental, but now, while the Queen and her favourite were away at Wanstead, there was another incident, and this time it was unmistakeably an attempt on Simier's life; he was fired on while walking in the grounds of Greenwich Palace. Again he escaped injury, but he was shaken and angry. The whisper ran around the court that the jealous, dangerous Earl of Leicester was behind the murder attempt, and Simier, knowing Leicester's reputation and well aware of his hostility to the French marriage, was ready to believe it. It was time for him to fight back, and for this he had the ideal weapon – he had found out Leicester's guilty secret. Simier, 'sage and discreet' indeed, with a talent for undercover dealings, had found out an item of information about his opponent's private life that could debar Leicester forever from the Queen's favour; now, in the interests both of his master's wooing and his own personal vengeance, the time had come for Simier to reveal what he knew. He told the Queen that Leicester was married.

It must have been one of the most agonizing moments of Elizabeth's life. All her greed for compliments and flattery, her love of hectic dalliance, and her vain posturing, signified not a secure, confident woman, but one who craved affection and dreaded being unloved and unsought after. She needed endless reassurances of her own ability to inspire love, and to old friends who provided her with a sense of stability she clung almost blindly – so that as a young girl she had not only kept her dear, fallible Kat Ashley with her after the affair of the Admiral, but had even welcomed back to her household the informer Parry. Robert Dudley had been by her side throughout her reign, almost her lover, always her dearest friend; he had sworn he would die for her, and she had believed him; through the twenty years of their relationship neither scandal nor jealousies nor quarrels had been able to part them for long, and her Robin's devotion had given Elizabeth the greatest emotional security she would ever know. She had carried on her political courtships confident in the knowledge that he was always close at hand, fuming with desire to marry her himself and gratifyingly jealous of those whom she seemed to favour. Of late he had appeared to accept the fact that he never would be her husband, but his position as her helpmeet had seemed to be unshakeable. He had put on weight over the years, his handsome face had become florid and his greying hair had receded, but Elizabeth's emotional dependence on her beloved Robin went far beyond physical attraction. For twenty years she had relied upon his love – and now, with a few whispered words from sly Simier, the relationship was ruptured and her security was shattered. For nearly a year, ever since the autumn of 1578, Leicester had been deceiving her. He had become the husband of another woman, the sensuous redhead Lettice Knollys, and then, while concealing the unforgivable fact of his own marriage, he had done all he could to hinder Elizabeth from taking a consort. It would have been a painful revelation for any woman; for one as emotionally demanding as Elizabeth it was almost unbearable.

In her first reaction she awoke echoes of her father Henry VIII – she cried that she would have Leicester committed to the Tower. Love was transformed into hate, and she wanted to hurt him as he had hurt her. But she was prevailed upon to modify the punishment, since lawful marriage was not a crime, and he was instead confined at Greenwich and then banished to his own house at Wanstead. It was not only Elizabeth's heart that was wounded; her pride had taken a painful blow. But, as Simier had probably calculated when choosing the moment for his disclosure, consolation was at hand. Alençon would know how to soothe and flatter the Queen into good spirits again, and if all went well, he might take Leicester's vacated place by her side, not as favourite, but as husband.

On 17 August 1579, a great foreign prince at last arrived to pay court to the Queen of England. She had always longed to be wooed in person by her illustrious suitors, and she found the experience every bit as sweet as she had expected. Alençon was not hideous at all, he was delightful; delicately built and somewhat scarred indeed, but with so much sex appeal that his imperfections were hardly noticeable. He was the embodiment of grace and charm, his manners were captivating, and, most appealing of all, he made it plain from the start that he was almost beside himself with passion for the forty-six-year-old Queen. Here was balm indeed for Elizabeth's bruised feelings.

Lacking normal relationships, she had always attached inordinate importance to the preliminaries and rituals of romance, so that the element of play-acting in her love-dealings was very strong. Now at last she had a noble suitor who was happy to enter into the spirit of the game, with enough conviction to make the pretence seem real. Officially Alençon's visit was supposed to be secret – the clandestine rendezvous which Elizabeth had so often suggested to her former suitors, without success. The news leaked out but remained un-acknowledged, thus adding a further layer of make-believe to the drama. 'On Sunday 23', wrote the Spanish ambassador, 'there was a great ball where the Queen danced much more than usual, Alençon being placed behind a curtain and she making signals to him.' That was a scene after Elizabeth's own heart. To know that the heir presumptive to the throne of France, a young and charming prince, was watching her with apparent adoration from amongst the hangings as she gaily leapt in the volta, or paced daintily through a galliard, was like a delightful dream come true for Elizabeth. She loved to show off, she was thrilled by the pretence of disguise, and it was delightful to her to send little signs to him as though in lovers' intimate communication, while the court looked on. Alençon had to have a pet name like all her favourites; she promptly christened him her 'Frog'. A 'Frog Galliard' was written for her to dance to, high and disposedly. A Frog he would a-wooing go, and it seemed that he had gone a-wooing with success.

Alençon's stay at Elizabeth's court was brief, but two weeks of his presence were sufficient to arouse a variety of strong emotions in many people. 'Leicester is much put out, and all the Councillors are disgusted except Sussex,' the Spanish ambassador Mendoza wrote with evident satisfaction. It was a bad time for the Queen's former favourite. Towards the end of August Mendoza reported: 'Leicester, who is in great grief, came hither recently, and when he came from his interview with the Queen, his emotion was remarked.' Leicester was not alone in 'cursing the French'. Among Elizabeth's lesser subjects discontent was growing as the likelihood of the French marriage increased. The old spectre of Mary Tudor's marriage to Philip of Spain was raised again, and the atrocities committed in France in the name of religion lent an edge of truth to anti-Catholic propaganda. Mendoza gave it as his opinion that revolution was in the air. Loyal Englishmen did not want a Catholic king and they did not want a French king; in Alençon they would have both.

For once Elizabeth seemed to be in earnest in her marriage negotiations. Alençon's wooing was exactly calculated to win her confidence and tempt her to take the step that she had resisted for so long; his protestations of passion combined the appeal of humble worship of her divine perfections with that of titillating eroticism, both of which delighted her. His courtship could not have been more ardent if she had really been a young and desirable woman, and since she was neither his words were doubly pleasurable to her. Simier bore witness to the Prince's feelings, informing Elizabeth that Alençon had hardly slept at all after leaving her, sighing and crying all night, and waking him, Simier, early in the morning to talk of her divine beauties and his pain at departing from her. Alençon wrote her four letters on 30 August and two more the next day, although just before the embarkation he was almost unable to write at all, he told her, on account of the copious tears that were flowing ceaselessly from his eyes. However, he managed to stop weeping for long enough to assure Elizabeth that he was 'the most faithful and loving slave on earth', and to conclude: 'As such, from beside the cruel sea I kiss your feet.' The young Prince was happy to offer such flattery for as long as Elizabeth was eager to receive it; though more than twenty years lay between them, they were well-matched partners in this splendid game of romance.

Love was in the air in that month of August, but so were

hostility and fear. Even while Alençon was sighing out his passion to the Queen at Greenwich, a pamphlet was being published and distributed in which very different passions were expressed. Entitled *The Discovery of a Gaping Gulf wherein England is like to be swallowed by another French marriage if the Lord forbid not the banns by letting Her Majesty see the sin and punishment thereof*, it was a long, vivid tract inspired by a combination of religious fervour and patriotic zeal, in which the appalling nature of the Queen's intended marriage was exposed in 'bitter scoffing style'. It sprang from the 'honest affectionate heart' of one who was 'Her Majesty's loving true servant', and who, loving his native England and idolizing his Queen, dreaded the prospect of Elizabeth's being 'led blindfold as a poor lamb to the slaughter' in shameful marriage with a French prince, a ruler of that race whose minds were known to be as diseased with Catholicism as their bodies were rotten with syphilis. Through many pages of historical and biblical allusion the writer warned against the coming of Alençon, 'the old serpent in shape of a man', who would so vilely corrupt 'our dear Queen Elizabeth' and despoil 'this English paradise', bringing with him his train of 'needy, spent Frenchmen' who were 'the scum of the King's Court, which is the scum of all France, which is the scum of Europe' to suck upon the poor honest English like horseleeches. The gravest aspersions were cast on the Prince's moral character, and his motives for wishing to marry a woman so much older than himself were discussed with a frankness that cared nothing for compliments to the Queen. 'Not one in a thousand of those younger men that seek their elder matches but doth it in side respects,' the writer pronounced, and went on baldly: 'It is quite contrary to his young appetites, which will otherwise have their desire.' The pamphlet was offensive, it was subversive, it was a monstrous encroachment on Elizabeth's royal prerogative; the Queen was enraged.

Copies of the publication were rounded up as swiftly as possible, before they could do further harm, and possession of them was strictly prohibited. The clergy were warned not to 'meddle with such high secular matters' in their sermons, 'nor intrude themselves into the Queen's affairs'; the Archbishop of

Canterbury was specially charged to quell any tendencies to subversive sentiments among the preachers, while the Lord Mayor was ordered to organize the confiscation of the pamphlets from members of 'the companies of the city' such as the Ironmongers' Guild and Grocers' Company. The author of the *Gaping Gulf* was soon apprehended – he proved to be a lawyer of strong Puritan affiliations, named John Stubbs. The devotion to the Queen that shone through his writings won him no mercy, and under a law passed in the previous reign to protect Mary Tudor's hated husband Philip of Spain from similar calumnies, he was condemned to lose his right hand. It was a barbarous punishment, from which mary expected him to be reprieved; that he was not did nothing to ease the stormy atmosphere gathering around the Alençon marriage. Nor were the mutters of discontent quietened by the scene that took place at the scaffold. In three blows Stubbs' right hand was severed; he raised his hat with the left, cried 'God save the Queen!' and fainted. Alençon, whom Stubbs' tract had so foully insulted, wrote to Elizabeth to express sincere sorrow at the man's punishment. As he well knew, the association of his name with public severities would not endear him to the resentful English.

Elizabeth's measures for suppressing the *Gaping Gulf* did not have the effect of silencing opposition to her marriage. According to the Spanish ambassador, the proclamation which she issued, 'instead of mitigating the public indignation against the French, has irritated it and fanned the flame'. Puritan feelings against her projected marriage found expression in a jingling little ballad:

> The King of France shall not advance his ships in English sand,
> Nor shall his brother Francis have the ruling of the land:
> We subjects true unto our Queen the foreign yoke defy,
> Whereto we plight our faithful hearts, our limbs, our lives and all,
> Thereby to have our honour rise, or take our fatal fall.
> Therefore, good Francis, rule at home, resist not our desire;
> For here is nothing else for thee, but only sword and fire.

Stubbs had in truth plighted one of his limbs in what he regarded as the service of the Queen. The danger of England falling under 'the foreign yoke' as a result of the match seemed very real; as Stubbs had somewhat insultingly pointed out, child-birth might well prove fatal at Elizabeth's age – 'the very point of most danger to Her Majesty for child-bearing' – and if she were to die giving birth the realm would be left under a French regency, with an infant half-Valois king or queen. For years Elizabeth had been under relentless pressure to take a husband, yet now that she was at last entertaining thoughts of marriage she found herself faced with resistance from her subjects and discouragement from her Councillors. With characteristic perception she had foreseen this situation years before; when pressed to marry by the presumptuous Parliament of 1566 she had observed angrily that many of those who were urging her to wed would be equally vociferous in criticizing whomever she chose for her consort – 'as ready to mislike him with whom I shall marry as they are now to move it' had been her bitter expression. Now, thirteen years afterwards, the truth of her words was becoming apparent.

Ultimately, Elizabeth's aversion to marriage and the realities of sex was too profound to permit her to accept Alençon or anyone else as a husband, but in the autumn of 1579 she had strong reasons for wishing to dally with the idea of marrying her charming French suitor. Leicester's faithlessness in abandoning his fruitless courtship of her for a normal marriage with another had lowered her morale, and left her, for the time being, without the sense of near-partnership that her relationship with him had given her for so long. But the illustrious Prince's impassioned wooing had both provided flattering evidence of her desirability and held out the tempting prospect of intimate companionship with a man who was her equal in blood and power. The idea of entering her old age as the cherished wife of an adoring young prince was very beguiling; even if at heart Elizabeth acknowledged the truth of her past observations about the likelihood that she would be courted for her possessions and not for herself, Alençon's protestations of disinterested love were ardent enough almost to be convincing, and the forty-six-year-old Queen found it very sweet to indulge in fantasies of accepting him. It was undoubtedly the last chance she would have of taking a husband and bearing children. After Alençon there would be no more serious suitors to the Queen of England, and she knew it.

Elizabeth appeared wrought up and emotional at this time; the tensions experienced by any woman approaching the menopause were heightened for her by the mingled excitements and anxieties of her final courtship. At the beginning of October she ordered her Council to discuss again the question of the Alençon match and give her their opinion of it. Meeting after meeting was held and on one occasion they were closeted in strict secrecy from eight o'clock in the morning until seven o'clock at night, which was most unusual, but all 'without proceeding to any full resolution'. Their final decision was that the Queen should 'do what best shall please her'. It should have been a safe enough verdict, but Elizabeth's mood was not what it had been at the time of the Parliament of 1566. She did not want her Councillors to maintain a respectful neutrality, leaving the decision to her, she wanted them to override her doubts and persuade her that it would be right for her to marry Alençon. She 'uttered many speeches', Burghley recorded, 'and that not without shedding of many tears', in her disappointment that her Councillors should have shown 'any disposition to make it doubtful whether there could be any more surety for her and her realm than to have her marry and have a child of her own body to inherit, and so to continue the line of Henry VIII'. She snapped that she must have been a fool to have entrusted them with debating the matter, 'for she thought to have rather had a universal request made to her to proceed in this marriage than to have made doubt of it'. The Spanish ambassador reported that after the interview she 'remained extremely sad', and 'was so cross and melancholy that it was noticed by everyone who approached her'. She told Walsingham, the arch opponent of the match, to get out of her sight, vowing that 'the only thing he was good for was a protector of heretics'. There were, indeed, good grounds for believing that he had been involved with the publication of the *Gaping Gulf*. To the Treasurer of the Household, who asked how she could contemplate marriage with a Catholic, she retorted angrily that 'he might pay dearly for the zeal he was displaying in the cause of religion, and it was a fine way to show his attachment to her, who might desire, like others, to have children'. The doubts and tacit discouragement of her ministers told her what she least wished to hear – that she was not 'like others'. She was not the radiant embodiment of femininity that Alençon's hot wooing implied, but a fading old maid almost past childbearing, whom an eligible foreign prince would only court out of sinister motives. It was not surprising that she should have appeared 'cross and melancholy' at this time.

Several times she declared defiantly that she was determined to marry Alençon, and the Spanish ambassador began to think optimistically that God might have ordained this marriage as a means of plunging England into civil war. On 20 November she instructed a select group of Privy Councillors to draw up the conditions of the marriage contract with Simier, and he left England four days later with an agreement. But the negotiations were by no means concluded. Elizabeth insisted that she must have two months in which to win her subjects over, and Simier had to sign a certificate before he departed, acknowledging this stipulation and agreeing that if she could not placate her subjects the marriage articles should be considered null and void. It was a loophole of which Elizabeth intended to take full advantage.

When Simier had gone the heady romance of her last courtship began to loosen its hold over Elizabeth. The *Gaping Gulf* had sneeringly called it 'a very French Popish wooing, to send smooth-tongued Simiers to gloss and glaver', but it had been a very successful kind of wooing. While Simier remained at her court he had provided a personal link with Alençon, staying by Elizabeth's side to flatter away her doubts with assurances of his master's passion for her, to remind her of all the Prince's charms, and to tempt her with talk of future joys; once he had departed, the sensual and emotional warmth went out of the affair. He continued to 'gloss and glaver' from a distance, in the lavish letters adorned with pink seals and lovers' knots which he sent Elizabeth day after day, but soon expressions of reproachful uncertainty began to appear among the compliments. Towards the end of January 1580, Simier wrote anxiously that he could tell that the Queen's change of heart had been brought about by the interference of those who wished to prevent the marriage, and in a meaningful reference to Leicester, whose coat of arms contained the bear and ragged staff, he begged Elizabeth to protect her monkey from the paw of the bear. He tried to play upon her pride, as well as her affection, musing provokingly: 'Who would have thought that a queen of the heavens and the earth, a princess of all the virtue in the world, could be mistaken in her knowledge of certain people who feel neither love nor affection otherwise than ambition for power impels them' – another aspersion on Leicester. But the situation had changed in Simier's absence. Without him beside her to plead Alençon's suit, Elizabeth was turning once more to her former favourite for admiration and companionship. As Leicester returned to her good graces, so did Walsingham, the other great opponent of the match. Lacking the persuasive presence of her suitor's representative, Elizabeth lost her desire for Alençon.

She still had need of her Frog, however, and it suited her purposes to have him poised, breathless with anticipation, on the brink of marriage with her. Philip of Spain was soon to acquire the throne of Portugal, and that increase in his dominions and power would make hostile Spain a still mightier threat to the security of Elizabeth's Protestant kingdom. It was ominous for the French, too, and caused Catherine de' Medici to wish to draw nearer to England, to redress the balance of power; however, marriage with Elizabeth was not the only means by which the House of Valois might be fortified. An alternative was 'the alliance of the Duke of Alençon with the King of Spain by marriage, and the joining of their forces to help each other'. If Alençon were to marry one of Philip's daughters, the combined weight of Spain and France, blessed by the Pope, might crush England in a triumphant crusade. Walsingham set little store by this threat, pointing out, with justification, that it had caused great fears before, in 1559, when King Philip had married Alençon's sister Elisabeth, *la fille de France*, yet nothing had come of it then, when England was so much weaker and more vulnerable than now. There was, however, no gainsaying the fact that Elizabeth's need for an ally against the rising menace of Spain in the 1580s was very great, and to this end she was fortunate in having an ardent French suitor to entice or rebuff as circumstances required.

She had asked for two months' grace, and before this period elapsed she produced an obstacle to the marriage – religion. In a letter full of verbal caresses she explained tenderly to Alençon that, though there was no prince in the whole world to whom she would rather give herself than him, her *treschère grenouille*, or with whom she would rather spend the years that were left to her, her people were adamant on the subject of religion; they would not tolerate a king-consort who openly worshipped according to the Roman rituals. If he were insistent on that point, Elizabeth wrote, they would have to give up the idea of marriage altogether, and agree to remain faithful friends. The truth was that she knew full well the negotiations would not end at this stage, she could continue to dally for many months more, but with her customary prudence she was establishing a solid obstacle behind which she could take shelter from the pursuit whenever it should become necessary. Alençon was not ignorant of her tactics, but there was little he could do against her pose of duty and conscience. Somewhat stiffly he wrote back that people were saying the Queen of England was merely using religion as a pretext for dismissing him, and that it was well known that her subjects were eager to see her married. In a brief post-script, referring to Elizabeth's envoy Stafford, he showed a measure of his displeasure : 'I find Sir Edward Stafford as cold as ice,' he wrote reproachfully.

Although Elizabeth was anxious to remain technically un-committed, she wanted the negotiations to prosper. The first flame of her excitement over Alençon had died, but she still felt a *tendresse* for her charming French Prince, so that pleasure was mingled with politics. In February 1580 Mendoza reported a discussion between the Queen, Cecil and the Archbishop of York, during which Elizabeth had asked for advice on her marriage, saying that she was between Scylla and Charybdis; 'If I do not marry him I do not know whether he will remain friendly with me; and if I do, I shall not be able to govern the country with the freedom and security I have hitherto en-joyed.' The Archbishop, knowing Elizabeth's inflammable moods where marriage was concerned, left the decision entirely in her hands, but Cecil, more forthright, advised her to accept Alençon if she wished, and if not, to put an end to the affair. He had not given the answer the Queen wished to hear. 'That', she retorted, 'is not the opinion of the rest of the Council, but that I should keep him in correspondence.' Throughout her reign she had profited from a policy of keeping her suitors 'in correspondence', and now she intended to do the same with her dear Frog Prince. 'For God's sake, Madame, lose no more time,' Simier wrote beseechingly, in April, but envoys and ambassadors had been begging Elizabeth for more than twenty years to lose no more time in taking a husband.

When, later that year, the civil warfare in France was brought to a halt, Henry III turned his thoughts again to forming an alliance with England by marrying his brother to the Queen. While he was fighting the Huguenots he could not have encouraged Alençon to become the husband of Elizabeth and master of a Protestant kingdom, but with the French at peace once more he welcomed the opportunity of passing the turbulent Prince, with his costly enterprises in the Netherlands, over to Elizabeth. If Alençon were her husband, England would be bound to stand with France against Spain, whose acquisition of Portugal had cast a shadow across Europe. Elizabeth had no intention of becoming irrevocably bound to any person or any course of action, but she had every reason for wishing to cultivate the friendship of the French. Preparations were made for the coming of an immense French embassy, which, with the envoys' trains, would consist of some five hundred people, and shortly before they arrived, in April 1581, Elizabeth paid a symbolic compliment to the Valois when she asked the French agent Marchaumont to perform the act of knighting Francis Drake, on board his little ship *The Golden Hind*, at Deptford. It was on this occasion that Elizabeth's garter slipped down, and was claimed for Alençon. The Queen coyly demurred, saying that she needed it to hold her stocking up, and she readjusted it on her leg in full view of the envoy. But afterwards it was sent as a love-token to her suitor, and he gave her endless thanks for the *belle jartière*, vowing that it brought him luck.

Elizabeth enjoyed any performance that focused attention

on her beauty and desirability, and she was in her element in the spring of 1581, when the French mission arrived in England to settle the marriage terms. A fantastical programme of merrymaking had been arranged for them, with the most sumptuous spectacles and diversions the English court could offer. A banqueting hall had been specially built, on the south-west side of Whitehall Palace; the huge edifice, gorgeously painted and decorated, was hung with greenery, the ceiling was painted with stars and sunbeams and the walls draped with cloth of gold and silver. The English nobility and Members of Parliament were charged to remain in London, and as the time for the visitors' arrival approached, tensions began to mount. People had not forgotten that the massacre of St Bartholomew's Eve had begun with a great gathering for a state occasion. Mendoza reported that the nobles were summoning all their kinsmen and followers together, partly for show, partly for protection, and that Leicester was endeavouring to collect the largest band of all. The Queen issued a special proclamation ordering her subjects to show great honour to the foreign visitors, and prohibiting any display of violence towards them on pain of death. Londoners who had hated Philip of Spain's Spaniards resented the impending arrival of hundreds of Frenchmen, and the prevailing mood was one of sullen mistrust. But the visit went ahead in magnificent style; two hundred guns pounded out a salute as the envoys' barges came gliding up the Thames, and soon the round of extravagant festivities was in progress.

On St George's Day, 23 April, a banquet was held in the new hall, and for the occasion Elizabeth was bedecked as gorgeously as the surroundings, in a golden dress studded with glittering jewels. The canvas outer walls of the hall were painted to represent stonework, and the Queen's elderly face was painted to represent beauty. Some of the highest members of the French nobility, with hundreds of their servants, had come to the English court for a mighty masquerade – a great expenditure of time and money for a marriage that would never take place. Leicester, who, with his fondness for the arts, would have been familiar with the English poets of the previous generation, might have echoed Wyatt's bitter words:

Who list to hunt, I put him out of doubt,
As well as I may spend his time in vain.

Alençon, like many suitors before him, was spending his time
in vain, pursuing the Queen of England.

A broad hint to that effect was given in a 'Triumph' that was
enacted for the visitors on 15 May, in the tilt-yard. In this
chivalrous spectacle Desire and his foster children, one of
whom was young Philip Sidney, endeavoured to storm the
Fortress of Perfect Beauty, using 'pretty scaling-ladders' and
'flowers and such fancies'. They addressed the Queen, pleading
with her to render up her beauty to the forces of desire, but at
last they were driven back by Virtue, leaving the maiden
fortress intact. The challengers were rebuked by an angel, who
proclaimed: 'If in besieging the Sun you understand what you
had undertaken, you would destroy a common blessing for a
private profit.' The symbolic reference to Alençon's wooing
was unmistakable.

The envoys found their mission almost impossible. Their
mouths were stopped with sweetmeats; they tried to talk
business and were given entertainments. Elizabeth was anxious
for an alliance with France, but she would not be tied to a
marriage pledge – she would only discuss that with Alençon
himself, she told them. A treaty was drafted for the marriage,
but Elizabeth was adamant that it should have no force as yet,
and that it was merely being drawn up for future use. Considering the 'growing greatness of Spain' it seemed necessary that
'some straiter league should be made between the two crowns
whatsoever became of the marriage', but the nature of that
league could not be agreed on while the envoys were insisting
that the basis for any alliance must be marriage. Henry III knew
that no paper treaty would bind the Queen of England; he
wanted her held fast in the arms of a Valois. Walsingham
stated Elizabeth's attitude succinctly in a letter he wrote from
France in August: 'The principal cause why I was sent over',
he reminded her, 'was to procure a straiter degree of amity
between the King and you without marriage, and yet to carry
myself in the procuring thereof, as might not altogether break
off the matter of the marriage.' It had been a difficult undertak-

ing, he added, 'considering the determination they had put on
here not to yield to a league without marriage, so long as there
was hope of marriage.'

The 'hope of marriage' which Elizabeth had so successfully
exploited throughout her reign was still very strong in Alençon's breast, even though the Queen was approaching her forty-
eighth birthday. The Prince's love-letters shamelessly ignored
reality, and in their eroticism they added a new dimension to
the fiction of Elizabeth's personal desirability. 'Kissing and
rekissing all that Your beautiful Majesty can think of', Francis
the Constant, 'he who burns with desire', waited for 'the sweet
consummation that I desire more than my life'. It must have
given this elderly maiden who so craved admiration a
delicious *frisson* to read that one of the greatest princes in
Christendom was almost beside himself with desire to be her
husband, 'in bed between the sheets in your beautiful arms',
after which happy event he had no doubt that she would soon
be nursing an infant Prince of Wales, 'made and forged by the
little Frenchman who is and will be eternally your humble and
very loving slave'. Alençon apologized charmingly for the
liberty of his style, but the frankness with which he expressed
his passion was excitingly novel for the Queen. A Valois prince
could be permitted freedoms which no lesser person might
assay. The fact that Elizabeth no longer had any intention of
marrying her Frog and sharing her great bed with him did not
detract from her pleasure in contemplating the prospect.

A gift of £30,000 helped to keep Alençon's desires at fever
pitch during the summer of 1581, and in October, after raising
the siege of Cambrai, he returned to England to pursue his
quarry in person once more. Catherine de' Medici had again
been talking of a Spanish bride for him, which called for the
appearance of great interest in her suitor from Elizabeth.
Alençon scarcely knew what to expect as he made the stormy
crossing to England. He needed money for his Netherlands
venture; whether or not he would obtain it by marrying the
Queen of England remained to be seen.

'The principal object of his visit is to ask for money,'
Mendoza stated baldly, but Elizabeth's intense pleasure in being
courted ensured an atmosphere of romance for the Prince's

visit. Alençon left his first interview with the Queen with his spirits high and his hopes rekindled. He was Elizabeth's ardent young lover again, sighing out the raptures which her aged face and figure inspired in him, whispering of the joys he longed to know in her withered arms, eager to hear her call him her Frog and tease him about the smallness of his fingers in her most archly coquettish manner. Scandal found fresh fuel in reports that the Queen had taken to visiting Alençon in his bedchamber, carrying little cups of soup to him while he was still in bed – 'There goes much babbling' ran a contemporary letter, 'and the Queen doth not attend to other matters, but only to be together with the Duke in one chamber from morning to noon, and afterwards till two or three hours after sunset. I cannot tell what a devil they do.' What a devil the Queen and her last suitor might or might not have done together, it certainly did not include sexual intercourse. Elizabeth's purpose was, as it had ever been, to provoke desire, not to satisfy it.

Rumours were rife; Elizabeth was treating Alençon with every sign of affection, and the courtship seemed to be prospering, but something was wrong. Leicester should have been glowering with jealous anger; instead, he was as courteous and affable as could be, and he announced in public that the only way for Elizabeth to 'secure the tranquillity of England' was for her to marry Alençon. Such complaisance could only mean that he was confident the Queen would do nothing of the sort. Walsingham, who had opposed the match so long and so vehemently, seemed equally well disposed towards Alençon. Elizabeth was enjoying a political pretence as she dallied with her French Prince, and they knew it; however, the remarkable scene which took place on 22 November was enough to shake their equanimity.

On 21 November Alençon and his company 'displayed, not discontent alone, but entire disillusionment as to the marriage taking place'. Their grim faces and resentful murmurs would not foster a spirit of amity between France and England; Elizabeth promptly took action to show her suitor how much in earnest she was. On the following day at eleven o'clock in the morning, she was strolling in a gallery of the palace with Alençon, while Leicester and Walsingham stood near. The

French ambassador approached, and told her that his master Henry III had ordered him to 'hear from the Queen's own lips her intentions with regard to marrying his brother'. Elizabeth did not hesitate. Regally, decisively, she spoke the words which one suitor after another had waited to hear, throughout the twenty-three years of her reign. 'You may write this to the King,' she told the ambassador clearly, 'the Duke of Alençon shall be my husband.' She turned to the astonished Alençon, kissed him on the mouth, and drew a ring from her finger which she gave to him, 'as a pledge'. Incredulous and delighted, he gave her a ring of his own in return, and then the Queen summoned her ladies and gentlemen from the presence chamber to the gallery, 'repeating to them, in a loud voice, what she had previously said'. The gloom of the day before had turned to rapture. Alençon and his followers were 'extremely overjoyed', and a messenger was immediately dispatched to carry the news to Henry III. Leicester and Walsingham must have exchanged anxious glances as the little French Prince proudly escorted his aged betrothed past the congratulating courtiers.

The Queen of England had capitulated at last. She had accepted the proposals of a suitor young enough to be her son; it must have been a strange, unreal sensation for her to hear herself agreeing, at last, to marry. But unreality was the keynote of the event. The Spanish ambassador, for one, sensed that Elizabeth's startling announcement was not what it seemed. 'People in London consider the marriage as good as accomplished, and the French are of the same opinion,' he reported, but in his view 'the display she has made is only artful and conditional'. The art lay in her ability to make Alençon believe that she was in earnest; the condition was whether or not her people would accept her decision. Mendoza thought that the scene in the gallery had been staged in the presence of Leicester and Walsingham as 'an artifice to draw Alençon on, and make him believe that the men who were most opposed to it are now openly in its favour'. She had put on a convincing show for the French, so that it appeared that she was determined to marry, but all the time she was comfortably certain that Parliament and public opinion would relieve her of the necessity of honouring her promise by showing implacable resistance to the marriage. As Mendoza put it: 'By personally pledging herself in this way, she binds him to her.' He explained: 'She rather prefers to let it appear that the failure of the negotiations is owing to the country and not to herself, as it is important for her to keep him attached to her, in order to counterbalance his brother, and prevent anything being arranged to her prejudice.' Strange as it might have seemed for Elizabeth to make a public announcement that she would marry, it was a characteristically clever move.

Instead of giving one of her ringing reprimands to any who dared to question her decision, she received such interference with a suspicious degree of equanimity. When one of her long-established favourites, Sir Christopher Hatton, burst into tears and sobbed that she might be deposed if she insisted on marrying against the will of the people, on whose affection the security of her throne depended, Elizabeth was not at all angered by his temerity, but answered him very tenderly. Leicester, who, despite his confidence that Elizabeth did not mean to marry, had been unnerved by the certainty of the French that the marriage would take place, went even further in his plain speaking. He asked Elizabeth point-blank whether she were 'a maid or a woman'. The effrontery of the question was appalling. To ask the unmarried Queen of England whether she was a virgin or not was insolence beyond belief – though the fact that Leicester should have been in doubt on the subject served to indicate that he himself had never physically possessed the woman he had courted for so long. Elizabeth had always set limits to how far Leicester might carry his intimacy with her, in every way, yet on this occasion no infuriated 'God's death, my Lord!' greeted his presumption. Quite tranquilly the Queen answered that she was still a maiden; possibly she was flattered to have been asked such a question at her age. Leicester then told her roundly 'that she had not acted wisely in carrying the matter so far and so ostentatiously', which Elizabeth seemed to agree with. Meekly she said that she would send Alençon a message to inform him that if she married him she was sure she would not survive for long. 'She would be very glad if he would allow her to defer the matter' was the

gist of the message, 'and she would be very much more attached
to him as a friend even than if he were her husband'.

It was put about that Elizabeth had spent the night of the 22
November in torments of indecision, while her waiting-women,
in floods of tears, begged her not to embark on the hazardous
undertaking of marriage and child-birth. But there was little
evidence to suggest that she still had any serious thoughts of
doing so. The real conflict that followed the scene in the gallery
was over the question of Alençon's departure. Elizabeth and
her ministers made it increasingly plain that they wanted him
to go, but having come so near to winning the great prize that
he had pursued for so long the Prince was determined to stay
on at court and secure his quarry or be compensated for his
loss. He had nothing to lose by remaining there, kept and fêted
at her expense, and he had high hopes of winning the Queen,
or, should the prize be denied him, receiving recompense. The
situation soon became embarrassing. Elizabeth's gallant guest
and his entourage remained resolutely where they were, while
Alençon insisted jocularly that the Queen had promised to
marry him, or created dramatic scenes in which he ranted that
he would kill himself, or carry her off by force. The pretence of
affection became very thin, though it was not abandoned;
Elizabeth used 'a hundred thousand false words and oaths' to
reassure her little Frog of her love for him, while he pouted
that he was hurt to find her so eager for his departure. When,
at long last, the moment of his leaving arrived, Elizabeth put on
a moving display of grief, although the Spanish ambassador
learned from his spies that in the privacy of her own chamber
she 'danced for very joy at getting rid of him'. When Elizabeth
Tudor could long for a suitor, a great prince who professed to
adore her, to leave her side, the end of an era had arrived.

Persuading Alençon to go away was an expensive business.
Elizabeth joined in the laughter when it was said that 'Alençon
was a fine gallant to sell his lady for money', and at first she
swore that she would neither marry him nor pay him, but on
15 December she agreed that he should be lent £60,000, to be
paid in two halves and repaid within six months. It was not
until 7 February that he finally embarked, at Sandwich.

Eager as Elizabeth had been for her suitor's departure, when he had gone she seemed to be stricken with a sense of what she had lost. She cried that she would give a million to have her Frog swimming in the Thames again, instead of in the stagnant waters of the Netherlands, and there were moments when she was painfully melancholy. It was not play-acting this time. Whatever his motives, Alençon had ardently wanted to marry her; he had flooded her with expressions of devotion and promises of a happy, fecund future. Now that he had gone the dream was over, and she knew that she could never have a husband and children, even if she had wanted to. The deep resistance to marriage which nothing had been able to overcome was in conflict with the fears of loneliness and yearnings for love which Elizabeth felt. She expressed her dissatisfied feelings in a revealing poem *On Monsieur's Departure* :

> I grieve, and dare not show my discontent;
> I love, and yet am forced to seem to hate;
> I dote, yet dare not say I ever meant;
> I seem stark mute, yet inwardly do prate.
> I am and am not – freeze and yet I burn,
> Since from myself my other self I turn.
> My care is like my shadow in the Sun –
> Follows me flying, flies when I pursue it . . .

In those lines she showed something of the conflict of her heart and mind, the confusion of her desires; she was a woman desperate to be loved, yet ever flying from the realities of commitment, unable to reconcile her differing needs. Doting, yet divided in her self, Elizabeth would remain a virgin all her life.

Though the last fierce flare of the emotion that Alençon had lit up in Elizabeth's heart in 1579 had died away, the ashes of the courtship continued to smoulder faintly. The Queen and the Prince continued to exchange ardent letters, and the marriage was talked of as a matter of expediency long after it had become impossible. Alençon's quest for glory in the Netherlands proved as unsuccessful as his wooing of Elizabeth. He played tennis in Antwerp while his soldiers grew mutinous; finally he had to flee the country, his ventures a failure. In the summer of 1584 he ended his ignominious career in death – he died of fever on 10 June. Elizabeth grieved for him. She went into mourning, and she wrote to Catherine de' Medici: 'Your sorrow cannot exceed mine, although you were his mother. You have another son, but I can find no other consolation than death, which I hope will soon enable me to rejoin him. If you could see a picture of my heart, you would see a body without a soul; but I will not trouble you with my grief, as you have enough of your own.' She was sincerely moved by Alençon's death. She had come near to marrying him, and for a time she had been happy in his company. She had received from him the passionate homage which she had always longed to win from a great prince; now, with his death, her last courtship was irrevocably ended, and she would never again receive sweet letters from her Frog. The last and most loving of the political suitors to the Queen was dead, and now there would be no more.

9

MISTRESS OF ENGLAND

'Some call her Pandora; some Gloriana; some Cynthia; some Belphoebe; some Astraea: all by several names to express several loves. Yet all those names make but one celestial body, as all those loves meet to create but one soul,' wrote the playwright Thomas Dekker. 'I am of her own country, and we adore her by the name of Eliza.' The almost mythical maiden who was the subject of those lines was then an old, old woman, whose sallow, lined skin was sometimes painted half an inch thick, right down to her sagging bosom, and whose thin cheeks had sunk where her teeth were missing. The physical realities of Elizabeth's appearance were irrelevant to the cult that had grown up around her. At an age when most noble-women were grandmothers or great-grandmothers several times over, surrounded and supported by their children and their childrens' children, Queen Elizabeth was still a virgin, set apart from the majority of mortals by her eternal maidenhood. She had never known the satisfactions of the wife and mother; instead, she clung greedily to the pleasures of youthful adulation, many years after such homage had ceased to be in any way appropriate to her fading charms. In a society which had, during Elizabeth's lifetime, worshipped the Virgin Mary, and which was still steeped in the medieval traditions of courtly love, the image of a virgin queen under whose benevolent rule England prospered, defying even mighty Spain's Armada, was easily assimilated. The special powers and properties belonging to virginity were well known to the literate members of Elizabethan society, and as a chaste maiden their Queen commanded a reverence that could easily spill over into idolatry.

Since she was a woman who craved admiration and attention, a vain, insecure and lonely woman, she cultivated such extravagant adoration.

Leicester, who knew the Queen better than anyone, understood her need for ardent love. When the Alençon match was in the air, he had written to Walsingham to warn him not to destroy her illusions about the French Prince's desire for her. 'You know her disposition as well as I,' he had written urgently. 'I would have you, as much as you may, avoid Her Majesty's suspicion that you doubt Monsieur's love to her, or that you had devotion enough in you to further her marriage; though I promise I think she has little enough herself to it. Yet what she would have others think and do, you have cause to know.' The fact that the Queen had no wish for marriage and sexual love did not lessen her desire that others should pine for her. It had been the same with all her suitors – she had revelled in their protestations of passion, while remaining elusive and unobtainable, only pretending to yield when there seemed to be a danger of their withdrawing from the pursuit. In her old age, when marriage had ceased even to be a remote possibility, Elizabeth's consuming need to be courted and adored was greater than ever, and the men who became suitors to the Queen in the last two decades of her life contributed their fantastical flatteries, in speech and in writing, to the mythology that was growing up around England's Gloriana. She was wooed now not as a wife, but as a chaste mistress in the courtly love tradition – she represented the fair and virtuous lady of chivalric legend, whose smile alone was sufficient to bind a knight to her service forever, in the kind of hopeless love that found informal expression in the sixteenth century verse which ran:

> I did but see her passing by,
> And yet I love her till I die.

Successful suitors to Elizabeth could hope for more substantial rewards than occasional kindly glances, however. To win her favour was to acquire influence and income; in the bright sunlight of the Queen's good graces a man could step from the shadows of insignificance into the forefront of court life, and there make his fortune. Elizabeth had become a haggard and temperamental old woman, but the image of herself that was reflected back to her by her courtiers and subjects was that of a radiant nymph, a paragon of beauty and virtue, and no one who had anything to gain from her favour would dare to shatter the magic glass.

By the 1580s, when Elizabeth's flare of feeling for Alençon had died away and her anger at Leicester's marriage had cooled, Leicester's position in her life was unassailable. The relationship which she had built up with him over the years had passed through passion to a deep and lasting tenderness that was closer to a normal loving partnership than anything she experienced in any of her other affairs. As long as Lady Leicester never showed her face at court Elizabeth could ignore her existence; she had indeed, had to become accustomed to the fact that most of her admirers were married men, and once her rage over his faithlessness in taking a wife had abated, her Robin was as high as ever in her favour. Yet his attentions alone had for years been insufficient to satisfy Elizabeth's hunger for male admiration. Even while he was by her side, eager to marry her, and foreign princes were making flattering proposals from abroad, she had delightedly flirted with a series of handsome young men. Her intimates had been given pet names; she called Leicester her 'Eyes', and charming Sir Christopher Hatton had become 'Lids', nicknames which they fondly represented in their letters by the symbols ÔÔ and △△. Hatton, who genuinely believed himself to be infatuated with the Queen, and remained unmarried for her sake, contributed a great many words and tears to the cult of her peerless beauty; in 1573, when she was only forty, and still busy with the first stage of her Alençon negotiations, Hatton had written passionately: 'I will wash away the faults of these letters with the drops from your poor Lids, and so enclose them. Would God I were with you but for one hour. My wits are overwrought with thoughts. I find myself amazed. Bear with me, my most dear sweet Lady. Passion overcometh me. I can write no more. Love me; for I love you,' and he had a great deal more to say in the same throbbing vein. Such outpourings of desperate love were highly acceptable to Elizabeth, as were the exquisite jewels and

presents which Hatton gave her; through the 1570s, while her
French marriages were under discussion, his star shone
brightly. It was he who broke down in tears after the scene in
the gallery when she promised, albeit falsely, to marry Alençon. But although his career advanced steadily – he was to
become Lord Chancellor in 1587 – Elizabeth's fancy for Hatton
fluctuated, and his constant uncertainty as to her feelings
towards him kept him in a state of anguished worship. 'I should
sin, most gracious sovereign, against a Holy Ghost, most dam-
nably, if towards Your Highness I should be found unthankful,'
he grovelled in the autumn of 1580, but his almost religious
devotion to the Queen could not save him from being obscured
by the shining meteor Sir Walter Raleigh, who rose at the
beginning of the 1580s, when Elizabeth's dealings with Alençon
were almost at an end and her sterile old age was upon her.

It was remarked that the good-looking West Country gentleman Raleigh had 'gotten the Queen's ear in a trice' after he
strode into court life. He was just the kind of man who had
always fascinated her, a virile, hardy adventurer who was also
artistic and intellectual in his tastes, and he shared Elizabeth's
love of magnificently showy clothes, in which he far out-
sparkled such former favourites as Hatton. Elizabeth was fascinated by him. A friend of Spenser and Marlowe, he too was a
poet, and he wooed the Queen with verses celebrating her
loveliness, depicting her as the Moon-Goddess, and delicately
dismissing the question of her age in such lines as :

> Time wears her not, she doth his chariot guide,
> Mortality below her orb is placed.
> By her the virtue of the stars down slide,
> In her is virtue's perfect image cast.

In his poetry she was half-divine, but she was a woman too, one
whose feminine beauties had set his pulses racing with desire :

> Those eyes which set my fancy on a fire,
> Those crispéd hairs, which hold my heart in chains,
> Those dainty hands, which conquered my desire,
> That wit, which of my thoughts doth hold the reins.

His words reassured her that it was not her sovereignty alone
that gave her power, but her own beauties of body and mind :

O eyes that pierce our hearts without remorse,
O hairs of right that wear a royal crown,
O hands that conquer more than Caesar's force,
O wit that turns huge kingdoms upside down.

Raleigh was a worthy admirer, and the Queen flirted delight-edly with him. In an obvious play on his christian name she nicknamed him 'Water', which prompted poor jealous Hatton to send her a little gold bucket, as a pointed gesture. As far as Elizabeth was concerned, the more admirers she had, looking languishingly at her and glowering at each other, the merrier; she had learned long ago, in the days of her serious courtships, that the presence of a rival did much to heighten a suitor's desire for her. She exulted in the knowledge that, despite her advancing age and dwindling charms, she could still rouse jealousy in her gallants; the total sterility of these post-menopausal love-dealings did nothing to lessen their intensity. Now that her failure to marry had been transformed from a fault into a virtue, Elizabeth could indulge her craving for the amorous pursuit without the fear of being captured, for all could see the *noli me tangere* that was 'graven in diamonds, in letters plain' about her inviolable beauties.

Raleigh became sickened with the sham by the time the Queen had done with him. In 1592, when the Queen was nearly sixty and he was in his late thirties, he committed the offence of loving and marrying one of her Maids-of-Honour. The punishment that had nearly fallen on Leicester in the same situation was meted out to Raleigh – he and his wife were sent to the Tower for having married without royal leave. The disgraced favourite poured out a highly coloured version of his feelings, in hopes that the letter would come to the Queen's eyes; hearing that she was going away on a royal progress through the realm, he wrote:

My heart was never broken until this day, that the Queen goes away so far off, whom I have followed so many years with so great love and desire, in so many journeys, and am now left behind her in a dark prison all alone. While she was yet near at hand, that I might hear of her once in two or three days, my sorrows were the less, but even now my heart is cast into the depth of all misery. I that was wont to behold her riding like Alexander, hunting like Diana, walking like Venus, the gentle wind blowing her fair hair about her pure cheeks like a nymph, sometime sitting in the shade like a goddess, sometime singing like an angel, sometime playing like Orpheus; behold! the sorrow of this world, once amiss hath bereaved me of all.

But he had lost his hold over Elizabeth's changeable fancy. He wrote in a very different style in his poem *The Lie*, expressing a fallen courtier's resentment and defiance:

> Tell potentates they live
> Acting on others' action
> Not loved unless they give,
> Not strong but by affection.
> If potentates reply,
> Give potentates the lie.

A contemporary wrote that Raleigh was one whom Fortune picked out to use as a tennis-ball, 'for she tossed him up of nothing, and to and fro to greatness, and from thence down'. Court favourites were vulnerable beings.

Only Leicester weathered all storms to retain his supreme place in Elizabeth's heart. There was an essential reality about their relationship that set it apart from all her other courtships and flirtations. Leicester was always uneasy at the emergence of a rival for the Queen's favour, just as he had feared and schemed through each of her political courtships, but she never lost her need for him, and no quarrel or jealousy could destroy the tender intimacy which had grown up between them over the years. Real affection, not merely an elaborate pretence of stylized adoration, shone through the letters that passed between them. 'Rob', Elizabeth wrote fondly in July 1586, when he was serving abroad as Governor of the Netherlands, 'I am afraid you will suppose by my wandering writings that a midsummer moon hath taken large possession of my brains this month, but you must needs take things as they come in my head, though order be left behind me.' She concluded lovingly: 'Now will I end, that do imagine I talk still with you, and therefore loathly say farewell ÖÖ ... With my million and legion of thanks, for all your pains and cares. As you know, ever the same, E.R.' Leicester had then little time left in which to take 'pains and cares' in serving his Queen. The fateful year 1588 saw the end of the long love-affair between Elizabeth and the most persistent of all her suitors. Within weeks of the glorious defeat of the Armada launched against her by another man who had once been a suitor to the Queen, her beloved Robin had left her side for ever. This time she could not call him back.

He had been ill, and he had gone to take the waters at Buxton; from Rycote, on 29 August, he wrote to the Queen whom he had for so many years hoped to make his wife. The vigorous, ambitious young Robert Dudley who had first taken up the pursuit when Elizabeth was a slender, graceful girl, was stout and white-bearded now, but his thoughts and his handwriting were still clear as he addressed her for the last time :

I most humbly beseech Your Majesty to pardon your old servant to be thus bold in sending to know how my gracious Lady doth, and what ease of her late pain she finds, being the chiefest thing in this world I do pray for, for her to have good health and long life. For my poor case, I continue still your medicine, and find it amends much better than any other thing that hath been given me. Thus hoping to find perfect cure at the bath, with the continuance of my wonted prayer for Your Majesty's most happy preservation, I humbly kiss your feet. From your old lodging at Rycote, this Thursday morning, ready to take on my journey, by Your Majesty's most faithful and obedient servant, R. Leicester.

He died six days later. Leicester's letter from Rycote, simple as it was, was more precious to Elizabeth than all the florid effusions of her other wooers; she kept it in a casket by her bed for the rest of her life. After her own death, in 1603, it was discovered. Pathetically, she had written on it : 'His last letter.'

Her grief at Leicester's death was intense. She shut herself away from the world in her despair, while England rang with rejoicings at the defeat of the Armada, and she did not come out until Burleigh finally had the door of the chamber forced open. Elizabeth had always clung tenaciously to her old and trusted friends, and the loss of her Robin, the dearest of them all, left her desolate. Time and again she had flirted with the idea of marrying him, pretending, to ambassadors and to herself, that she only refrained from doing so because he was her subject and her inferior; perhaps in the first dark distress of his death she wished with all her heart that she had married him, and that she might now have had a son of his, to be her comfort and her successor. By rejecting all her suitors she had protected herself from the horrors that her childhood had taught her to expect from marriage, but she had made herself vulnerable to loneliness. Lacking husband, child or lover in the fullest sense of the word, she could only grasp at artificial substitutes for those natural sources of emotional satisfaction. Leicester had, within the limitations that her personality imposed, fulfilled the role of a husband for Elizabeth; in her relationship with his stepson, Robert Devereux, Earl of Essex, she found a curious outlet for a measure of her dormant maternal feelings.

Essex had made his début at court in 1587, as Leicester's protégé; if Leicester had hoped to see the boy outshine bright Raleigh he was well-satisfied. Essex was in his twentieth year, but he had already been to the wars, fighting valiantly at Zutphen, where Sir Philip Sidney was killed, and besides strength and courage he possessed the magnetic qualities of beauty, wit and charm. With his height, his thick curling hair and his red lips he drew interested glances from all the women of the court, and Elizabeth's keen eyes were on him at once. Soon he was riding with her, sitting by her; soon he was privileged to be the subject of the scandalous whispers that had always surrounded the Virgin Queen. 'At night', wrote one of Essex's servants, 'my Lord is at cards, or one game and another with her, that he cometh not to his own lodging till birds sing in the morning.' Strolling back through the quiet galleries of the palace as the dawn broke, Essex must have been whistling like the birds, in the exhilaration of youth and hope and confidence, knowing that the elderly woman whom he had just left had power over all England, and that he was gaining power over her.

Significantly, he was given the post of Master of the Horse when Leicester vacated it; it seemed that young Essex was destined to wear the mantle of his stepfather. He was anxious to do so. He showed himself flatteringly belligerent towards his rivals for the Queen's affection; during the winter that followed the defeat of the Armada and Leicester's death, Essex twice hazarded his life in jealous quarrels with other royal favourites. In the tilt-yard one day, handsome Sir Charles Blount acquitted himself superbly, and Elizabeth, who loved to preside at the jousts, as though the contenders were doing battle for her smiles, graciously sent the young man the reward of a golden queen from her set of chessmen. Elated, Blount obeyed the dictates of courtly tradition by tying the favour ostentatiously to his arm; when Essex spied this proof of the Queen's interest he was furious. 'Now I perceive every fool must have a favour,' he sneered, at which, not surprisingly, Blount challenged him to a duel. Instead of emerging as a contemptuous victor, Essex found himself wounded in the thigh, and, still more galling, Elizabeth was not sorry. 'By God's death', she said sharply, 'it was fit that some one or other should take him down and teach him better manners, otherwise there will be no rule with him.' The lesson in manners was not sufficient, however, for within a month Essex had challenged Raleigh to fight over some minor dispute. Dangerous as such aggression could be amongst her courtiers, Elizabeth was no doubt secretly gratified that the handsomest young men at court should be moved to fight over her. She had yet to discover the truth of her words, that there would never be any ruling Essex.

Like a wayward but lovable child he was forgiven again and again when his reckless pride and troublesome personality led him to flout authority. He was greedy for power just as Elizabeth was greedy for admiration; in their strange relationship each sought to feed on the other, and each, ultimately, was left hungry. Fascinated as she was by him, Elizabeth gave way to him and put up with his escapades from the outset. When, in defiance of her express refusal of permission, he slipped away to join Drake's expedition in 1589, she summoned him back with royal anger. 'Our great favours bestowed on you without deserts, hath drawn you thus to neglect and forget your duty,' she trounced him, but once he was back by her side her anger could not last. In 1591, when he begged for hours to be permitted to command the force bound for France, Elizabeth finally gave him his way. She forgave him when, against all her known wishes, he bestowed knighthoods upon his followers. And Essex, when kept in good humour, rewarded her with exquisitely wrought proofs of his love. From France he wrote:

The two windows of your Privy Chamber shall be the poles of my sphere, where, as long as Your Majesty shall please to have me, I am fixed and unmoveable. When Your Majesty thinks that heaven too good for me, I will not fall like a star, but be consumed like a vapour by the sun that drew me up to such a height. While Your Majesty gives me leave to say I love you, my fortune is as my affection, unmatchable. If ever you deny me that liberty, you may end my life, but never shake my constancy, for were the sweetness of your nature turned into the greatest bitterness that could be, it is not in your power, as great a Queen as you are, to make me love you less.

There was no doubt that Essex was a man of remarkable talents, for all his faults. Elizabeth was not merely attracted by his looks and his challenging charm, she also recognized in him talents that should be fostered. The great statesmen of the older generation were dying off; with maturity, Essex might climb high to become a brilliant servant of the realm. But, prudent in all matters of state, Elizabeth steadfastly resisted his attempts at political manoeuvring, blocking one after another of his attempts to have his own candidates appointed to public offices. There was no way in which she could stem the flood tide of Essex's ambition, however. Reckless, self-confident, heedless of warnings, Essex in many ways resembled the first man to whom Elizabeth had ever been attracted, her first real suitor, Thomas Seymour. By coincidence, he, like Seymour, was to hold the post of Master of the Ordnance. He, like Seymour, could never be content with a measure of success, a portion of power, but was driven always to strive for more, until, in striving, he would lose everything he had. Essex, like Seymour, would follow blindly the path of pride and ambition, until it ended at the block.

Essex's wilfulness made his moments of adoring compliance all the sweeter for Elizabeth; again and again she forgave him for his offences, and brought him back to her side. But the dangerous aspects of his nature were not to be quelled. When the appointment of a new Lord Deputy for Ireland was being discussed, in the summer of 1598, Essex pressed to have a friend of the Cecil faction appointed. The reason for his nomination was obvious – the man was known to be his enemy, and he was anxious to have him removed to a distant and dangerous post. Smiling, the Queen refused the suggestion, but instead of yielding Essex became angry. He argued vehemently, until Elizabeth was thoroughly annoyed with him. In the petulant gesture of a thwarted child, Essex turned his back on his sovereign; the Queen, furious at the insult, boxed his ears resoundingly, and told him to get out. At that Essex lost control entirely; in an instant his hand was on his sword.

Such an action constituted the most blatant transgression of every rule and principle of a subject's conduct towards his sovereign. Essex was shouting that he would not endure such treatment from anyone, would not have suffered it even at Henry VIII's hands; such violent insolence could only be answered by an extreme form of punishment. As the news of the young Earl's incredible temerity spread, his enemies must have rejoiced, sure that this display must damn him at last in the eyes of the Queen. But Elizabeth's righteous wrath as a sovereign was, again, less potent than her intense feelings for Essex. A period of disgraced retirement to the country followed; soon Elizabeth wanted him back. By the autumn he had returned to court and the Queen's favour, and by the following spring, 1599, he was riding out of London at the head of a mighty army as Elizabeth's commander in Ireland, bound for fresh glories.

He was too volatile and irresponsible even to make a success of his military career. As his failures in Ireland mounted, he became increasingly fearful for his position in Elizabeth's heart. He determined, in flagrant disobedience of his instructions, to return unexpectedly to court, where he could woo the Queen again with his fair looks and persuasive words, and rekindle the heat of her feelings for him. On 24 September he left for England; on the morning of 28 September he reached Nonsuch Palace. Once there, he did not pause. Without stopping even to change his rumpled, sweat-stained clothes or take off his muddied boots he strode past the startled attendants to burst unceremoniously into Elizabeth's bedchamber. There he fell to his knees to kiss her hand; he raised his eyes; he was looking at an old woman not yet attired for the day, bare alike of the trappings of regality and of femininity. The sixty-six-year-old woman at whose feet he knelt had not yet put on her 'crisped hairs', the great wig of red-golden curls, nor her alabaster complexion, nor the massive ruff that should stand out like a fine halo about her face, nor the sparkling jewels that should lend their radiance to her as she moved. She sat there, startled, a plain old woman.

The Queen was calm, but this time Essex had gone too far. His disobedience in returning without permission was an offence not merely against herself but against the security of her realm. Not all his charm could disguise the infamy of his actions in Ireland, and in a profoundly significant phrase, Elizabeth swore that if it had been her own son who had transgressed so in his conduct, she would have committed him to the highest tower in England. Yet still she was not severe. He was reprieved from state trial, and judged instead by a special commission, after which he was confined in relative comfort and suspended from his offices. Elizabeth still believed that he might be reformed through chastisement. The smell of treason that lingered about his handsome form was still faint enough to be covered by more pleasing scents.

Through the spring and summer of 1600 Essex remained in confinement. Elizabeth had been merciful to him, and she missed him, but his offences were too great for him to be allowed to return to court. Essex sought to recapture her favour with mounting anxiety as the year drew on. He put his talent for writing sweet, glib letters to good use: 'Haste, paper, to that happy presence whence only unhappy I am banished,' he wrote in September, 'kiss that fair correcting hand which lays now plasters to my lighter hurts, but to my greater wound applieth nothing. Say thou comest from shaming, languishing, despairing SX.' The boyish impetuousness of the fluent phrases and the punning signature concealed agonies of worry. The lease of his principal source of income, the duties on sweet wines, was about to run out; if the Queen chose not to renew it he would be in heavy financial difficulties. This time Elizabeth was determined to have the ruling of him. She chose not to renew it. Deprived of his income, debarred from her presence, Essex turned in the fury of his rash pride to a desperate alternative – open rebellion.

Gloriana's last knight abandoned her service, to use his sword against her. All his vows of love had been empty words. He turned his eyes away from the fading woman who had been seated so long upon the throne of England towards the man who was to succeed her there, James vi of Scotland, Mary Stuart's son. Once more Elizabeth's acute perception was to be proved. For years she had resisted naming her successor, insisting that to do so would be to hold her winding-sheet up before her eyes, since her heir, once known, would become the focus of discontent in her realm. She knew the truth of what she said, since in her sister's reign she had held that dangerous post, and she knew what plottings there had been then; she refused to place another in that position. Now her words were to be proved valid. Flaming with dissatisfied ambition and pride, her own beloved Essex plotted with his band of reckless, improvident friends. Elizabeth was one of those potentates who were, as Raleigh had written so bitterly: 'Not loved unless they give.' Essex and his party withdrew their love and their allegiance from the Queen who did not give enough. No chivalrous passion for Gloriana would move Essex if he saw a higher profit in another cause.

His glittering charm had won him popularity such as Leicester had never enjoyed, amongst his contemporaries and the common people, but London did not rise in his support. The rebellion failed, just as, years before, Wyatt's rebellion to put Elizabeth on the throne had failed. Once again, Elizabeth had seen love end in the darkness of betrayal and violence; once again a man for whom she had held romantic feelings went to the block. The headless body of Essex, who died by her command, was to lie beneath the flagstones of the chapel in the Tower, near to the headless body of her own mother, Anne Boleyn, who had died by her father's command. Essex's treason had at last left her no alternative but to send him to execution, to die as her first love, Thomas Seymour, had died. Love and guilt; love and fear; love and death; the conclusion was as inevitable as it had been when she was a girl of fifteen.

But now she was an old woman of sixty-eight, and there could be no more love-affairs. No more suitors would court the Queen of England with words of love, and now her own subjects were covertly turning their eyes from her, and looking northwards to James of Scotland. Burghley's son Robert Cecil, Elizabeth's Principal Secretary as his father had been, was communicating with James in coded letters, and sending him envoys selected for their discretion, so that the foundations of service to the next sovereign were being laid while the present sovereign yet lived. Potentates, Raleigh had warned, were 'not strong but by affection'; her courtiers' affections were beginning to slide away from Elizabeth to her successor, as she had always known they would. Essex had rebelled to put James on the throne, just as Wyatt, years before, had rebelled to put Elizabeth on the throne. Memories must have glowed and flickered through the Queen's mind in the last months before she died.

Reassurance was what she had always craved from her suitors. Her unstable childhood and troubled adolescence had left her with insatiable need for assurances that she was loved and wanted. No protestation of passion could be too fulsome for her; as long as men sought her, with words of love and desire, she could feel reassured, though she could never dare to put their promises to the test of marriage. She could never truly give love, but she needed to receive it, and the homage of her suitors provided her with a rich diet of the emotional sustenance she craved. As a child she had cried that she would never marry, and she had had little cause as an adult to change her mind, but with her antipathy to the realities of marriage and sexual union went an intense need for the elaborate pretence of love. She would always avoid capture, but she was excited and delighted by the rituals of the chase, whether her pursuer was an unknown foreign prince such as the Archduke Charles, or a well-loved companion such as Robert Dudley.

For years Elizabeth's subjects had expected her to marry. Parliament had urged and exhorted her to the limits of her patience, almost overstepping the bounds of their duty in their insistence that she must take a husband. For the sake of the realm, for the weal of the kingdom, they had pressed her to marry with all speed. In a different manner, though with equal conviction, the greatest of all her ministers, Cecil, had believed that the Queen should accept one of her suitors, preferably a Habsburg, for her consort; he had seen 'no continuance of her quietness' if she remained single. The need to keep loyal discontent at bay had played a part in Elizabeth's courtships; after the Parliament of 1566 she had shown a livelier interest than she felt in the wooing of the Archduke Charles. But as the years passed and England remained secure under its virgin sovereign, public attitudes began to alter. The coming of a foreign consort began to be regarded less as an insurance and more as a threat to England's independence, while Elizabeth's isolation on the throne awoke feelings of protective loyalty that involved a sense of national pride and resentment at the prospect of co-rule by a representative of a foreign power. Under the married Queen Mary England had been torn by discontent and rebellion; under the virgin Queen Elizabeth the realm had achieved unity and prosperity. Thus it was that when Elizabeth found herself giving serious thought to Alençon's proposals, the mood of her subjects had changed; instead of welcoming the match, with its promise of heirs of the Tudor line, they muttered ominously against it.

In giving sound advice to his son, William Cecil made one observation which might, in retrospect, have been offered to the Queen; he commented that marriage was 'like unto a stratagem of war, in which a man can err but once'. Had Elizabeth chosen a consort, and chosen wrongly, her error would have been final and devastating. Had she accepted a Catholic, she might have faced Protestant rebellion; had she wed a Protestant, such as Eric of Sweden, Catholic plots in favour of Mary Queen of Scots might have acquired overwhelming support. If she had chosen either a Habsburg or a Valois, she would have committed herself irrevocably to one side or the other, and she could not have preserved the fragile balance between the two great powers as she did, inclining freely now to one, now to the other, as her country's need dictated. In remaining uncommitted, as a woman and thus as a queen, in dallying with her suitors and at last rejecting them all, she avoided the error of choosing wrongly, and kept herself free to exploit the asset of her marriageable status in the glittering game of her great courtships. From her weakness emerged political strength.

The cult of Gloriana drew a shining veil over the ugly aspects of her old age. As the Faerie Queene of England she was not a wrinkled old woman who had an unsuitable craving for the flattery and caressing attentions of handsome, vigorous young men, but an eternally radiant embodiment of beauty and virtue to whom the homage of gallant knights was due by right, and for whom no praise could ever be adequate. She was living proof of the magical properties of virginity, the pure maiden of all legend; under her shining banner England won prosperity and victory. In her personal relationships at the end of her life the veil became threadbare; glimpses of an old woman who was not loved unless she gave showed through the fine network of duty and service. Essex took arms against his Queen, shattering the magical looking-glass which reflected her image of lovely perfection, and showing the sham and pretence to a woman whose love-dealings had, almost all her long life, been founded on make-believe.

Yet the achievements of the reign of the Virgin Queen were real and solid enough. Appalling dangers had been averted; England was a prospering, independent nation. In eluding all the suitors who had pursued her down the years of her reign, in the greatest hunt in history, Elizabeth had not erred. From the rich and glorious literature produced by her subjects under her peaceful sovereignty, one sentence in particular might stand as an epitaph for the Queen who was courted from infancy to old age by the finest men in Europe, and yet rejected all her suitors to die a maid. It was the playwright Lyly, Shakespeare's friend, who, in a panegyric on the glories of Elizabeth's reign, wrote truly and lovingly: 'This is the only miracle virginity ever wrought: for a little island, environed round about with wars, to stand in peace.'

INDEX